THE ELECTIONS
OF 1988

THE ELECTIONS OF 1988

Michael Nelson, editor
Vanderbilt University

A Division of
Congressional Quarterly Inc.
1414 22nd St. N.W., Washington, D.C. 20037

Printed in the United States of America

Second Printing

Library of Congress Cataloging-in-Publication Data

The Elections of 1988.
    1. Presidents—United States—Election—1988.
2. United States. Congress—Elections, 1988.
3. Elections—United States. I. Nelson, Michael,
1949-
JK1968 1988   324.973′0927   89-684
ISBN 0-87187-494-6

To five wise teachers

Eugene Perticone
Jack Edwards
David Holmes
Francis Rourke
Erwin Hargrove

CONTENTS

PREFACE

In planning this book, it was not my intention to develop any particular themes or to suggest any to the writers. What I did set out to do, beginning well over a year before election day, was to assemble the most suitable authors in the country—scholars and journalists with well-established expertise and a demonstrated ability to write clearly and engagingly—and to commission them to describe and analyze the elections of 1988, especially the presidential election, as a set of distinct events and in broader historical and theoretical contexts. This charge the authors have fulfilled.

Moreover, to my delight, from the authors' separate labors two important themes emerged, one normative, the other empirical and analytical. The normative theme can be stated as follows: Did the 1988 campaign (and does modern political campaigning in general) fulfill even minimally the requirements of democratic government, especially the requirement that important issues of public policy be brought before the voters? Paul Quirk, the author of chapter 3 on the general election campaign, says no, as does Thomas Patterson, who assesses the role of the mass media in chapter 4. In sharp contrast, Jean Bethke Elshtain, appraising the election's issues and themes in chapter 5, finds considerable merit in the conduct of the campaign.

The other authors latched on to a more empirical and analytic theme: Where is the American party system headed, and with what consequences for government and public policy? Rhodes Cook describes the parties' presidential nominating processes in chapter 2 as increasingly candidate-centered affairs. "Split-level realignment" and the divided control of government that it portends are the concerns of Francis Rourke and John Tierney, the authors of chapter 1 on the political setting of the election; Gary Jacobson, who writes about Congress in chapter 6; Erwin Hargrove, the author of chapter 7 on the presidency; and me in chapter 8, which discusses certain constitutional aspects of the election. Since 1968 the American political system has settled into a historically unprecedented pattern: Republican dominance in presidential elections, Democratic control of Congress. All of these chapters deal with the causes and consequences of this split-level realignment, among other things.

No reader will agree with all of the interpretations in this book; indeed, no reader could, since the perspectives of different authors on the same topics are as diverse as they are insightful and provocative. This is as it should be: elections are not so one-dimensional as to be captured easily by a single line of interpretation. Better that readers should experience a variety of viewpoints than have one imposed on them.

I am grateful to a number of people—including the nine authors—for working hard and well to produce this book on a timely basis. At CQ Press, I especially thank Nancy Lammers, Carolyn Goldinger, Barbara de Boinville, Nola Healy Lynch, and Janet Schilling for their patience, talent, and thoroughness in editing the manuscript. Thanks, too, to Joanne Daniels, director of CQ Press, and David Tarr, director of the Book Department. Finally, I am ever grateful to my wife, Linda Nelson, and my children, Sam and Michael, for their steadfast love.

Michael Nelson

1. THE SETTING: CHANGING PATTERNS OF PRESIDENTIAL POLITICS, 1960 AND 1988

Francis E. Rourke and John T. Tierney

The conduct and outcome of presidential elections are shaped, to a large degree, by the times in which they occur. Look at the examples of Herbert Hoover, who won a landslide victory in the prosperous year of 1928, then was defeated overwhelmingly in the midst of the depression in 1932; Jimmy Carter, who was elected in 1976 but defeated in 1980; or Benjamin Harrison and Grover Cleveland (Harrison defeated Cleveland in 1888, then Cleveland defeated Harrison in 1892).

Thanks to the two-term limit imposed on presidents by the Twenty-second Amendment, Ronald Reagan was retiring and no incumbent president was running in 1988. This fact alone brings to mind the elections of 1960, which came at the end of the presidency of Dwight D. Eisenhower. The Democrats won in 1960, and their victory was the sixth in the eight most recent presidential elections. In contrast, their defeat in 1988 was their fifth loss in the last six presidential elections. Yet Democrats maintained their majorities in Congress in both 1960 and 1988. In this essay, Francis Rourke and John Tierney attribute the changing fortunes of the Republican and Democratic parties between 1960 and 1988 to alterations that have occurred in the conduct of presidential campaigns and the composition of the two political parties. They draw particular attention to the new phenomenon of "split-level realignment" (Republican dominance of the presidency, Democratic control of Congress). In doing so, they introduce a theme that is returned to in later chapters by Gary Jacobson, Erwin Hargrove, and Michael Nelson.

Both before and while it was in progress, the presidential campaign of 1988 frequently was compared with the campaign of 1960, which matched Democrat John F. Kennedy against Republican Richard Nixon. The similarities are obvious. In 1988, as in 1960, a Republican vice president was facing a Democratic challenger from Massachusetts, and the Democrat sought to win the election by forging a Boston-to-Austin alliance through the selection of a Texan (Sen. Lyndon B. Johnson in 1960, Sen. Lloyd Bentsen in 1988) as his vice-presidential running mate. The Democratic candidate in 1988, Gov. Michael S. Dukakis, tried to capitalize on the resemblance between the two elections by invoking memories of Kennedy on the campaign trail.

Dukakis's Republican opponent, George Bush, had less reason for such nostalgia—Nixon, after all, lost the 1960 election. But Bush's selection of Dan Quayle, the forty-one-year-old senator from Indiana, as his running mate (regarded among Republicans as well as Democrats as one of the great mysteries of modern American politics), may perhaps be understood as an effort to give his campaign the image of youthful vigor that Kennedy's candidacy had brought to the Democratic ticket.

The similarities between 1960 and 1988 on matters of age and geography lie on the surface of politics. A more fundamental resemblance between the two elections is that in both cases voters faced the certainty of change in national leadership no matter which candidate was victorious. A venerable and generally well-liked Republican incumbent was leaving the presidency after eight years in office: Dwight D. Eisenhower in 1960 and Ronald Reagan in 1988. Each departure was required by the terms of the Constitution's Twenty-second Amendment, which stipulates that no one can be elected president more than twice. Eisenhower was the first president to feel the effect of this amendment, and Reagan was the second. Since the two-term limit became part of the Constitution in 1951, voters have been unable to escape the necessity of change in the White House after a president has served two terms in office, even if they are sufficiently satisfied with the performance of the incumbent to prefer continuity. In 1989, as in 1961, a new president would take office, either the Republican vice president or his Democratic adversary.

Implicit in the enactment of the Twenty-second Amendment was the assumption that an incumbent president running for reelection has an advantage over the other political party's nominee, so much so that the opportunity for change in national politics and policies had to be buttressed by reworking the nation's fundamental law. For most of American history, the desire for healthy competition in the quest for the presidency was achieved not by law but by the force of custom. Incumbent presidents did not seek nor were they offered renomination after two terms. The political consensus that sustained this no-third-term tradition was shattered in 1940, when Franklin D. Roosevelt sought and received the Democratic presidential nomination for the third time in a row. Roosevelt followed this break with tradition with a successful fourth-term candidacy in 1944.

The ratification of the Twenty-second Amendment represented the use of law to restore the customary process by which Americans choose a president—setting a limit on the tenure in office to which any chief executive can aspire. To be sure, many voters need no legal compulsion to vote for change after a president has served two terms. Some political scientists have argued that toward the end of any incumbent's second term a certain restlessness begins to stir within the electorate, a "coalition of the discontented" slowly forms,[1] and the prospect of political change begins to look more and more appealing to a growing number of voters. In view of the penchant for novelty that surfaces everywhere else in American life, it would be surprising if every president were not judged to be somewhat "out-of-date" after eight years in office. From this perspective, the eight-year limit in office coincides with a natural political cycle in which the voters are ready for change at just the time the president is required to depart.

The Twenty-second Amendment makes its own contribution to the phases through which this cycle runs. Toward the end of the second term, a president is, in political parlance, a "lame duck," a much less formidable figure than at earlier stages of the presidential career. Other actors in the political system know that the president's days in office are numbered, and they are less inclined to cultivate good will or to fear displeasure from the White House. To some degree, therefore, the president's ability to mobilize support or to overcome political opposition is diminished during the twilight of the second term precisely because the Twenty-second Amendment makes it clear to all that the second term is also the last hurrah. With the president's ability to shape the political life of the country reduced, the election of a new chief executive may seem not a misfortune but an opportunity for the country to move on to greater accomplishments under new leadership.

Ronald Reagan's last days in office were in many ways as disappointing as those of other lame-duck presidents, including Eisenhower.[2] In the congressional elections of 1986, Democrats retrieved the control over the Senate that they had lost in 1980 and strengthened their majority in the House of Representatives. Shortly thereafter, the Iran-contra affair began to take its toll on the reputation of the Reagan administration, when it was revealed that the United States had sold arms to the government of the Ayatollah Ruhollah Khomeini in Iran in an effort to secure the release of American hostages from captivity in Lebanon. Some of the proceeds from this sale were then used to provide military support for the forces seeking to overthrow the Sandinista government in Nicaragua, in defiance of a congressional statute that prohibited such support.[3]

In the wake of these events, the initiative on at least the domestic front shifted from the White House to Congress. New laws were enacted over Reagan's veto, most notably the Civil Rights Restoration Act of 1988; Republicans joined Democrats to strengthen the enforcement of statutes to protect the rights of women and minority groups. Reagan also felt obliged to accept legislation that he would have preferred to veto, such as a plant-closing law that required large companies to give sixty-days' notice to their workers before shutting down a facility. Finally, Reagan encountered increasing opposition in the Senate to his appointments to high office. Robert Bork, whom he nominated to the Supreme Court in 1987, would have given Reagan a powerful and possibly decisive voice on the Court in behalf of his social agenda, perhaps leading to a reversal of the Court's positions on issues like abortion and affirmative action. But after a bitter and highly visible fight, the Bork nomination was rejected by the Senate.

Nevertheless, Reagan, like all lame-duck presidents, was able to use his veto power to defeat some legislation he opposed. For example, in August 1988 Reagan vetoed the fiscal 1989 defense authorization bill, arguing that, if enacted, it would signal a basic "change away from strength and proven success and back toward the weakness and accommodation of the 1970s." Like other lame ducks before him, Reagan maintained presidential primacy in foreign affairs. Indeed, Reagan's major foreign policy accomplishment came in the last year of his administration, when he successfully concluded negotiations with the Soviet Union to ban intermediate range nuclear missiles from Europe. Senate ratification of this pact was ensured by the Democratic majority's strong commitment to disarmament. Thus, Reagan may have devised a formula for success as a lame duck that eluded Eisenhower and other second-term presidents—confront your political opponents in Congress with policy proposals they have long favored.

Continuity and Change in 1988

No matter how Reagan's last days in office are viewed—either as the ultimate triumph of his presidency or as a period in which he governed effectively only by deferring to the opposition—in 1988 both major political parties perceived a strong desire for change in the American electorate. Reagan acknowledged this desire in his address to the Republican National Convention in New Orleans when he said, "We are the change." He urged the voters to "give custody of this office to someone who will build on our changes, not retreat to the past— someone who will continue the change all of us fought for."

With these bold words the president sought to portray his party not only as a vehicle for continuity—a claim the Democrats could

hardly dispute because the Republicans occupied the White House—
but also as a better instrument to bring about the kind of change the
voters were seeking. The Republican platform sounded much the same
theme.

> An election is about the future, about change. But it is also
> about the values we carry with us as we journey into tomorrow and
> about continuity with the best from our past.
> On the threshold of a new century, we live in a time of
> unprecedented technological, social, and cultural development, and a
> rapidly emerging global economy. This election will bring change.
> The question is: Will it be change and progress with the Republi-
> cans or change and chaos with the Democrats?

Moreover, in his acceptance speech, the convention's presidential
nominee, George Bush, sought to present himself as the candidate best
able to provide the voters with both change and continuity. He did so by
borrowing and giving a new twist to a well-worn metaphor that
Franklin Roosevelt had used earlier in behalf of his own presidential
candidacy after the outbreak of World War II. As Bush put it:

> We will surely have change this year, but will it be change that
> moves us forward? Or change that risks retreat?
> In 1940, when I was barely more than a boy, Franklin
> Roosevelt said we shouldn't change horses in midstream.
> My friends, these days the world moves even more quickly, and
> now, after two great terms, a switch will be made. But when you
> have to change horses in midstream, doesn't it make sense to switch
> to one who's going the same way?

Shifting Tides

As the candidate of the Democratic party, which had not elected a
president since 1976, Dukakis had little trouble presenting himself as
an agent of change. Electing the candidate of the party not in power is
the normal way voters bring about changes in government policies and
practices in a democratic society. But, like Kennedy before him,
Dukakis faced the problem that the change he represented might strike
voters as excessive or threatening. Consequently, the strategy he
initially adopted was to avoid promising any dramatic alterations in
policies or programs, suggesting instead that he was the candidate best
equipped to manage the government effectively. "Competence," not
"ideology," was Dukakis's main theme during the early stages of his
campaign for the presidency.

The emphasis Dukakis put on managerial skill made a great deal
of sense during the primary season in the spring, when memories of the
Iran-contra affair were still fresh. The investigations of the affair had

depicted Reagan as a president largely detached from his job and uninformed about the activities of his own subordinates in the executive branch. The accuracy of this portrait was subsequently confirmed through the early publication of the memoirs of some of his principal aides, such as White House chief of staff Donald Regan and Larry Speakes, de facto press secretary. These "insider" accounts of the president's inattention to the duties of his office, coming from people close and loyal to him, were widely discussed in the news media. Particularly embarrassing was the revelation that the president's schedule sometimes was shaped by consultations between his wife and her astrologer.[4]

By the time the election campaign was in full swing after the Republican convention in August, however, Dukakis's "competence" strategy, which had appeared so promising, seemed to have lost its luster. Memories of Reagan's limitations as a manager gradually faded as the voters' attention shifted to the campaign to choose his successor. Moreover, Dukakis's own reputation for competence suffered when Massachusetts suddenly confronted a serious budget crisis.

Even more damaging to the Democratic nominee's prospects was that both competence and ideology suddenly became less important than "likability" as the standard by which presidential candidates were measured, and Dukakis never quite met public expectations in this regard. (It was perhaps one indication of Reagan's effect on the presidency that the likability for which he was renowned should become so important in the selection of his successor.)

In any case, as the campaign progressed, the polls showed that the voters' enthusiasm for change had begun to wane. In the spring of 1988, the stock market crash of October 19, 1987, was still a recent event, and there was widespread apprehension that a serious downturn in the economy might follow. By election day, however, the country was congratulating itself that the market's fall seemed to have had no lasting economic effects. In the meantime, good things had begun to happen elsewhere. In May the United States and the Soviet Union had signed a significant arms reduction agreement, and in September the United States had gone back into space with the launch of a newly designed space shuttle, the *Discovery*. Two of the chinks in Reagan's armor thus were sealed: he was no longer vulnerable either to the charge of being indifferent to the need to negotiate arms agreements or to the complaint that the *Challenger* disaster had left the Soviets in sole command of outer space.

In addition, candidate Bush was highly successful in diverting voter attention from troublesome areas in which the Reagan administration had faced a strong demand for change during its last years in office: the failure of the war against drugs, the continuing problem of budget deficits, the explosive growth of the national debt, and the declining ability of American products to compete effectively in world markets. Instead, relying on a tightly scripted series of sharp attacks, the Bush campaign was able to convince many voters that a Dukakis victory might bring about changes of a threatening sort—especially a softness on crime as symbolized by the Massachusetts prison furlough policy (similar to the practice of other state and the national penal systems), which had allowed weekend freedom for a criminal who subsequently assaulted and terrorized a 'young couple in Maryland. The Bush organization also was adept at defusing issues on which it might be vulnerable to demands for change. The charge that Bush, like Reagan before him, would be negligent on environmental protection was addressed by pointing to the pollution that had persisted in Boston Harbor during the Dukakis administration.

Differing Historical Contexts

Campaign tactics aside, the question remains: Why was Kennedy able in 1960, while Dukakis failed in 1988, to convince the voters that he rather than his opponent best represented the change the Twenty-second Amendment demanded? The answer seems to lie mainly in differences between the times in which the two elections occurred.

In 1960 the United States was just emerging from a severe economic recession that already had given the Democrats an over-whelming victory in the congressional elections of 1958. The economic discontent that so often has fueled Democratic campaigns since the days of the New Deal worked very much in Kennedy's favor in 1960. Equally important, Soviet sputniks were circling the globe in 1960, while the American space program was still struggling—literally—to get off the ground. The 1960 election gave the Democrats an opportunity to do something they have not been able to do since—run a campaign based on strong nationalistic appeals to the pride of Americans in their country and to their enduring belief that the United States is destined to be first in all things, celestial as well as terrestrial. This appeal was buttressed by the argument, spurious as it eventually proved to be, that a "missile gap" between the United States and the Soviet Union seriously endangered American national security.

In short, what Kennedy had going for him in 1960 were what are often described as "gut" issues—issues so viscerally powerful that a political newcomer can use them to overcome whatever reluctance voters may have to risk change. A campaign run, as Kennedy's was, on the theme of getting the country moving again was highly credible when the United States was suffering from economic strains and was seemingly being outstripped in space and in national defense by the Soviet Union.

In 1988 Dukakis carried the Democratic banner at a time when the nation was enjoying an extended period of economic prosperity, something for which the incumbent Republican administration claimed much credit. Moreover, the Soviet Union no longer seemed to be outstripping the United States. Instead, the chief goal of Soviet policy was to catch up with the United States and other advanced industrial societies.

If there was a gut issue available for Dukakis, it was the extent to which the United States had fallen behind, not the Soviet "evil empire" of Reagan's legendary rhetoric, but Japan and the capitalist powers of the West. A case could be made for the proposition that the United States had been fighting in the wrong trenches for the past three decades. If nothing else, this approach would have given Dukakis a nationalist appeal equal in its emotional potency to the flag and Pledge of Allegiance issues that Bush used so effectively against him. As he fell behind in the polls, the Massachusetts governor did begin to sound the theme of economic nationalism. But by then it was too late for nationalism to be for him what it had been for Kennedy—the driving force behind an ultimately victorious campaign.

The Changing Presidential Campaign

As we have seen, Kennedy had advantages in 1960 that were denied to Dukakis in 1988. These advantages illustrate how much American politics had changed in the intervening years. In 1960 the Republican party was still haunted by its image as the party of the Great Depression of the early 1930s. The Democrats, in contrast, basked in the reputation of being the party that had presided over both the recovery from that depression and the American triumph in World War II. To be sure, they had lost the 1952 and 1956 presidential elections. But they had done so under the leadership of Adlai Stevenson II, perhaps the most widely respected loser of presidential elections in modern American history and a candidate who had energized many active supporters for future work within the party.

It is suggestive of the different political settings in which Kennedy and Dukakis ran that in 1960 the two most recent Democratic presidents to whom voters could look to forecast the kind of leadership Kennedy would bring to the country were Franklin Roosevelt and Harry S Truman. When the Massachusetts governor ran in 1988, the two most recent Democratic presidents were Johnson and Carter. Although history may treat them more kindly than their contemporaries did, today Johnson is best remembered for America's ill-fated involvement in Vietnam and Carter for the humiliating seizure of the American Embassy in Tehran by Iranian militants and a domestic economy beset by inflation.

The Democrats also were hurt by changes that had taken place since 1960 in the conduct of presidential campaigns. One striking feature of the Kennedy-Nixon race was that in 1960 traditional party organizations at the local level were still viewed as largely controlling the outcome. A major player in the Kennedy victory was Mayor Richard J. Daley of Chicago. He headed one of the most formidable of the old-style political machines and was widely credited with putting his state in the Democratic column—whether by fair means or foul was a matter of continuing dispute between partisans of Nixon and Kennedy.

The Republican party came to believe that the Democrats' superior grass-roots organizations had played a significant role in Nixon's defeat. Not long after the election, it appointed a committee headed by Ray Bliss, the Republican party chair in Ohio, to probe the causes of the election failure. The committee's principal conclusion was that the Republicans had lost the presidency in 1960 because their party's organization lagged behind the Democrats in the major cities of the country.[5]

The Republican Edge: White House Experience

By 1988 the political parties' view of what it took to win a presidential election had changed quite radically. Not grass-roots machinery but skill at using the media was regarded as the first requirement for success at the polls in a national campaign. The Republicans were widely credited with being far more talented in this regard than the Democrats. With only a month to go before election day, a neutral observer outlined some of the ways the Republicans had demonstrated their superiority in media strategies during the 1988 campaign.

> Political professionals in both parties generally believe that Mr. Bush's camp has been more adept in using television advertising, more disciplined at finding effective issues and sticking with them for several days at a time, more skillful at controlling damage and more creative in coming up with new speeches and new lines. The Dukakis campaign has paid a back-handed compliment to the skills of the Bush staff by running a series of television advertisements that attack not Mr. Bush, but the professionals who are managing his campaign.[6]

One indication of the change that had taken place in the nature of presidential campaigning between 1960 and 1988 was that the individuals who were credited with having political savvy in 1988 were not the local party leaders like Daley, but the political advisers skilled at identifying and molding the opinions of a national electorate in a media age. The chief architect of the Bush campaign in 1988, for example, was James A. Baker III, who had honed his skills in media manipulation in three earlier presidential contests.

More important than his campaign experience, however, was that Baker also had played a major role during the Reagan administration in designing strategies to ensure that the president's policies were treated favorably by the news media. For Baker and others in the Bush campaign, the 1988 election was simply a continuation of what they had been doing at the White House for eight years. Samuel Kernell and others have described the importance modern presidents attach to the task of winning public support to ensure the success of their policies—"going public," Kernell calls it.[7] One consequence of going public as a strategy to maintain presidential power is that it gives White House aides considerable practice at hand-to-hand combat with the media, experience that proves extremely useful in a presidential campaign.

Considering that, as of 1988, Republican presidents had occupied the White House for sixteen of the past twenty (and twenty-four of the past thirty-six) years, the aptitude they have shown for media management in recent presidential campaigns can fairly be said to exemplify the "practice effect"—individuals and organizations are better than their competitors at doing the things they do more often. Studies have shown, for example, that the best place to go for open-heart surgery is the hospital where this operation is performed most frequently. By the same token, the best place to find the skills necessary to deal with the media in national political campaigns is among people who have worked at the White House and been continuously involved in shaping the news in ways that will be beneficial to the president.

In sum, significant changes have occurred in the style and tactics of presidential campaigns since 1960 when Kennedy defeated Nixon. The Republicans no longer need worry as much as they once did about their weaknesses in local party organizations. The Democrats, however, have real cause for concern. The news media—particularly television—have become the principal channels through which presidential candidates seek to exploit the hopes and fears of the electorate—finding and pushing its "hot-buttons"—and the Republicans, as the incumbent party, bring to their campaigns all the skills that now are necessary to manage public relations for the White House. The Democrats, in contrast, are obliged on very short notice to put together an "instant" organization to manage the campaign, what Alvin Toffler describes as an "adhocracy." [8] Inevitably, it is a less professionally skilled operation than that of their opponents.

The Incumbent as Campaigner

One measure of the great improvement in campaign management the Republicans have achieved since 1960 is the skillful use they made of the popular incumbent president in behalf of the Bush-Quayle ticket in 1988. After the 1960 election many observers suggested that Nixon's failure to make sufficient use of Eisenhower in his campaign had contributed to his defeat. Only at the end of October was the president's help really solicited; only then did a surge toward Nixon occur. Not surprisingly, when the votes were counted, there was widespread speculation that an earlier and stronger Eisenhower presence in the presidential campaign would have put Nixon over the top.

No such unwillingness marked the 1988 campaign of George Bush; from the outset the powers and popularity of the Reagan presidency were fully exploited in behalf of the Bush candidacy. Several of Reagan's appointments in 1988 were tailored to help Bush, most notably the selection of Lauro F. Cavazos to be the secretary of education. Cavazos was the first Hispanic to serve as a member of the cabinet, and soon after his appointment he joined Bush at a campaign appearance in Texas, where the Hispanic vote is substantial. Reagan made other decisions that helped the vice president's election effort. In an apparent response to pleas from the Bush organization, the president allowed a Democratic plant-closing bill to become law rather than veto it. A number of regulatory decisions on environmental policy were altered to prevent damage to the Bush campaign.

The Bush headquarters also made frequent use of the president's talent for crowd-pleasing oratory. Reagan's appearances on the campaign trail raised money and ignited enthusiasm among the Republican faithful. Equally important, he often lavished praise on the vice president for his role in the administration. His support for Bush was a far cry from Eisenhower's inadvertent devaluation of Nixon's performance as vice president. Asked at a press conference to identify a significant contribution that Nixon had made to the work of his administration, Eisenhower replied offhandedly that if he were given a few days, he might be able to think of something.

Perhaps the greatest service Reagan performed for the Republican ticket was to postpone certain politically unpopular decisions until after the election. In the week that followed Bush's victory, the Reagan administration took several steps that, an administration official conceded, had been delayed because they might have had a damaging effect on the Bush candidacy.[9] Among other things, eighty-three thousand farmers were notified that they might soon face foreclosure proceedings, and it was revealed that the Social Security Administration was working on a plan to make it more difficult for people to appeal agency decisions that denied them disability or retirement benefits.

The Character of the Campaign

In retrospect the changes in the style of partisan political combat that took place between the 1960 and 1988 presidential campaigns can be best described in military terms, as a shift from ground war to air war. The media, particularly television, became the principal instrument through which each side sought victory at the polls. The ground forces—namely, grass-roots party organizations—still played an important role in getting out the vote on election day, but the attitudes that voters took with them to the polls already had been shaped largely by what had appeared on television.

As in previous campaigns, television came under severe criticism for its role in the 1988 election. Among other charges, it was accused of trivializing the contest for the presidency by featuring thirty-second "sound bites"—snapshots of the candidates attacking each other on the campaign trail—rather than discussions of the issues that were of most serious consequence to the voters. In their defense, the television networks could well argue that their coverage reflected the campaign the candidates were conducting, a campaign in which little was said about the issues.

The 1988 campaign may be best remembered for its negative character. At the outset, Bush's strategists recognized that their candidate drew a highly negative rating from voters, while Dukakis was viewed quite favorably. Their solution to this problem was to attack the Democrat's competence and character, a strategy that succeeded perhaps beyond their wildest dreams. By late October, Dukakis's negative ratings among voters had climbed dramatically. Even Reagan was drawn into this strategic design, referring to Dukakis at one point in the campaign as an "invalid."

To be sure, Bush's strategy of accentuating the negative forfeited the opportunity to win the sort of mandate for his administration that more positive appeals might have engendered. It also ran the risk of antagonizing Democrats in Congress, who strengthened their majorities in the House and the Senate, and whose support Bush surely would need to put some of his policies and programs into effect. But these disadvantages aside, negative campaigning had one essential virtue in the eyes of Bush campaign aides—it worked. Since rewarded behavior tends to be repeated, the strategy may well become a model for future presidential campaigns.

The Electoral Connection

When John Kennedy mounted his successful campaign for the White House in 1960, the Democratic coalition that Franklin Roosevelt had cemented together almost three decades earlier was still largely intact. Unionized workers, southerners, northern blacks, urban ethnics, and middle-class liberals formed the principal building blocks of Roosevelt's New Deal coalition. What held these disparate constituencies together was a shared set of attitudes: belief in the desirability of an active central government, faith in the ability of government to understand and solve social and economic problems, and approval of the robust power that such a government must have.

Kennedy carried all the populous Democratic strongholds in the North and East, but lost Ohio. With the help of his running mate, Lyndon Johnson, Kennedy carried seven southern states, including Johnson's home state, Texas. The Democratic ticket also was victorious in two western states—Nevada and New Mexico. Even so, cracks were beginning to appear in the Democrats' traditional coalition. Richard Nixon carried four states from the traditionally Democratic South and almost all of the West.

The cracks evident in 1960 have since become chasms. The South has been virtually realigned into a Republican monolith, as has the Rocky Mountain region. By 1988 the Republican base in presidential elections—defined as those states the party's presidential candidates had carried in every election since 1968—was more than two hundred electoral votes.

What has happened since 1960 to give the Republicans the distinct advantage they now seem to have in presidential elections? The changes can best be understood in terms of the shifting support of broad constituencies, activated by or reacting against sweeping new social movements that emerged in American society.

Civil Rights and the Democrats

The Democrats' potent electoral coalition, which had brought it victory in almost all of the presidential and congressional elections from 1932 to 1964, began to crumble in the mid-1960s on the shoals of civil rights for blacks. Although committed to eliminate from American democracy the stigma of racial discrimination, Kennedy had decided early in his presidency not to push immediately for the passage of civil rights legislation, preferring to advance the cause through assorted executive actions until he felt that the time was ripe politically for legislative initiatives. Not until 1964 did the power and the will coincide to produce the landmark Civil Rights Act, which aimed principally to eliminate racial discrimination in public accommodations and employment. The Voting Rights Act, passed in 1965, greatly enhanced the legal protection for blacks to participate in elections.

Although public opinion polls showed that most Americans favored these legislative efforts to secure the constitutional rights of blacks in the South, popular support for civil rights began to erode after 1964. One reason was that each summer from 1965 to 1968 television screens in living rooms across America carried pictures of ghetto riots by blacks in New York, Los Angeles, Chicago, Cleveland, and many other major cities. Although arising from several sources, urban violence was a manifestation—to whites—of a disturbing change that had occurred in the civil rights movement: the nonviolence that had characterized Martin Luther King's leadership had begun to give way to the more revolutionary impulses of militant blacks such as Stokely Carmichael and H. Rap Brown. The peaceful litigation strategies pursued by the National Association for the Advancement of Colored People (NAACP) were increasingly overshadowed by the more violent confrontational tactics of organizations like the Black Panthers.

By 1966 the cause of civil rights was losing momentum for another reason. The Johnson administration's efforts to secure cultural equality for blacks—embodied chiefly in ambitious inner-city programs created by the Economic Opportunity Act of 1964—did not sit well with many working-class and lower-middle-class ethnic whites, who believed that they would bear the costs of these redistributive programs to help blacks. Equally jarring to some elements of the traditional Democratic coalition were the administration's attempts to bar racial discrimination in the sale or rental of private housing (a practice widespread in the North) and to use "affirmative action" programs to correct past injustices by treating blacks preferentially.

All these policies had a profoundly divisive effect on the Democratic coalition, alienating the white South (once solidly Democratic) and leading to massive defections among working-class Democrats in the North. The Johnson administration's programmatic response to the civil rights movement—namely, policies aimed at promoting racial equality and participatory democracy—disturbed many Democrats, who saw them as threatening to take away gains they had won under the New Deal. The federal government, which under the New Deal had been seen as a source of assistance for the average American, now came to be looked upon by many as the cause of deprivations.

The political harm to the Democratic party first became evident in the 1966 congressional elections, when the Republicans added forty-seven seats to their minority in the House. Polls indicated that many northern white voters thought the Johnson administration was moving too far and too fast in its efforts to help blacks.[10] Moreover, the violence in the inner cities each summer increased the demand for "law and order" and lowered voters' willingness to expend tax dollars for any program that seemed to be rewarding black rioters.[11] The presidential campaign of Republican Richard Nixon in 1968 and that of the independent candidate, Alabama governor George Wallace, successfully exploited these social issues, driving wedges into the traditional Democratic coalition.

Vietnam's Political Legacy

Issues of civil rights and civil disorder were by no means alone in producing new cleavages within the Democratic party. At least as important in that regard was the Vietnam War. Although the Johnson administration's conduct of the war triggered prolonged and acrimonious controversy among the foreign policy elites, the public at large gave the administration firm and even enthusiastic support during the war's early years. But public support began to erode when an American victory seemed elusive and the costs escalated in terms of casualties abroad and disruption at home, including the mobilization of some reserve units, tougher policies on draft deferments, a surtax on incomes, and a decided tilt toward guns in the federal budget's ratio of guns to butter. By 1968 nearly half of the public regarded American military intervention in South Vietnam as a mistake, doubling the number holding that opinion three years earlier.[12]

As with so many other controversies in American political life, however, the fight over Vietnam took place not between the two parties but within the majority party.[13] It was mainly among Democrats that the antiwar movement found candidates to carry its banner. Senators Eugene McCarthy and, later, Robert F. Kennedy led the challenge against President Johnson on the war issue—not just on the floor of the Senate but in presidential primaries as well. McCarthy, waging a campaign supported largely by antiwar activists, ran almost even with Johnson in the hard-fought New Hampshire primary in 1968. The senator's showing was widely interpreted as a moral victory and was credited with dissuading the president from continuing his fight for renomination. When antiwar activists withheld their support from the eventual Democratic nominee, Hubert H. Humphrey, it increased the likelihood that Nixon would defeat the divided opposition without bearing the onus of having to attack the president.[14]

In terms of longer lasting effects, the antiwar demonstrations of the late 1960s and early 1970s and the antiwar candidacy of Democratic senator George McGovern in 1972 also produced a backlash of nationalist sentiment from which the Republicans eventually profited. The Democrats began to be seen as lacking in patriotism and as weak on national defense, a perception that, as noted earlier, has hurt them ever since in presidential politics.

Religion and Politics

Issues of civil rights, war and peace, and national defense were not solely responsible for reshaping the political behavior of the electorate in the late 1960s and early 1970s. The almost simultaneous rise of new social issues had at least as powerful an effect, cutting across all constituency groups but having a particularly strong effect on white evangelical Protestants in the South. Social issues helped to give rise to one of the most powerful movements in modern American politics, the religious Right.

When Kennedy ran for president in 1960, white evangelical Protestants, who comprised about 20 percent of the national electorate, tended to be politically passive but supportive of the Democratic party, especially in the South. By the time Dukakis ran almost thirty years later, Democratic strategists knew that white evangelicals would be among their stiffest opponents, having realigned solidly in support of Reagan and the Republican party.

As A. James Reichley has shown, the transformation of white evangelicals from a passive component of the Democratic coalition to one of the driving forces of the Republican Right has been slow but steady. After supporting Jimmy Carter (a born-again Baptist) in 1976, they became disenchanted over what they considered to be his abandonment of their social agenda. A wide variety of modern trends contributed to their growing uneasiness. As Reichley notes:

> [E]vangelicals in the 1970s felt that their entire way of life, which they tended to identify as the American way of life, was threatened by such by-products of modernity as increase in divorce, rising crime, rapid increase in the percentage of children born out of wedlock, widespread use of recreational drugs, and virtually unrestricted availability of pornography. These symptoms of social decay, they were told by their preachers, were caused by the dominance of a philosophy called "secular humanism" in major universities, the national media, the federal government, and the federal courts.[15]

Particularly threatening to traditional moral values, in the view of evangelicals, were policies such as the prohibition of officially sponsored prayer in public schools, abortion on demand, the proposed Equal Rights Amendment, and demands for gay rights.

During the late 1970s, popular television preachers like Jerry Falwell and Pat Robertson began calling for political action by evangelicals. In 1979 Falwell founded the Moral Majority, an organization that, like other New Right groups, built a strong financial base through sophisticated direct mail fund-raising operations and well-developed grass-roots political organization. The religious Right played an important role in helping Reagan win the White House in 1980. Four years later, the movement was even more active. Evangelical churches engineered ambitious voter registration drives that brought hundreds of thousands of new voters into the electorate in 1984; on election day white evangelicals gave Reagan an astonishing 80 percent of their vote.

Although not nearly as monolithic in their voting as evangelicals, Roman Catholics also have moved to the right since 1960. Catholics never gave a majority of their votes to a Republican presidential candidate until 1972, but they have done so in every election since then, save for 1976. In 1988, 52 percent of Catholic voters chose Bush. The abortion issue accounts for only a small part of the changing Catholic vote; polls show it to be decisive with about one Catholic voter in ten. But the consequence of the decline in Catholics' longstanding loyalty to the Democratic party has been the loss of a solid bloc of reliable support the party once enjoyed in the major industrial states of the Northeast and Midwest. Even the Hispanic vote in Texas is increasingly up for grabs, making it more and more difficult for the Democrats to win the third most populous state.[16]

"New Politics" and the Business Community

Another important element in reshaping the Democratic party's identity—and in inspiring opposition forces to mobilize—was the emergence in the late 1960s and early 1970s of a broad constellation of citizens' organizations. Most of these organizations were committed either to securing the rights of particular groups in society (such as women, the handicapped, and nursing home patients) or to advancing broad public interests (such as consumer rights, environmental protection, and occupational health and safety) against what typically were depicted as the narrow, self-interested claims of powerful corporate interests.

Adopting the tactics of older, more established interest groups, citizens' organizations and public interest groups used every political weapon available. They lobbied legislators, monitored and participated in the administrative process, pursued strategies of litigation, and brought their message to the public, often as dramatically as possible, through finely tuned direct mail campaigns and the skillful use of other new technologies of persuasion. The combination of zeal and practical political skills brought these "new politics" organizations success along two principal avenues, one involving efforts to advance or protect rights (for example, freeing women from credit discrimination and from discrimination in educational institutions), the other involving federal regulations that affect the conditions under which goods and services are produced, the physical characteristics of consumer products, and the disposition of waste from the manufacturing process.

The success of these citizens' groups came to be identified primarily with the Democratic party, which was the principal source of their support in Congress. Yet that association redounded somewhat to the party's disadvantage in presidential elections. As had been true of earlier social movements, the efforts of the new politics organizations generated a backlash from which the Republican party benefited.

The reaction was nowhere more apparent than in the business community. The antagonism between business and labor that traditionally has been fundamental to the politics of industrial democracies was overshadowed in the 1970s by an even more bitter struggle between business and the axis of interests grouped under the public interest umbrella.[17] Part of the explanation for the hardened antagonism between business and citizens' groups was the changing nature of governmental regulation in the early 1970s. Unlike earlier attempts to regulate railroad freight rates or drug safety, regulatory innovations in the fields of occupational health and safety and environmental preservation were not industry-specific. Rather, they affected business as a whole, thus generating antagonism from all sectors of the business community.

With abundant incentive to protect its interests, American business countermobilized in the late 1970s. Corporations created their own lobbying operations in Washington or hired lawyers and lobbyists to represent their interests. Seduced by Reagan's pledge in 1980 to lift the regulatory crown of thorns that (at least in the eyes of business organizations) had been pressed onto the corporate brow by Democrats, the business community firmly reunited under the Republican banner in 1980. As never before, Republicans had access to seemingly limitless campaign funds and thus to the technological means of victory in modern presidential politics: computers, high-speed printers, opinion and tracking polls, television advertising, and telephone banks.[18]

Business was not alone in reacting negatively to the efforts of citizens' groups. Less easily traced, but probably no less important in its electoral consequences, was a reaction among working-class Democrats, who came to regard "public interest" activism as adverse to their welfare. Many such workers believed that the costs of federal requirements to clean up the air and water and make workplaces and consumer products safer fell disproportionately on their shoulders in the form of lost jobs and income and higher taxes and prices. Moreover, the new politics organizations came to be identified (not always correctly) in the minds of many Americans with the encroaching power of the government into matters of personal behavior or preference, through policies ranging from the proposed saccharin ban at the national level to state-level "bottle-return" regulations, antismoking statutes, and laws to require the use of seat belts or motorcycle crash helmets.

Even as the Democratic party was hurt in presidential elections by its association with the new politics groups, it did not often receive offsetting support from them. Most of these organizations are not particularly effective at delivering large blocs of voters on election day. But this did not prevent them from insisting that the party platform reflect their interests. In 1984, for example, the list of organizations that sought to have their concerns incorporated into the Democratic party platform included environmental groups, gay rights advocates, feminists, peace activists, blacks, senior citizens, Hispanics, and Asian-Americans. As the party tried to accommodate all these demands, its message got muddled and its 1984 candidate, Walter Mondale, was branded a captive of "special interests."

Finally, these new politics organizations, simply by adding to the heterogeneity of interests in the Democratic party, have made it more difficult for Democrats to achieve unity in presidential campaigns. Their disunity provides Republicans with increased opportunities to promote and exploit divisions within the Democratic coalition, especially on social issues.

Epilogue: Perspectives on 1988

The millions of Americans (half the electorate) who failed to vote on November 8, 1988, were wrong if they believed that elections do not matter. Every presidential election opens or closes the door to change in American society in a variety of ways. Elections are the engines that drive the political process, advancing some ideas, retarding others, and sometimes providing mandates for significant social or economic change.

In recent years, one of the principal questions that observers of American politics have asked is whether the nation is undergoing a major shift from Democratic to Republican dominance of its political life. From the 1930s to the 1960s, the Democrats were preeminent, controlling the principal elective institutions in Washington and the states most of the time. Moreover, the Democratic party enjoyed almost a two-to-one edge over the Republicans among voters who were willing to state an allegiance to one party or the other.

But in 1980 the Democrats' seemingly commanding posture in Washington fell before a new Republican juggernaut. Reagan won the presidency, and the Republican party captured control of the Senate and took thirty-three seats away from the Democrats in the House (more than either party had lost in any other presidential election since 1948). Reagan was reelected in 1984, carrying every state but Minnesota. With the 1988 victory, the Republicans had won seven of the last ten presidential elections.

But the Republicans' impressive strength in the presidential arena was not replicated elsewhere in the political system. Even after its defeat in the 1988 presidential election, the Democratic party still held twenty-eight of the nation's fifty governorships, controlled a majority of state legislatures, and, even more important, had secure majorities in both houses of Congress. The Democrats actually gained seats in Congress in 1988 (five in the House, one in the Senate), dealing Bush a setback of the sort normally reserved for midterm elections. Assessing the results during the week following the election, Kevin Phillips, one of the nation's leading Republican political analysts, described the Republican house as a facade with nothing of substance behind it: "The truth is that, for Bush-era Republicanism, the White House is not just a President's mansion; it is becoming the GOP's only major fort on the battlefield of politics." [19]

It is not altogether clear why the American electorate has delivered such a split verdict. At a minimum, the voters have a less than total trust in either political party. Therefore, some suggest, they have added what one observer has called "a new ad hoc element to the Founding Fathers' system of checks and balances." [20] A better explanation is that each party has political advantages and disadvantages that result in Democratic victories in congressional races and the election of Republicans to the White House.

Voters seem to rely on the Democratic party in Congress to defend government benefits or services on which they are particularly dependent. The Democrats excel at serving a variety of local interests through the time-honored device of providing casework and other services to individual constituents. Even more important, the Democratic party provides a political umbrella under which a wide range of programmatic groups can gather, including blacks, women, environmentalists, consumers, and senior citizens. Faithfully delivering on its commitments to these interests, the Democratic party has become the institutional embodiment of "interest group liberalism" in American society.

But the same heterogeneity of organized constituencies that is a source of strength for the Democratic party in Congress also weakens the party in the presidential arena, where diversity generates considerable friction between groups with conflicting views on particular issues. During the 1988 Democratic nominating contest, New York mayor Ed

Koch said it would be "crazy" for any Jew to vote for the black candidate, Jesse Jackson, in the state's presidential primary. (Jackson was widely regarded in the Jewish community as unsympathetic to Israel in its struggle with the Palestinians.) Other conflicts have erupted in the Democratic party between trade unions that represent workers in defense plants and peace groups anxious to limit military spending, or between "right-to-lifers" who oppose abortion and "prochoice" groups that support the right of women to elect such a procedure.

While constantly struggling to accommodate such diverse interests within its ranks, the Democratic party finds that its heterogeneity renders it vulnerable to external attack from Republicans eager to drive wedges between Democratic constituencies. Nowhere is the Republicans' success at this more evident than with respect to abortion, school prayer, and other social issues, which Republican candidates have skillfully used to separate evangelical Protestants and traditional Catholics from their Democratic moorings.

In trying to handle their internal divisions, the Democrats face difficulties not unlike those encountered long ago by the Austro-Hungarian empire. Acceptance of heterogeneity is useful for territorial expansion because it permits a variety of diverse constituencies to be encompassed within a single sovereign unit. But heterogeneity also becomes a source of internal tension, division, and possible insurrection—as disadvantageous for a political organization like the Democratic party as it has been for empires in the past.

The Republican party, much more homogeneous than its rival, faces no similar balkanization by interests. The internal fault lines within the Republican party tend to be ideological. For example, in the 1950s conservative Republicans complained that the party was dominated at the national level by liberals whose policy preferences were scarcely distinguishable from those of the Democrats. Decades later, conservatives still were complaining, in the wake of the 1988 election, that the "moderate" Bush would bear careful watching. Still, despite the recurring tensions between its two ideological camps, the Republican party has managed to keep its divisions from tearing it asunder in every presidential election except 1964.

The Republican party's strength in presidential politics also has been increased by the lock it seems to have acquired on nationalist fervor in the United States. If there is one issue that can give a party the edge in the presidential electoral arena, nationalism is that issue; it carries a strong emotional appeal that cuts through a variety of constituencies and often transcends the more particular concerns that members of those constituencies may have. In recent presidential elections, Republican campaign strategists have been more successful than the Democrats at manipulating symbols like the flag and at using gauzy rhetoric ("morning in America," for example) to inspire and capitalize on nationalist sentiments.

The Republican edge on nationalism has been reinforced by their most recent exercises of national power abroad, such as the invasion of Grenada in 1983 and the air raid on Libya in 1986. These produced much flag-waving and a large resurgence of national pride, at very little political cost. The Democrats, by contrast, seem to specialize in high-cost exercises abroad—wars in Korea and Vietnam and President Carter's highly controversial grain embargo. Such ventures may have projected an image of American strength abroad, but at home they imposed considerable costs on the president and his party.

Will control over national policy making divided between a Democratic Congress and a Republican president prevent the United States from dealing with its most serious social and economic problems during the Bush presidency? Historically, divided government in the United States has not made political deadlock inevitable. In fact, in the two most recent periods when the nation had a Republican president and a Democratic Congress, there have been significant policy break-throughs. The collaboration between President Nixon and the Democratic 91st and 92d Congresses between 1969 and 1972 produced landmark legislation in environmental and consumer protection, occupational safety and health, and general revenue sharing. During the final two years of the Reagan presidency, there were major policy achievements, such as welfare reform and arms control, even though the Democrats controlled both houses of Congress.

Even as divided or "coalition" government does not ensure policy deadlock, having the same party in control of both branches provides no guarantee against it. Indeed, the most recent period of interbranch control by one party—the Carter administration—was one of frequent stalemate. Carter failed to secure passage of most of the major domestic legislation he proposed, including welfare reform, energy reform, and hospital cost containment.

Still, even if the partisan cleavage that now separates the president from Congress does not lead to stalemate, the particular issues and policy problems that await action in the wake of the 1988 election may make their own contribution to political paralysis. The budget deficit is the most troublesome of the many issues that face the president and Congress; many observers are convinced that it can be solved only by some combination of tax increases and spending cuts, the very things that elected officials least like to do. Equally formidable are policy problems such as acid rain that will continue to divide Congress internally, not so much by party or ideology as along geographic and regional lines.

For George Bush, as for other presidents, the challenge will be to find support for his policy initiatives in the ranks of both parties. The Democratic 101st Congress faces a task no less formidable—to defend the interests and welfare of its constituents without prejudicing the country's ability to find solutions for its most pressing problems. The ability of the White House and Congress to shape national policy effectively through some mix of combat and compromise will go a long way toward determining the fate of the political parties in the presidential election of 1992, an event that was already on the minds of both Democratic and Republican politicians even before Bush was inaugurated as president January 20, 1989.

Notes

1. A somewhat different term, "coalition of minorities," is used in this connection by John Mueller in *War, Politics, and Public Opinion* (New York: John Wiley & Sons, 1973), 205.
2. For an analysis of the "lame duck" experience, see Michael B. Grossman, Martha Joynt Kumar, and Francis E. Rourke, "Second-Term Presidencies: The Aging of Administrations," in *The Presidency and the Political System*, 2d ed., ed. Michael Nelson (Washington, D.C.: CQ Press, 1988), 207-228.
3. See *Report of the Congressional Committees Investigating the Iran-Contra Affair*, S. Rept. No. 100-216; H. Rept. No. 100-433, 100th Cong., 1st sess., 1987.
4. Donald T. Regan, *For the Record: From Wall Street to Washington* (San Diego: Harcourt Brace Jovanovich, 1988); and Larry Speakes, *Speaking Out: The Reagan Presidency from Inside the White House* (New York: Scribner, 1988).
5. This story is told in greater detail in Francis E. Rourke, "Urbanism and the National Party Organizations," *The Western Political Quarterly* 18 (March 1965): 149-163.
6. E. J. Dionne, Jr., "The Debates: Revival for Democrats," *New York Times*, October 7, 1988, B4.
7. Samuel Kernell, *Going Public: New Strategies of Presidential Leadership* (Washington, D.C.: CQ Press, 1986). Also see Sidney Blumenthal, *The Permanent Campaign: Inside the World of Elite Political Operatives* (Boston: Beacon Press, 1980).
8. See Alvin Toffler, *Future Shock* (New York: Random House, 1970), 112-135.
9. Steven V. Roberts, "Sensitive Issues Put on the Shelf to Protect Bush," *New York Times*, November 16, 1988, A29.

10. For Gallup poll data tracking opinion on the matter, see James L. Sundquist, *Politics and Policy: The Eisenhower, Kennedy and Johnson Years* (Washington, D.C.: Brookings Institution, 1968), 498.
11. Sundquist, *Politics and Policy,* 286.
12. See *Gallup Opinion Index,* Report No. 35, May 1968, 21.
13. Samuel Lubell's argument that the major controversies in American political life take place not between the two parties but within the majority party can find no better illustration than the fight over Vietnam. See Samuel Lubell, *The Future of American Politics* (New York: Harper, 1951), 200-205.
14. Francis E. Rourke, "The Domestic Scene," in *America and the World: From the Truman Doctrine to Vietnam* (Baltimore: Johns Hopkins University Press, 1970), 165.
15. A. James Reichley, "Religion and the Future of American Politics," *Political Science Quarterly* 101 (1986): 25.
16. This discussion of the Catholic vote also draws on Reichley, "Religion and the Future of American Politics," 31-35.
17. For data substantiating this point, see Kay Lehman Schlozman and John T. Tierney, *Organized Interests and American Democracy* (New York: Harper and Row, 1986), 285-286.
18. Benjamin Ginsberg and Martin Shefter, "A Critical Realignment? The New Politics, the Reconstituted Right, and the Election of 1984," in *The Elections of 1984,* ed. Michael Nelson (Washington, D.C.: CQ Press, 1985), 21.
19. Kevin Phillips, "A Shaky G.O.P. Victory," *New York Times,* November 17, 1988, A31.
20. R. W. Apple, Jr., "The People Are Yearning for a Leader, but Expecting Much Less," *New York Times,* November 6, 1988, E1.

2. THE NOMINATING PROCESS

Rhodes Cook

The question of who becomes president in a given election year can be approached in the manner of Sherlock Holmes solving a case. "Eliminate the impossible," Holmes always said, "and whatever is left, however improbable, is the answer." Perhaps the greatest influence in this process of elimination is the decision of many potential candidates not to run. The Democrats, in particular, were distressed in 1988 by the refusal by some of their leading political figures to contend for the presidency, including Gov. Mario Cuomo of New York, Sen. Edward Kennedy of Massachusetts, and Sen. Bill Bradley of New Jersey.

Those who did campaign for the Republican or Democratic nomination for president faced what Rhodes Cook describes as "an unmistakable five-stage structure." First comes the "exhibition season," the preelection year phase of the nominating campaign in which the candidates jockey for position. Next are the "media fishbowl" contests: the Iowa caucuses and New Hampshire primary. Third is "Super Tuesday," the crowded day of mainly southern primaries and caucuses in early March. Then the extended "mop-up stage" unfolds, in which each party's presidential nomination is clinched by the winning candidate in the remaining state contests. The final "convention" stage is as much the beginning of the general election campaign as the culmination of the nominating campaign.

Each presidential nominating campaign is a trek into the unknown, but no campaign in recent times started out looking as thoroughly unpredictable as the one in 1988. Not since President Lyndon B. Johnson's decision to withdraw from the 1968 election had there been a presidential race without the long shadow of an incumbent's reelection campaign falling over either the Democratic or Republican field. Never before had so many states packed their primaries and caucuses so densely into the opening weeks of the election year. Never had a black candidate been as strongly positioned to compete for a presidential nomination as the Reverend Jesse Jackson was in the Democratic party.

Yet the surprise for many people was that the 1988 nominating process was not the disaster they expected it to be. Some feared that momentum would sweep a successful dark horse from the back of the pack to the verge of nomination before that candidate came under sustained scrutiny. Others worried that the glut of early events would produce a different result—a hopelessly muddled race that would be resolved only after bitter party infighting.

Neither of those situations occurred. By the time the nominating process had run its course, it had yielded two clear winners— Republican vice president George Bush and Democratic governor Michael S. Dukakis of Massachusetts—who had begun the year at or near the top of their parties' public opinion polls. The 1988 process even offered something to those who had dreaded a front-runners' cakewalk devoid of suspense. Despite their strong organizations and ample campaign coffers, both Bush and Dukakis suffered at least one scare before they got a grip on their nominations.

Satisfaction with the 1988 nominating process, however, did not extend to all quarters. Many states felt overlooked, as Iowa and New Hampshire continued to draw a disproportionate share of attention with their media-grabbing events at the start of the nominating season. Jackson, Dukakis's prime challenger, maintained, as he had when he first ran for president in 1984, that aspects of the Democratic party rules were unfair to him.

For these and other reasons, it seems safe to predict that the nominating campaign in 1992 will be different from 1988, just as 1988 was different from the nominating contests that preceded it.

The Constant Is Change

One of the striking features of the presidential nominating process is its ongoing change, with aspects of both the parties' rules and the calendar order of primaries and caucuses noticeably different from election to election.[1] Compared to nominations, the process of electing a president is a model of stability, with a one-day, fifty-state vote every fourth year on the first Tuesday after the first Monday in November.

The major impetus for change in the nominating process has come from the Democrats, who began revising their delegate-selection rules after the party's tumultuous 1968 convention in Chicago, at which Vice President Hubert H. Humphrey was nominated without having run in a single primary state. Convention delegates in 1968, as in previous elections, had been chosen mostly by established party leaders within each state, in many cases during the year before the election.

When liberals, opposed to the war in Vietnam, cried foul at Humphrey's nomination, party regulars grudgingly agreed to create a commission to review the party's nominating rules. The McGovern-Fraser commission (named for its leaders, Sen. George McGovern of South Dakota and Rep. Donald Fraser of Minnesota) undertook an overhaul of the process that has yet to be completed. Rewriting their rules every four years since 1968, the Democrats have transferred power in their nominating process from party kingmakers to citizens at the grass roots. The overwhelming majority of convention delegates now are chosen in primaries that are open to any and all voters who call themselves Democrats. Since the 1970s, there has been a steady growth in the number of primaries—from seventeen in 1968 to thirty-seven in 1980 and, after a brief downturn in 1984, up to thirty-eight in 1988.

To a significant degree, the Republican nominating process also has been changing since 1968. In many states where Democratic-controlled legislatures have established presidential primaries for their party, the Republicans have been pushed to hold a primary as well. When southern Democrats decided they would try to maximize their influence over the party's 1988 nomination by having all their region's presidential primaries on the same day (March 8, the much-heralded Super Tuesday), Republicans—operating in the minority—were almost powerless to stop them.

The Weight of the Primaries

The effect of the proliferation of primaries cannot be understated. In 1968, when party and elected officials still controlled the nominating process, the relatively small number of primaries played little more than an advisory role in helping them make up their minds. Democratic leaders were interested to find out through the 1960 primaries, for example, that Massachusetts senator John F. Kennedy, a Roman Catholic, could win votes from religiously conservative Protestants in states like West Virginia. In 1968 former vice president Richard Nixon used the primaries to demonstrate to Republican leaders that, even though he had lost the 1960 presidential election and the 1962 gubernatorial election in California, voters did not see him as a "loser." But in both cases, party leaders decided how much weight should be attached to the verdict of the primaries.

Now that primaries dominate the nominating process, candidates spend as much time courting grass-roots party activists in Iowa and New Hampshire as they do the governor of New York or the state party chairman in California (see Table 2-1). The national party convention no longer determines the nominee; rather it serves mainly as

Table 2-1   1988 Contest Primary-Dominated

In every Democratic and Republican nominating campaign since 1972, more delegates have been chosen in primaries than in caucuses. But in 1988, the primary-caucus ratio was particularly one-sided.

Thirty-five Republican primaries (in thirty-three states plus the District of Columbia and Puerto Rico) selected more than three-fourths of the 2,277 Republican delegates to the party's national convention. That percentage included roughly 100 Republican delegates in six primary states who were selected at party conventions or state committee meetings and were not required to reflect their state's primary results.

Meanwhile, delegates elected in thirty-four Democratic primaries (thirty-two states plus the District and Puerto Rico) cast nearly two-thirds of the 4,162 votes at the Democratic National Convention. The rest of the delegates were almost equally divided between those elected in caucus states and those guaranteed delegate slots by virtue of the party or elected position that they hold, the so-called superdelegates.

Source of delegates	Delegates	Percentage of convention
Democrats		
Primaries	2,771	66.6%
Caucuses	746	17.9
Superdelegates	645	15.5
Republicans		
Primaries	1,751	76.9
Caucuses	526	23.1

a backdrop for the coronation of the candidate who emerges on top in the primaries.

Even the Democratic party's efforts to "undemocratize" the presidential nominating process by restoring, at least in part, a role for party leaders has had little effect. Beginning in 1984 the party created several hundred "superdelegate" slots for Democratic members of Congress and state party leaders. These delegates do not have to run in their state's primary or caucus and can vote for any candidate they wish. Although the superdelegates occupied roughly 15 percent of the seats at the 1984 and 1988 Democratic conventions, they did not steer the nominating contest in a direction of their own choosing. Almost unanimously, they fell in line behind the front-runner in the primaries, former vice president Walter F. Mondale in 1984 and Dukakis in 1988.

Although the ranks of participants in the nominating process are far larger than twenty years ago, those who vote in the primaries still are only a fraction of the number who cast ballots in the November presidential election. In 1988, 35 million votes were cast in the primaries—23 million on the Democratic side, 12 million on the Republican—compared to more than 91 million in the general election. Activity in the states that choose their delegates in party caucuses (caucuses, like primaries, are open to all party members but they require that participants attend a meeting rather than just pull the lever in a voting booth) probably did not involve more than 2 million additional voters. One of the characteristics of the smaller primary and caucus electorate, most analysts agree, is that the nominating process is more apt to be dominated by ideological activists—liberals in the Democratic party, conservatives in the Republican party.

The Only Strategy: Start Early

The modern nominating process frequently is described as "wide open." Many candidates can run, and it is impossible to predict with much certainty who will win.

When it comes to devising a strategy to win a party's presidential nomination, however, the modern process is anything but wide open. Candidates have no choice but to adopt nearly the same approach— start early, organize early, and try to put the opposition away before the primary season is more than a few weeks old.

In this respect, as in many others, presidential politics once was very different. As late as 1968, candidates had plenty of flexibility in deciding how to run their campaigns. They could enter the race early or late; they could run in some or all of the limited number of primaries that were held or they could skip them all. Still, it was difficult for any-one outside a small circle of established political figures to be considered seriously for president.

The sanctity of the small circle of prospective candidates and the strategic flexibility of candidates within that circle were destroyed by the reforms that followed the Democrats' 1968 convention. As power moved from party committee rooms to the grass roots, the barriers to running for president came down. Party "outsiders," George McGovern in 1972 and Jimmy Carter in 1976, proved conclusively by sweeping to the Democratic nomination that the nominating process was beyond the control of any power bloc within the party. McGovern had his base in the insurgent anti-Vietnam War wing of the party; Carter was a one-term former governor of Georgia. Neither was particularly well known when they began their campaigns.

But McGovern and Carter understood the dynamics of the revamped nominating process and, unlike their opponents, made major efforts in Iowa and New Hampshire. Both ran well in those early contests, gaining a bonanza of favorable media attention and a surge of

Figure 2-1   Presidential Primaries: More and Earlier

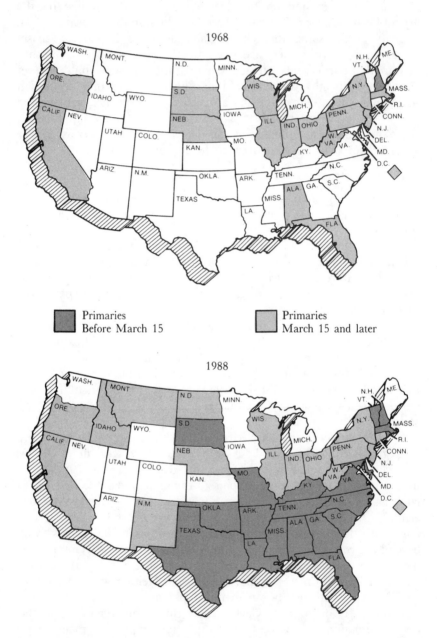

1968

Primaries
Before March 15

Primaries
March 15 and later

1988

NOTE: Both maps include "binding" primaries that selected delegates and "nonbinding" primaries that were beauty contests only. Neither Alaska nor Hawaii holds presidential primaries. South Carolina held a primary for Republicans only.

publicity, financial contributions, and organizational volunteers that carried each of them to further primary victories and, ultimately, to the nomination.

The imperative to start campaigning early is a legacy of McGovern and Carter that has come to dominate the entire process. It is an imperative that obsesses not only the candidates but also the states. In an effort to increase their influence in the nominating process, a growing number of states has moved primaries and caucuses to dates near the beginning of the delegate-selection season. In 1968 only New Hampshire held its primary before the middle of March; in 1984, seven states did, and in 1988 there were twenty. Add another ten or so caucus states—including Iowa—that held their events by mid-March 1988 and it is easy to see why candidates in 1988 were gearing up earlier than ever (see Figure 2-1).

The Nominating Process: An Overview

Although the nominating process has continued to evolve during the last twenty years, some basic patterns have developed that give it an unmistakable five-stage structure.

The first stage is the "exhibition season," the period that lasts from the day after a general election to the start of primary and caucus action more than three years later. The exhibition season is a time for potential candidates to test the political waters, raise money, and begin to organize their campaigns around the country, wooing important individuals and interest groups and honing basic campaign themes.

The second stage is the "media fishbowl," in which the voters finally get involved and those in Iowa and New Hampshire begin to winnow the field of candidates. Third is Super Tuesday, the crowded day of primaries and caucuses in early March for which only the best-financed candidates can prepare adequately. The fourth stage of the nominating process is the "mop-up" stage, the spring primaries in which each party's nomination is clinched. Whether the mop-up stage concludes in harmony or bitterness may affect the nominee's chances in the general election.

The fifth and final stage is the "convention" stage, the month or more after the primary season ends in early June, when attention shifts to discussions of the party platform and the party's nominating rules for the next campaign, as well as to the choice of vice president. Culminating the fifth stage—and the nominating process—is the convention itself, the four-day summer gathering of politicians and media from around the country at which nominations are ratified and the party tries to show its most attractive face to the world.

The Exhibition Season

During the long exhibition season candidates can exert the most control over their destiny. The exhibition season is a building and testing period, in which candidates are free to fashion campaign themes and to discover which constituencies are receptive to their appeals.

The candidates are not entirely free, however: they must spend much of their time raising money in the relatively small amounts permitted by the Federal Election Campaign Act (FECA). Prior to the passage of the FECA in 1974, well-connected candidates could raise campaign funds quickly by tapping a handful of large contributors. The current system slows down the fund-raising process by placing a $1,000 limit on individual contributions and a $5,000 limit on contributions from political action committees (PACs). The FECA also allows only individual contributions of $250 or less to be matched by public funds. Indeed, even candidates who do not participate in the public financing system still are bound by the FECA's contribution limits.

Two kinds of candidates have special advantages when it comes to raising money for the campaign—those with national stature and those who can compensate for the absence of such stature through their access to a lucrative fund-raising constituency. In 1988 Republicans Robert Dole of Kansas, the Senate minority leader, and Vice President Bush clearly had national stature and were able to raise all the money the law allowed. Although they were not well known nationally (at least not in political circles), Dukakis and the Reverend Pat Robertson were nearly as successful as Bush and Dole in early fund raising. Robertson, for many years the host of "The 700 Club" on television, tapped into the fundamentalist Christian community in his quest for the Republican nomination, and Dukakis was able to exploit his Greek heritage and his status as the sitting governor of a populous state. Dukakis drew a rich lode of financial support from his fellow Greek-Americans around the country and from residents of Massachusetts and those who did business with the state.[2]

As the exhibition season neared its close at the end of 1987, Bush ($18.1 million), Robertson ($14.2 million), Dole ($13.2 million) and Dukakis ($10.2 million) were the front-runners in collecting individual campaign contributions, much of which the federal government would match under the FECA.[3] As a result, when the voting in the early primaries and caucuses began, they were free to campaign full time while their rivals still were hunting for money. In addition, they were financially in position to compete in more of the myriad early primaries and caucuses than their rivals.

Jockeying for Position. The exhibition season is about more than money; it is also the time for candidates to woo the support of interest groups that can provide their campaigns with organizational muscle. In recent years, Democratic candidates have sought the support of the AFL-CIO, the National Education Association (NEA), the National Organization for Women (NOW), and other liberal groups that can provide a campaign with active support at the grass roots. In 1988, however, Republican presidential candidates matched the Democrats at the interest group game, making stops at numberless meetings of conservative organizations in quest of the grass-roots help their activist members could provide.

As Mondale discovered in 1984, too close an identification with interest groups can be a mixed blessing. Support from the AFL-CIO, the NEA, and NOW was a boon to Mondale in caucus states, where turnout is traditionally low and a candidate's organizational strength is crucial. But the interest group endorsements also enabled Mondale's rivals to label him the "special interest" candidate, a charge that particularly hurt him in primaries that took place outside the heavily unionized, industrial Northeast and Midwest.

In 1988 Democratic candidates were more coy than Mondale had been. They solicited the help of interest group activists, but avoided making a full-court press for the public endorsements of their national organizations.

The Early Bench Marks. The bench marks of candidate success during the exhibition season are campaign fund-raising reports, public opinion polls, straw votes at state party gatherings, and, in 1988, press reviews of the candidates' performances in the plethora of debates that dotted the preprimary calendar.

These early bench marks are the less-than-perfect harbingers of what will happen in the primaries and caucuses that follow. Success at meeting some of the challenges of the exhibition season is difficult to quantify—notably, the building of organizations that can turn out the vote in Iowa and New Hampshire and the development of campaign themes that can appeal to the voters there. The quantifiable bench marks are sometimes irrelevant by the time the voting actually takes place.

Polls taken before the presidential election year rarely reflect much more than "name identification," the share of the voters who have heard of each candidate. Straw votes at state party gatherings reveal the preferences of only the most dedicated political activists. Fund-raising problems during the exhibition season are not always insurmountable—they often will disappear if the candidate wins an early primary or caucus.

Still, even well-constructed campaigns can find it difficult to survive without some success in the widely monitored early bench marks. Candidates who are not receiving favorable debate reviews or who are not among the leaders in public opinion surveys must survive the scarcity of media attention and volunteer help needed to succeed. Without a cadre of talented and hard-working supporters in the early primary or caucus states, some candidates are essentially out of the race before the first vote is cast.

The Media Fishbowl

The exhibition season is a model of order and decorum compared to the topsy-turvy media fishbowl stage of the presidential nominating contest that follows. For long-shot candidates, this turbulent period is the one remaining chance to make a breakthrough and emerge as a serious contender. To the front-runner, the media fishbowl offers the opportunity for an early knockout and a quick finish to the campaign.

The delegate-selection contests that are most closely watched during the media fishbowl stage are in Iowa and New Hampshire. These two states have had competition for the coveted lead-off spot in recent years: in 1988 Republican caucuses in Michigan, Hawaii, and Kansas were held before the February 8 precinct caucuses in Iowa. (Michigan Republicans, hoping to grab the media spotlight from Iowa, actually began their caucuses in 1986!) But the early Republican events were conducted in a confusing fashion and received scant attention.

It is during the media fishbowl stage when the electronic and print media probably have their greatest influence. Their interpretations of who won and who lost various delegate-selection contests help to winnow the field of candidates. Low vote totals are fatal; but the media can describe even candidates who run fairly well as losers if they do not do as well as they were expected to do. Conversely, a candidate who does not win, but does better than expected, is likely to be portrayed as a winner.

Robertson, for example, received reams of favorable media attention when he finished second in the Iowa caucuses with 25 percent of the vote simply because no one expected him to do that well. But the media generally regarded Illinois senator Paul Simon's second-place finish on the Democratic side, with 27 percent of the caucus tally, as a loss because he had been given a fair chance of winning before the vote. Poor media reviews, damaging enough in their own right, also can mean dwindling finances if they discourage potential contributors, which in turn can force a candidate to fold the campaign within days of the Iowa vote.

In every recent presidential nominating campaign, the requirements for success in the media fishbowl have been the same: a candidate must "win, place, or show" in Iowa and New Hampshire. Since 1976 every Democratic and Republican nominee has won at least one of the two states and finished no lower than third in the other. McGovern, the Democratic nominee in 1972, was widely perceived to have been the winner in Iowa and New Hampshire: even though he lost both states to the early front-runner, Maine senator Edmund S. Muskie, he ran much stronger (and Muskie much less strong) than had been expected.

Many Democrats complain that Iowa and New Hampshire are inappropiate places for their party to start its nominating process. Both are wildly unrepresentative of the party and the nation—neither has big cities or a sizable minority population, and they nearly always vote for Republican presidential candidates in the general election. (Iowa has voted Republican in eight, and New Hampshire in nine, of the last ten presidential elections.) Moreover, in Iowa and New Hampshire relatively small numbers of voters have an enormous effect on the nominating process. In Iowa, roughly 235,000 voters turned out for the Democratic and Republican caucuses in 1988, and about 280,000 voters participated in the Democratic and Republican primaries in New Hampshire. In comparison, more than 5 million voters participated in the California primary on June 7, but they had little influence on the nominating process because both parties' contests already had been settled by then.

Still, many in the political community regard Iowa and New Hampshire's small populations as a virtue rather than a vice. Because both states can permit a candidate to overcome low name identification and limited financing with personal effort and an effective organization, they have carved out reputations as launching pads for long-shot candidates. New Hampshire, in particular, lacks strong interest groups such as labor, which can skew the race to the candidate they support. Finally, Iowa and New Hampshire test the candidates' ability to compete in two totally different systems of delegate selection—the small-turnout world of the Iowa caucuses, where the key to success is either a passionate message or a superior organization, and the proportionately larger-turnout world of the New Hampshire primary, where a candidate must demonstrate broad acceptability among a wider range of voters.[4]

Super Tuesday

The big prize for the winner in Iowa or New Hampshire is not delegates, but momentum. A win in Iowa provides a candidate with a boost in New Hampshire, and a win in New Hampshire can boost a candidate in the states that immediately follow. One of the big questions in 1988, however, was what would happen to this momentum once it hit Super Tuesday on March 8, only three weeks after the New Hampshire primary.

Super Tuesday was not wholly a 1988 phenomenon. A small-scale southern primary took place in early 1980 and 1984 that involved three states—Alabama, Florida, and Georgia. But weary of taking a back seat to the early media fishbowl events and of being saddled with northern liberal presidential nominees who seemed to be a drag on the ticket, Democratic state legislators across the South expanded the event to include almost every state in the region. A few states in other regions joined in, with primaries in Massachusetts and Rhode Island and caucuses in several western states.

No one was quite sure what the effect of Super Tuesday would be. Many southerners hoped that it not only would force candidates to come to the South and "talk southern," but also that it would reduce the Iowa and New Hampshire events to the status of small-scale warm-up acts. Others argued that Super Tuesday could just as easily enhance the influence of Iowa and New Hampshire. A burst of momentum based on a victory in one of those two states, critics suggested, could enable the winners to sweep through the vast block of states that were voting on March 8.

Which prediction was right? In a sense, both were. On the Republican side, Vice President Bush, who had rebounded from an Iowa loss to win New Hampshire, swept the South on Super Tuesday and essentially wrapped up the nomination. But the Democratic race became more muddled. The two candidates with southern ties—Tennessee senator Albert Gore, Jr., among white voters, and Jackson mainly among blacks—emerged with strong showings on Super Tuesday that enabled them to challenge Rep. Richard A. Gephardt, D-Mo., and Dukakis, the winners in Iowa and New Hampshire, respectively.

The Mop-up Stage

In recent elections, the last twelve weeks of the primary season often have been anticlimactic. The period from mid-March to early June is the mop-up stage of the nominating contest: the front-runner concentrates on the gradual accumulation of enough delegates to make a nominating majority, and the other surviving candidates try desperately to catch the front-runner.

In the not-too-distant past, the situation was entirely different. The spring solstice was the beginning, not the end, of the nominating process. In 1968, for example, Sen. Robert F. Kennedy of New York entered the Democratic presidential contest in mid-March in the wake of Minnesota senator Eugene J. McCarthy's strong showing against President Johnson in the New Hampshire primary. The eventual nominee in 1968, Hubert Humphrey, entered the race more than a month later.

But a late start no longer is feasible, partly because the FECA now makes it so difficult to raise money quickly and partly because there are not as many delegate-winning opportunities available for a candidate who starts late. Almost half the states had voted by mid-March 1988, and filing deadlines had passed in a number of the later-voting states, including delegate-rich New York and Pennsylvania.

Even for those who already are in the race, recovery from early defeats is difficult. Theoretically, a candidate could make a comeback after Super Tuesday. A number of populous states have yet to vote. In addition to New York and Pennsylvania, these include Illinois, Ohio, New Jersey, and California. To "backload" the process further, Democrats in 1988 moved the selection date of their roughly three hundred congressional superdelegates from a week before the Iowa caucuses to April 19-20. Still, no candidate in recent years has mounted a successful comeback during the mop-up period. Since 1976 the candidate who had amassed the most delegates by mid-March has won the party's nomination. Both major party candidates continued this pattern in 1988.

The mop-up stage poses challenges even to the front-runner, however. Not the least of these is money. The public financing system establishes state and national spending limits. The individual state limits are of little concern after the media fishbowl stage because only in Iowa and New Hampshire do candidates usually spend close to the maximum allowable amount. But the national limit—nearly $27.7 million in 1988—may be a problem, especially for the early leader who spent heavily in the exhibition season to organize nationally.[5] Indeed, a challenger who did not spend money early because the money was not available may now be able to outspend the front-runner in the closing primaries.

By itself, a monetary disadvantage is not fatal to the front-runner in the mop-up stage or afterward. The front-runner who continues to receive favorable media treatment need not depend on spending large sums of money. For example, Jackson outspent Dukakis by $1.5 million to $1.2 million in the largest of the late primary states in 1988—Pennsylvania (April 26), Ohio (May 3), and California and New Jersey (June 7). But Dukakis easily won all four events.[6]

Although the nominee may be all but chosen when the mop-up stage begins, the way the race ends can be important in the November general election. Front-runners—and most party leaders—want the nominating contest to end quickly and without acrimony so that the competing forces will have time to mend fences and the victor will have time to develop a strategy for the general election. The longer the battle for the nomination drags on, the less chance the party has to win.

The mop-up stage also can be crucial to the long-term political future of the runner-up. It is important to finish respectably enough to remain a major player on the national scene. Bush did that in 1980, defeating Ronald Reagan in several late primaries, including Pennsylvania and Michigan. Bush's late spurt helped to earn him the vice-presidential nomination.

On to the Convention

Even if the nominating *contest* is effectively over by the end of the primary season in early June, the nominating *process* is not. If the race has been bitter, the losing side may mount a last-ditch fight at the convention over issues such as the delegates' credentials—as McGovern's foes did in 1972—or convention rules—as Reagan did against President Gerald R. Ford in 1976 and Sen. Edward M. Kennedy of Massachusetts did against President Carter in 1980. But whether the political hatchets from the primaries and caucuses have been buried, the period leading up to the conventions is also the opening round of the fall campaign. The front-runner's decisions no longer are geared toward nomination, but toward election.

The preconvention period is concerned with image, issues, and strategy: image, in terms of how the front-runner is mending fences with the defeated rivals, especially the concessions that may have to be made as the price of a united party; issues, as the views of the nominee and the other candidates are reflected in the party platform; and strategy, as shown in the nominee's choice of a vice-presidential running mate. Because a front-runner usually selects someone who will buttress the ticket's support in a state or constituency group where the presidential nominee's own appeal is weak, the vice-presidential selection can be the first real clue to the fall campaign strategy.

Different Playing Fields

Democratic and Republican candidates play basically under the same rules when it comes to the calendar of primaries and caucuses and the campaign finance laws that regulate fund raising and spending. But the two parties' candidates are on different playing fields when it comes to winning delegates. The Republican party allows a winner-take-all system of delegate selection in its various state primaries and caucuses; the Democratic party is more oriented to proportional representation, with the delegates divided to reflect each candidate's share of the primary or caucus vote. The result is that a Republican candidate who registers a string of early successes in the media fishbowl and Super Tuesday states, as Bush did in 1988, is more apt to score a quick knockout than a Democratic candidate who gets off to a similarly fast start.

On Super Tuesday alone, Bush won every delegate at stake in six southern primary states, including those in the two most populous, Texas and Florida. In contrast, virtually every Democratic delegate chosen that day was allocated on the basis of proportional representation, further delaying the emergence of a clear winner on the Democratic side. Subsequent Democratic primaries in Illinois, Pennsylvania, and New Jersey were modified winner-take-all contests that offered the victorious candidate the chance to reap a large windfall of delegates. But those states stood virtually alone as exceptions to the Democratic rule of proportional representation.

The System in Action: The Republicans

From the very beginning, the 1988 Republican nominating contest was Bush's to lose. He had enlisted more big-name support within the party, raised more money, and built more of a national organization than any of his competitors. In addition, nearly every national poll showed Bush with a significant lead over Dole, while the rest of the Republican field trailed far behind.

It also was to Bush's advantage that the 1988 Republican race was rather mundane, at least compared to the party's great ideological fights of the past. The pivotal Republican nominating contests of 1952 (Ohio senator Robert A. Taft versus Gen. Dwight D. Eisenhower), 1964 (Arizona senator Barry M. Goldwater versus New York governor Nelson A. Rockefeller) and 1976 (Reagan versus Ford) were ideologically driven, the insurgents against the establishment. But in 1988 no strong insurgent wing was at work within the Republican party. Factions existed, but they lacked effective champions. Rep. Jack F. Kemp of New York and former Delaware governor Pierre S. "Pete" du Pont IV sought to lead "movement" conservatives, but they lacked the stature of Goldwater or Reagan. Robertson tried to mobilize the religious Right, but the size of that bloc, as well as its sentiments, was quite unclear; virtually every other candidate drew some support from religious conservatives. Finally, no prominent moderate Republican stepped forward to lead the faction that once had dominated the Republican party.

Dole, to be sure, was a threat to Bush, but Dole's differences with the vice president centered on background and personality, not ideology. As a result, the core message of both campaigns emphasized the candidates' managerial and leadership skills, not any sharply defined ideological differences.

As vice president, Bush enjoyed one enormous asset that Dole lacked—a close identification with President Reagan, who was still widely popular among Republicans as his second term wound down. The Reagan connection enabled Bush to reach out to the Republican Right, which had viewed him with suspicion since he ran against Reagan for the presidential nomination in 1980.

Trouble in the Media Fishbowl

Despite all his advantages, Bush quickly ran into trouble. He barely survived a complicated and confusing lead-off contest in Michigan by breaking up a coalition between Kemp and Robertson forces and forging his own alliance with Kemp. On February 8, the vice president suffered a major defeat in Iowa, where the final tally read 37 percent for Dole, 25 percent for Robertson, and 19 percent for Bush.

Bush, whose connection with Reagan was a liability in a state that largely opposed the administration's controversial farm policies, had expected to finish behind Dole. Dole, after all, represented nearby Kansas in the Senate, which enabled him to campaign with the slogan, "I'm one of you." But finishing behind Robertson was a surprise, particularly in a state that Bush had won in 1980. Robertson's "invisible army" of conservative evangelical Christians was strongest in Democratic areas of Iowa where there was a low Republican turnout; Dole won elsewhere, while Bush found no base at all. Of Iowa's ninety-nine counties, the vice president failed to carry a single one, and he emerged from the caucuses desperately searching for a constituency.

Bush found not just a constituency, but a broad one in New Hampshire, which probably saved his candidacy. Early polls had shown the vice president with a large lead in the first primary state, but once he lost Iowa, his edge quickly eroded. Bush moved on a number of fronts to recover. The aloof, front-running campaign style of Iowa was replaced with a more personable, down-home manner. He ran negative ads blasting Dole as a closet proponent of increased taxes, and Gov. John H. Sununu staked his prestige on Bush's behalf. But Bush's greatest advantage was that he now was running in a nonfarm state where the Reagan connection was an advantage. On February 16 he swamped Dole, 38 to 28 percent, carrying virtually every constituency group in the state (see Table 2-2).

Nearly everything that happened the night of the New Hampshire primary worked to Bush's advantage. Making a live split-screen appearance with the vice president on NBC, Dole reminded voters of

Table 2-2 1988 Republican Primary Results

State	Turnout	Bush	Dole	Robertson	Kemp	Others	Uncom- mitted
N.H. (2/16)	157,644	37.6%*	28.4%	9.4%	12.8%	11.8%	x
S.D. (2/23)	93,405	18.6	55.2*	19.6	4.6	0.6	1.3%
Vt. (3/1)	47,832	49.3*	39.0	5.1	3.9	2.7	x
S.C. (3/5)	195,292	48.5*	20.6	19.1	11.5	0.3	x
Ala. (3/8)	213,561	64.5*	16.3	13.9	4.9	0.3	x
Ark. (3/8)	68,305	47.0*	25.9	18.9	5.1	1.0	2.1
Fla. (3/8)	901,222	62.1*	21.2	10.6	4.6	1.4	x
Ga. (3/8)	400,928	53.8*	23.6	16.3	5.8	0.5	x
Ky. (3/8)	121,402	59.3*	23.0	11.1	3.3	1.4	1.8
La. (3/8)	144,781	57.8*	17.7	18.2	5.3	1.0	x
Md. (3/8)	200,754	53.3*	32.4	6.4	5.9	2.0	x
Mass. (3/8)	241,181	58.5*	26.3	4.5	7.0	2.3	1.4
Miss. (3/8)	158,526	66.1*	16.9	13.5	3.5	x	x
Mo. (3/8)	400,300	42.2*	41.1	11.2	3.5	0.7	1.4
N.C. (3/8)	273,801	45.4*	39.1	9.8	4.1	0.5	1.0
Okla. (3/8)	208,938	37.4*	34.9	21.1	5.5	1.0	x
R.I. (3/8)	16,035	64.9*	22.6	5.7	4.9	0.8	1.1
Tenn. (3/8)	254,252	60.0*	21.6	12.6	4.3	0.6	0.9
Texas (3/8)	1,014,956	63.9*	13.9	15.3	5.0	0.7	1.2
Va. (3/8)	234,142	53.3*	26.0	13.7	4.6[a]	0.8	1.6
Ill. (3/15)	858,637	54.6*	36.0	6.8	1.5	1.0	x
P.R. (3/20)	3,973	97.1*	2.7	0.1	x	0.1	x
Conn. (3/29)	104,171	70.6*	20.2[b]	3.1	3.1	x	3.1
Wis. (4/5)	359,294	82.2*	7.9	6.9	1.4	1.0	0.7
Pa. (4/26)	870,549	79.0*	11.9	9.1	x	x	x
D.C. (5/3)	6,720	87.6*	7.0	4.0	x	1.4	x
Ind. (5/3)	437,655	80.4*	9.8	6.6	3.3	x	x
Ohio (5/3)	794,904	81.0*	11.9	7.1	x	x	x
Neb. (5/10)	204,049	68.0*	22.3	5.1	4.1	0.5	x
W.Va. (5/10)	143,140	77.3*	10.9	7.3[c]	2.7	1.8	x
Ore. (5/17)	274,486	72.8*	17.9	7.7	x	1.5	x
Idaho (5/24)	68,275	81.2*	x	8.6	x	x	10.2
Calif. (6/7)	2,240,387	82.9*	12.9	4.2	x	x	x
Mont. (6/7)	86,380	73.0*	19.4	x	x	x	7.5
N.J. (6/7)	241,033	100.0*	x	x	x	x	x
N.M. (6/7)	88,744	78.2*	10.5	6.0	x	2.4	2.9
N.D. (6/14)	39,434	94.0*	x	x	x	6.0	x
National Total	12,169,088	67.9*	19.2	9.0	2.7	0.7	0.5

[a] Kemp withdrew from the race March 10.

[b] Dole withdrew from the race March 29.

[c] Robertson suspended his campaign May 16.

NOTE: Results are based on official returns. An "x" indicates that the candidate or uncommitted line was not listed on the ballot. Republicans did not hold a preference vote in New York; the April 19 primary was for election of delegates only. An asterisk (*) indicates the winner.

his "hatchet man" image by tartly telling Bush to "stop lying about my record." Meanwhile, Robertson flunked his first test with voters in a broadly based primary electorate, finishing fifth, and none of the other contenders did well enough to gain momentum from the results.

A week later, Dole scored his last victories of the campaign in two other farm states, South Dakota and Minnesota, but these were barely noticed. After New Hampshire, political attention turned to the South, where Bush had both an organization in place and Reagan's popularity to rely on.

Super Tuesday Knockout

The tone for the March 8 Super Tuesday vote was set on Saturday, March 5, when South Carolina Republicans held the second presidential primary in the state party's history. Reagan had won the first in 1980, overwhelming Bush and former Texas governor John B. Connally and setting the stage for a Reagan sweep of a trio of southern primaries three days later.

In 1988—aided by his association with Reagan, as well as by momentum gained in New Hampshire and the support of Gov. Carroll A. Campbell, Jr.—it was Bush's turn to win in South Carolina. Although Dole, Robertson, and Kemp all made major efforts in a bid to slow Bush down before Super Tuesday, the vice president won nearly half the vote, while his closest rival, Dole, received barely 20 percent.

The rest of the South proved easy pickings for Bush. It was the region where Reagan had run best in the 1984 general election and where he still recorded his highest presidential approval scores among voters. Bush had effectively organized the South to muster the normally small Republican primary vote. The delegate harvest he reaped on Super Tuesday—Bush won sixteen states to one for Robertson (the Washington State caucuses) and none for Dole—gave the vice president such a commanding lead that the Republican race was essentially over. According to the Associated Press, Bush finished Super Tuesday with 704 of the 1,139 delegates needed to nominate; Dole had 164; Kemp, 39; and Robertson, 17.

Ironically, Dole's main problem in the South was the same one Bush had faced in 1980: conservatives dominate the region's Republican party. Just as Bush had been seen as the moderate alternative to the conservative Reagan in 1980, Dole was widely perceived as the moderate alternative to Bush in 1988. In the South, that did not win Dole many votes. He lost all but five primaries on Super Tuesday by a margin of at least 2-to-1, and in only three states—Missouri, North Carolina, and Oklahoma—was he able to finish within ten percentage points of Bush. North Carolina was the home of Dole's wife, Elizabeth, one-time secretary of transportation, who was widely considered one of his major assets as a candidate. Missouri and Oklahoma border Dole's home state of Kansas, and in both Dole ran best in the counties nearest to Kansas.

For his part, Robertson was unable to win even a majority of the votes cast by white fundamentalists or evangelical Christians.[7] Robertson was hurt by a number of problems, which ranged from fellow televangelist Jimmy Swaggart's admission in late February that he had visited prostitutes to controversies stirred by Robertson's own actions. Robertson's assertion at a New Hampshire debate that there were Soviet missiles in Cuba was bluntly denied by the Reagan administration. And his decision to drop a libel suit against former Republican representative Paul N. McCloskey, Jr., of California—who charged that Robertson had bragged of being spared combat duty in the Korean War through the intercession of his father, Sen. A. Willis Robertson of Virginia—left the impression with many voters that Robertson was no fighter. He did not come close to winning any southern primaries and finished second in only two, Texas and Louisiana. Robertson's delegate count for the day, once expected to be in the hundreds, was instead in single digits. He remained a candidate until May, but served more as a nuisance to Bush than a threat.

Kemp fared even worse than Robertson. His hopes of energizing his campaign evaporated with a fourth-place finish in South Carolina. On March 8 Kemp's share of the vote hovered around 5 percent in every state. Two days later, he bowed out of the race, joining du Pont and former general Alexander M. Haig, Jr., on the sidelines.

Dole's withdrawal soon followed. He had hoped to slow Bush's momentum in the March 15 Illinois primary, but the "I'm one of you" theme that had worked so well in Iowa was muted in more heavily industrial Illinois. Dole also suffered from the "loser" image his succession of primary defeats had earned him and from Gov. James R. Thompson's open support for the high-flying Bush. The vice president won the Illinois primary by nearly twenty percentage points, and two weeks later Dole left the race. On April 26 in the Pennsylvania primary, Bush won the delegates needed to seal the nomination formally.

In a sense, Bush may have been almost too effective in dispatching his opposition. After locking up the Republican nomination, he fell out of the national headlines. Meanwhile, on the Democratic side, Dukakis was putting together a string of primary victories over Jackson. Polls showed Dukakis moving into a lead over Bush that the Democrat did not relinquish until the Republican convention in August.

Still, Bush had wrapped up the nomination in convincing fashion

Table 2-3   1988 Republican Primary Vote

Vice President George Bush recovered quickly from his loss in the February 8 Iowa caucuses to dominate voting in the primaries that followed. His win in New Hampshire a week later reestablished him as the front-runner in the Republican race; his sweep of the Super Tuesday primaries March 8 essentially erased any doubt that he would be the nominee.

The chart below breaks down the Republican primary voting by time period and by region. The megastate vote is based on primary returns from California, Florida, Illinois, New Jersey, Ohio, Pennsylvania, and Texas; the Republican primary in New York was for delegates only, while Michigan held a caucus. Totals in the chart are based on official returns.

	Turnout	Bush	Dole	Robertson	Kemp
Total	12,169,088	68%*	19%	9%	3%
Time periods					
Pre-Super Tuesday	494,173	39*	31	15	10
Super Tuesday	4,853,084	57*	24	13	5
Post-Super Tuesday	6,821,831	78*	15	6	1
Regions					
East	2,029,059	72*	17	7	3
Midwest	3,187,678	67*	23	8	2
South	4,190,106	58*	21	14	5
West	2,758,272	81*	13	5	0
Territories	3,973	97*	3	0	0
Megastates	6,921,688	74*	16	8	2

NOTE: An asterisk (*) indicates the winner.

(see Table 2-3). His only stumble was in the farm states, and the only big question mark about his candidacy was whether he would be as appealing to general election voters as he had been to the Republicans who turned out in the primaries.

The System in Action: The Democrats

The race for the Democratic presidential nomination in 1988 underscored an obvious fact about the nominating process—who wins depends on who runs. Three of the Democrats' best prospects stayed on the sidelines—Gov. Mario M. Cuomo of New York, Sen. Sam Nunn of Georgia, and Senator Kennedy. Each cited a variety of reasons for not running. Kennedy and Nunn pointed to their work in the Senate—Kennedy as chair of the Judiciary Committee, Nunn as the head of Armed Services. Cuomo mentioned the disruption of family life that a presidential campaign would cause and the difficulty of governing his state while running for president.

Left unspoken by all three was that the modern nominating process—long, tiring, and studded with primaries and caucuses—is geared as much to an aspiring dark horse with little to lose as it is to a prominent public officeholder who must balance official responsibilities with frequent campaign appearances in the hamlets of Iowa, New Hampshire, and elsewhere.

The Exhibition Season: Hold Outs and Drop Outs

Without Cuomo, Kennedy, and Nunn in the race, the role of Democratic front-runner fell to Gary Hart, the former senator from Colorado. Hart had nearly won the nomination in 1984, when a surprising string of early caucus and primary victories carried him from dark-horse status to within a whisker of the party's nomination. Even after his momentum slackened on Super Tuesday, Hart doggedly pursued Walter Mondale through the mop-up stage of the primary season and finished with a flourish by posting a big victory in California. Altogether, Hart won more than 1,200 delegates in 1984, almost one-third of the convention total.

Initially, the main question about Hart in 1988 was whether he could succeed as a front-runner. As McGovern's campaign manager in 1972 and as a candidate in 1984, Hart had seemed most comfortable in the role of a political insurgent who relied on anti-establishment themes to win votes. Intent on being the Democratic nominee in 1988, however, he began to open lines of communication to traditional elements in the party that had opposed him in the past. For example, Hart made overtures to organized labor, which had resented his 1984 criticism of Mondale as a captive of special interests. And he released a host of major policy statements to forestall any recurrence of Mondale's taunt from the previous campaign: "Where's the beef?"

Still, Hart was a shaky front-runner when he announced his candidacy on April 13, 1987. He was beset by angry creditors, who complained that he was lackadaisical in paying off 1984 campaign debts that still totaled more than $1 million. And he faced continuing doubts about his personal character. In 1984 Hart's momentum had been slowed after his victory in the New Hampshire primary when it was revealed that he had changed his name (from Hartpence), age (to appear a year younger), and even the handwriting in his signature.

Hart opened another area of his personal life to scrutiny shortly after his announcement, when he complained of being the victim of rumors that he was a womanizer and challenged reporters to follow him and see for themselves how he really lived. Within days, the *Miami Herald* had a story based on its reporters' surveillance of Hart's

Washington, D.C., town house. The *Herald* reported on May 3 that Hart had hosted Donna Rice, a twenty-nine-year-old model and actress over the weekend while his wife, Lee, was in Colorado.

The *Herald* story sent shockwaves through the Democratic campaign. Hart protested that he was the victim of inaccurate reporting, maintained that he had done nothing immoral and challenged the paper's ethics in publishing the story without interviewing all the parties involved. Nonetheless, Hart's campaign quickly unraveled. Informed that additional damaging stories about his personal life were about to be published, Hart quit the race May 8, 1987.

Hart's withdrawal was not quite the end of the saga. He astonished the political community by reviving his candidacy in mid-December. But Hart's renewed effort was largely ignored by fellow Democrats, and he was treated as nothing more than a political curiosity. After failing to win a single delegate, Hart exited the race for good after Super Tuesday.

The "Seven Dwarfs"

Hart's departure left the Democratic race without a front-runner. The field of candidates consisted of a governor (Dukakis), a former governor (Bruce Babbitt of Arizona), a House member (Gephardt), three senators (Gore, Simon, and Joseph R. Biden, Jr., of Delaware), and Jesse Jackson. As a group, they became known, somewhat disparagingly, as the "seven dwarfs."

Soon there were six. Biden quit the race in September 1987, buffeted by charges that he had plagiarized the speeches of Robert Kennedy and British Labour party leader Neil Kinnock, even to the extent of falsifying events in his life history. The episode cut short a promising candidacy. At the time he shut down his campaign, Biden had raised more money than any other Democrat except Dukakis. After a slow start, he also was showing progress in the Iowa polls.

But, like Hart, Biden lacked a dedicated personal constituency to act as a safety net in his time of political crisis. Of the Democratic candidates, only Jackson had run for president before and only he had an identifiable constituency, among fellow blacks, whose support he could count on through thick and thin. The other candidates were self-starters who, lacking any wide or deep base of support, had to construct a coalition as they campaigned.

Biden's exit reflected badly on Dukakis, because it was his campaign manager, John Sasso, who had provided the media with videotaped examples of Biden's plagiarism, then lied about doing so. (Sasso resigned from the campaign.) But of the candidates who remained in the race, Dukakis was as well positioned as any to win the nomination. He had money, a positive reputation in neighboring New Hampshire, and was a more than adequate debater in a Democratic contest that featured numerous debates among the candidates.

Dukakis was especially well suited to a marathon-style nominating campaign in which there were no dominant candidates and few cutting issues. The qualities he offered were nonideological: his even temperament, independence, energy, engaged leadership, credibility on economic issues, and, as the campaign moved into the large industrial states, his ethnicity. In his call for competence, Dukakis could point to his state's economic comeback, a development he attributed to his leadership as governor and that he referred to constantly as the "Massachusetts miracle." This theme worked because the other Democratic candidates were on a basically similiar wavelength. Only Gore—and then only occasionally—used the numerous debates to draw a sharp distinction between himself and the other candidates on the issues. Gore enunciated more hawkish positions than his rivals on a handful of defense and foreign policies, including support for both the Reagan administration's 1983 invasion of Grenada and its policy, begun in late 1987, of escorting ships in the Persian Gulf.

Strategically, Gore also disagreed with the premise that Iowa would be more important than ever in 1988. He publicly wrote off the state in November 1987, claiming that the caucuses were dominated by a small band of liberal activists who were unrepresentative of Democrats nationally. Playing to his regional base, Gore decided to aim for the votes of conservative white southerners on Super Tuesday.

Iowa and New Hampshire: Regional Winners in the Media Fishbowl

Except for Gore, the Democratic candidates virtually encamped in Iowa. Gephardt was there so much, wrote the *Des Moines Register* in early 1987, that he looked "like a candidate for sheriff." [8] During the course of the campaign, Gephardt gradually honed an effective, angry-voiced populist message that emphasized his tough trade-protection bill and his farm bill, which aimed to boost agricultural prices through strict government controls on production. On caucus night, Gephardt forged a winning coalition of distressed farmers and blue-collar laborers who resented foreign competition.

But Gephardt quickly found that in 1988 Iowa did not produce the sort of momentum he needed. Past Democratic winners had headed out of Iowa at full throttle, but Gephardt's showing was neither a surprise—as Hart's second-place finish in 1984 had been—nor decisive—like Jimmy Carter's triumphs in 1976 and 1980. With 31 percent of the caucus vote, Gephardt finished narrowly ahead of Simon

(27 percent) and Dukakis (22 percent), a modest victory in a state where he had emphasized his Midwestern roots and invested heavily in time and money. Criticism of his nationalist appeals, not celebration of his victory, dominated postcaucus reporting in the media.

In New Hampshire Dukakis had the strong regional advantage. In the absence of a Gephardt surge, he took full advantage of it. Although Dukakis's victory was long assumed, he still won in impressive fashion, defeating the runner-up Gephardt, by 36 percent to 20 percent. Dukakis carried not just the bustling communities along New Hampshire's southern border, where the "Massachusetts miracle" had had its greatest effect on the local economy, but also in mill towns far to the north, where his visibility was far lower.

The voting in Iowa and New Hampshire claimed one casualty, Babbitt, and one near-casualty, Simon. Babbitt's sense of humor and unabashed call for a tax increase to cut the huge budget deficit had made him a media favorite, but he finished fifth in Iowa and sixth in New Hampshire and quit the race. Simon did much better, but failed to meet media expectations. He finished second in Iowa (where many thought he would win) and third in New Hampshire, where his goal was second.

Simon failed as a candidate because he was unable to break out of the liberal box that many Democrats believed had harmed their party's chances of winning in recent elections. Although he portrayed himself as a traditional "jobs and butter" Democrat in the Humphrey mold, his intellectual, bow-tie-and-horned-rimmed-glasses manner was much more appealing in academic communities than in blue-collar neighborhoods. After finishing fourth in the Minnesota caucuses on February 23, Simon effectively withdrew by announcing that he would skip Super Tuesday to concentrate on making a last-ditch stand in his home state of Illinois on March 15.

Although Iowa and New Hampshire got the Democratic race off to a muddled start, there were hints soon afterward that Dukakis and Jackson would be the two finalists. They ran first and second in pre-Super Tuesday voting in Minnesota, Maine, and Vermont.

Super Tuesday: The Big Split

Clarity did not come as quickly to the Democratic race as to the Republican. On March 8 Democrats displayed their penchant for noisy and crowded nominating battles with a fractured result that left the race as garbled after the vote as it had been before.

Four Democrats—Dukakis, Gephardt, Gore, and Jackson—came into Super Tuesday with their presidential ambitions still alive. All but Gephardt came out claiming to be the day's big winner. Dukakis won the most delegates and the most states, carrying eight primaries and caucuses that ranged geographically from New England to Hawaii to the "crown jewels" of the South, Texas and Florida. Jackson won the most Democratic primary votes—more than 2.5 million—and ran first in four Deep South states and in Virginia. Gore, for his part, could point to a convincing victory in his battle with Gephardt for the support of conservative white voters; they helped him to carry six states (most of the border states and Nevada), while Gephardt won only his home state of Missouri.

Despite these varied claims, there was a feast-or-famine quality to the vote each "winning" candidate received on Super Tuesday that cast doubts on his ability to broaden his base in the primary voting to come. Jackson was the candidate of the black South: he won a virtually unanimous share of the region's large black vote but less than 10 percent of the white vote.[9] Gore capitalized on his southern roots and the alliances among courthouse politicians that his most potent ally, Tennessee governor Ned McWherter, had forged over the years: Gore carried areas that were overwhelmingly white and culturally southern, but ran less well in areas that were black or ethnically diverse. Dukakis emerged as the champion of the "non-South" South, from the Research Triangle area in central North Carolina to the Hispanic barrios of Texas to the condos of south Florida. He carried the southern two-thirds of Florida and Texas, where he was able to capitalize on his ethnicity, northern roots, and ability to speak fluent Spanish. But elsewhere in the South Dukakis made little impression, failing to win even one congressional district between the Washington Beltway and the outskirts of New Orleans.

The only candidate not to find a base on Super Tuesday was Gephardt, who had come under sharp attack from Simon, Dukakis, and Gore after his Iowa win for alleged flip-flops in his voting record on issues such as the MX missile and the environment. Nor did Gephardt fare well on the nation's editorial pages, where writers wondered how a consummate Washington insider who chaired the Democratic Caucus in the House of Representatives could campaign credibly as a populist outsider. Having devoted much of his money to winning Iowa, Gephardt did not have enough in reserve to defend himself adequately.

To one degree or another, money was a problem for all the Democrats on Super Tuesday. Unlike the Republican Bush, none had the funds or organization to blanket the fourteen southern and border states that were the centerpiece of the March 8 vote. Each candidate had to target his appeals to particular areas and voting groups.

As an event, Super Tuesday was only a marginal success for its southern Democratic sponsors. The southern regional primary did not place native son Gore on the road to the nomination, nor did it thwart the ambitions of more liberal candidates like Dukakis and Jackson. Although twice as many votes were cast in the Democratic primaries as were cast in the Republican contests, less than 25 percent of the region's voting-age population bothered to vote at all. By comparison, recent presidential elections have brought between 50 and 55 percent of the voting-age population to the polls.

Mop-up I: From Fogginess to Confusion

As the Democratic contest moved north into the major states of the industrial Frost Belt, Dukakis appeared to have the inside track on the other candidates: he was heading into seemingly favorable terrain with a certain degree of momentum from Super Tuesday and, equally important, with some of the fruits of momentum, money in the bank and especially strong organization. Yet Dukakis lost two big states in a row, which raised doubts about the future of his candidacy and spurred talk within the political community of a primary season that would end with no winner. Pundits speculated that the Democrats might have the first multiballot nominating convention since 1952.

Dukakis's loss in the March 15 Illinois primary was, in truth, not a big surprise. Although he mounted a media blitz to warn of the evils of a brokered convention (the implicit result of a Simon victory), the Dukakis ads were no match for the network of supporters that Simon had built up during more than thirty years in Illinois politics. Simon won easily with 42 percent of the popular vote; Jackson, carrying Chicago on the strength of a large black turnout, had 32 percent, and Dukakis finished third with 16 percent.

Dukakis's loss to Jackson in the Michigan caucuses on March 26 was more damaging. In a state that is only 13 percent black, Jackson took 53 percent of the caucus vote, nearly twice as large a share as Dukakis received. Gephardt, who had declared Michigan a make or break state for his candidacy, finished third and withdrew from the race.

The Michigan caucuses briefly put the Democratic nominating contest into an entirely new light. For the first time, Jackson's nomination was discussed in the political community as a real possibility. Yet there were hints in the Michigan results that his victory there would be difficult to duplicate in the large northern primary states to follow, namely, Wisconsin, New York, Pennsylvania, and Ohio. Jackson had rolled up his margin of victory in Michigan in areas where the voters were economically pinched—predominantly black, inner-city Detroit and hard-hit communities like Flint and Battle Creek. Unemployment rates there were still in double digits, something not common in other parts of the region.

What is more, Michigan was the only one of the nation's ten most populous states to hold a caucus instead of a primary in 1988. Because caucus turnouts are traditionally very low (only 3 percent of the voting-age population participated in the Michigan Democratic caucuses), the candidate who inspires the most intense support usually is the most successful. In Michigan, that candidate was Jackson, as it was in Alaska and Vermont, states with few blacks whose caucuses he also won. But Jackson's performance in the higher turnout primaries was closely related to the racial composition of the electorate. Except for the District of Columbia and Puerto Rico, Jackson's primary victories in 1988 came exclusively in the South, and never in a state with a population less than 19 percent black.

Mop-up II: Dukakis's Breakaway

As Jackson moved on to Wisconsin, he was fighting not only his Democratic rivals, but also the high expectations spawned by his victory in Michigan. Jackson had thrived as a "protest candidate" through whom voters could "send a message." But with his win in Michigan, he came under the intense media scrutiny that is accorded a potential president of the United States. On the eve of the April 5 Wisconsin vote, Jackson found himself being criticized on editorial pages across the country for having sent a letter to the embattled Panamanian general, Manuel Antonio Noriega, which some interpreted as an interference in American foreign policy.

Against the new critical backdrop, some of Jackson's potential supporters in Wisconsin backed away. Meanwhile, the low-key Dukakis was increasing the voltage of his attacks on the "human legacy" of the Reagan years and stepping up his grass-roots campaigning, especially among students and blue-collar workers. On primary day, a lopsided share of the late deciding voters cast their ballots for Dukakis, and the Massachusetts governor swept all but one of Wisconsin's seventy-two counties en route to a decisive 48 percent to 28 percent win over Jackson.

Wisconsin was a high-stakes contest for Dukakis. Already shaken by the losses in Illinois and Michigan, his campaign might have begun to unravel with another defeat. But with the victory, Dukakis regained the look of a winner. The delegate count was still close: Dukakis, 741 and Jackson, 705, according to a post-Wisconsin tally by the Associated Press. But Dukakis's victory had shifted the pressure to Jackson to win the next major primary in New York.

With its substantial numbers of blacks and liberals, the twin cornerstones of his political success, New York was about as favorable terrain as Jackson would find in the remaining primaries. Of all the large states, Jackson had run best in New York in 1984, where he took 26 percent of the primary vote against Mondale and Hart.

Still, New York posed problems for the Jackson campaign. The Jewish vote, which Dukakis had won in Florida, accounted for one-fourth of the Democratic primary turnout. The Hispanic vote, which Dukakis had won in Florida and Texas, was another 5 percent to 10 percent. And in Wisconsin, Dukakis had won easily in the suburbs, industrial centers, and rural areas, all of which were important components of the Democratic electorate in New York.

To win New York, Jackson needed someone to take a large chunk of the white vote that might otherwise go to Dukakis. But Simon already had suspended his campaign after a distant fourth-place finish in Wisconsin, and Gore's campaign was not in much healthier condition. Although he was adequately financed, Gore lacked a coherent message. In the South, Gore's theme had been a stronger national defense; in Wisconsin, he called for higher dairy price supports; in New York, he campaigned as an adamant defender of Israel's get-tough policy with the Palestinians.

An endorsement from New York City's outspoken Democratic mayor, Ed Koch, backfired for Gore. Koch said that any Jew would be crazy to vote for Jackson (who had called New York City "Hymie-town" in 1984), then claimed that Jackson was a liar who would bankrupt the nation if he were elected president. Koch's vitriolic comments helped to keep the city's disparate voting blocs polarized.

As primary day approached, Koch's brickbats were increasingly viewed as verbal overkill. When the voting took place on April 19, the order of finish within multi-ethnic New York City was Jackson narrowly ahead of Dukakis and Gore a weak third. Statewide, however, Dukakis was far ahead, with 51 percent to 37 percent for Jackson and 10 percent for Gore. Within days, Gore quit the race. Forced to run one-on-one against Dukakis in the remaining primaries, Jackson's last real hope of winning the nomination had passed.

Mop-up III: Dukakis Wins

The death knell for Jackson's candidacy was sounded the following week in the steel country of western Pennsylvania, a region dotted with closed factories and displaced workers. The severe economic conditions provided a suitable backdrop for Jackson's populist message. But western Pennsylvania is also a region of ethnic lodges, veterans' organizations, old-style machine politics, and conservative racial views. When the primary ballots were cast on April 26, Dukakis swept many of the "steel counties" with more than 80 percent of the vote.

After winning Pennsylvania, it was not difficult for Dukakis to lock up the Democratic nomination. He won eleven of the last twelve primaries, losing only in the heavily black District of Columbia. And with a steady stream of superdelegates publicly declaring their support, Dukakis surpassed the required nominating majority of 2,082 convention delegates when California, New Jersey, New Mexico, and Montana all voted on the final day of the primary season (see Tables 2-4 and 2-5).

Table 2-4   1988 Democratic Primary Vote

This chart breaks down the 1988 Democratic presidential primary vote by time period, region, and racial composition of the primary state. The vote in the category marked "Territories" is from Puerto Rico; the megastates' vote is based on primary returns from California, Florida, Illinois, New Jersey, New York, Ohio, Pennsylvania, and Texas, and on the caucus vote from Michigan.

Totals are based on official returns from all states except California, Montana, Ohio, and West Virginia, where results are unofficial.

At the bottom of the chart is the total number of districts carried by the various Democratic candidates in both primary and caucus states. The number of districts adds up to 445—10 more than the nationwide total of congressional districts because in New Jersey and Texas the vote was tabulated according to state legislative districts.

	Turnout	*Dukakis*	*Jackson*	*Gore*	*Gephardt*	*Simon*	*Hart*
Total	23,318,128	42%*	29%	14%	6%	5%	2%
Time periods							
Pre-Super Tuesday	245,909	39*	11	6	24	11	4
Super Tuesday	9,704,383	26	27*	26	13	2	3
Post-Super Tuesday	13,367,836	54*	31	5	1	6	1
Regions							
East	5,872,836	58*	29	6	3	2	1
Midwest	5,316,816	42*	27	6	8	14	1
South	7,882,767	23	28	30*	10	2	3
West	3,889,531	61*	34	2	0	1	0
Territories	356,178	23	29*	14	3	18	8
Racial composition							
Over 20% black	3,309,606	20	38*	28	7	1	3
Under 20% black	20,008,522	46*	28	11	6	5	2
State size							
Megastates	13,013,439	49*	31	7	4	6	1
Districts won	445	271	88	52	14	20	0

NOTE: An asterisk (*) indicates the winner.

Table 2-5 1988 Democratic Primary Results

State	Turnout	Dukakis	Jackson	Gore	Gep-hardt	Simon	Hart	Others	Unc.
N.H. (2/16)	123,512	35.7%*	7.8%	6.8%	19.8%	17.1%	4.0%	8.8%	x
S.D. (2/23)	71,606	31.2	5.4	8.4	43.5*	5.6	5.4	0.5	x
Vt. (3/1)	50,791	55.8*	25.7	x	7.7	5.2	4.0	1.6	x
Ala. (3/8)	405,642	7.7	43.6*	37.4	7.4	0.8	1.9	0.8	0.4
Ark. (3/8)	497,544	18.9	17.1	37.3*	12.0	1.8	3.7	2.0	7.1
Fla. (3/8)	1,273,298	40.9*	20.0	12.7	14.4	2.2	2.9	0.8	6.2
Ga. (3/8)	622,752	15.6	39.8*	32.4	6.7	1.3	2.5	0.5	1.2
Ky. (3/8)	318,721	18.6	15.6	45.8*	9.1	2.9	3.7	0.9	3.3
La. (3/8)	624,450	15.3	35.5*	28.0	10.6	0.8	4.2	5.5	x
Md. (3/8)	531,335	45.6*	28.7	8.7	7.9	3.1	1.8	1.3	2.8
Mass. (3/8)	713,447	58.6*	18.7	4.4	10.2	3.7	1.5	1.2	1.7
Miss. (3/8)	359,417	8.3	44.7*	33.5	5.5	0.6	3.9	0.9	2.6
Mo. (3/8)	527,805	11.6	20.2	2.8	57.8*	4.1	1.4	0.9	1.3
N.C. (3/8)	679,958	20.3	33.0	34.7*	5.5	1.2	2.4	0.6	2.4
Okla. (3/8)	392,727	16.9	13.3	41.4*	21.0	1.8	3.7	1.9	x
R.I. (3/8)	49,029	69.8*	15.2	4.0	4.1	2.8	1.5	1.0	1.7
Tenn. (3/8)	576,314	3.4	20.7	72.3*	1.5	0.5	0.8	0.3	0.5
Texas (3/8)	1,767,045	32.8*	24.5	20.2	13.6	2.0	4.7	2.2	x
Va. (3/8)	364,899	22.0	45.1*	22.3	4.4	1.9	1.7[a]	0.9	1.7
Ill. (3/15)	1,500,930	16.3	32.3	5.1	2.3	42.3*	0.9	0.7	x
P.R. (3/20)	356,178	22.9	29.0	14.4	3.0[b]	18.2	7.5	5.0	x
Conn. (3/29)	241,395	58.1*	28.3	7.7	0.4	1.3	2.4	1.0	0.8
Wis. (4/5)	1,014,782	47.6*	28.2	17.4	0.8	4.8[c]	0.7	0.3	0.3
N.Y. (4/19)	1,575,186	50.9*	37.1	10.0[d]	0.2	1.1	x	0.1	0.7
Pa. (4/26)	1,507,690	66.5*	27.3	3.0	0.5	0.6	1.4	0.8	x
D.C. (5/3)	86,052	17.9	80.0*	0.8	0.3	0.9	x	0.1	x
Ind. (5/3)	645,708	69.6*	22.5	3.4	2.6	1.9	x	x	x
Ohio (5/3)	1,383,572	62.9*	27.4	2.2	x	1.1	2.1	4.4	x
Neb. (5/10)	169,008	62.9*	25.7	1.5	2.9	1.2	2.5	0.4	2.8
W.Va. (5/10)	340,097	74.8*	13.5	3.4	1.8	0.7	2.7	3.2	x
Ore. (5/17)	388,932	56.8*	38.1	1.4	1.7	1.2	x	0.7	x
Idaho (5/24)	51,370	73.4*	15.7	3.7	x	2.7	x	x	4.5
Calif. (6/7)	3,138,748	60.9*	35.1	1.8	x	1.4	x	0.8	x
Mont. (6/7)	121,871	68.7*	22.1	1.9	2.8	1.3	x	x	3.4
N.J. (6/7)	654,302	63.4*	32.7	2.8	x	x	x	1.1	x
N.M. (6/7)	188,610	61.0*	28.1	2.5	x	1.5	3.7	1.5	1.7
N.D. (6/14)	3,405	84.9*†	15.1†	x	x	x	x	x	x
National Total	23,318,128	42.5	29.1	13.7	6.0	4.6	1.8	1.3	1.0

[a] Hart withdrew from the race March 11.
[b] Gephardt withdrew from the race March 28.
[c] Simon suspended his campaign April 7.
[d] Gore suspended his campaign April 21.

NOTE: Results are based on official returns. The percentages do not always add to 100.0 percent because of rounding. "Unc." means uncommitted. An "x" indicates that the candidate or the uncommitted line was not listed on the ballot. No Democratic candidates filed to be on the ballot for the June 14 North Dakota primary; a dagger (†) indicates write-in votes; an asterisk (*) indicates the winner.

Despite Dukakis's strong finish, doubts remained about how strong a vote-getter he really was. Dukakis finished the primaries with 42 percent of the nationwide Democratic primary vote, far below Bush's 68 percent share on the Republican side. He did not inspire passionate support even among many of those who voted for him. He ran poorly among blacks, southern whites, and young voters. (A *New York Times* survey found that Dukakis ran no better than even with Jackson among voters under age forty-five.) If Dukakis had a base, it was among fellow suburbanites and ethnics. Born and raised in Brookline, Massachusetts, just outside Boston, Dukakis won the votes of Democratic suburbanites from Nassau County, New York, to Orange County, California. He also drew 75 percent of the Jewish vote, 60 percent of the large Catholic vote (30 percent of all Democratic primary ballots), and 48 percent of the vote cast by Hispanics.[10]

Even though he lost, Jackson established himself as a major player on the American political scene. After a brief effort to forge a multiracial "rainbow coalition," Jackson's campaign for the 1984 Democratic nomination had been largely symbolic and aimed primarily at blacks. His 1988 campaign was far more sophisticated in terms of fund raising and organization and offered as its theme an expansive message, directed mainly to the economically dispossessed of all races. The benefits of Jackson's new strategy and stature were obvious at the ballot box. In 1984 he won 18 percent of the primary vote and 12 percent of the delegates and carried only two primaries, Louisiana and the District of Columbia. In 1988 he won 29 percent of the primary vote, 29 percent of the delegates, and seven primaries.

Jackson extended his vote-getting appeal particularly in the nation's urban centers. He won a number of cities in 1984, but not nearly as many as in 1988. The list of those he carried reads like a roll call of America's best-known cities: Atlanta, Baltimore, Chicago, Dallas, Detroit, Houston, Memphis, Milwaukee, New Orleans, New York, St. Louis, and San Francisco. Cities with black majorities Jackson won easily. Those with large ethnic elements, such as Milwaukee and New York, he carried by narrower margins.

The Convention Season

On June 8, the day after he locked up the nomination with primary victories in California and New Jersey, Dukakis secured the endorsements of Simon, Gephardt, and Babbitt. One defeated rival who did not fall into line was Jackson, who announced that he was pressing on to the Democratic convention and would continue to seek support from uncommitted delegates. Jackson began to spell out the issues that he wanted to see addressed in the platform and party rules. He also indicated that as the runner-up in the nominating campaign, he deserved an offer to be Dukakis's vice-presidential running mate.

As events transpired, Jackson got much of what he wanted on the rules, a little on the platform, and nothing at all on the vice presidency. The Dukakis forces had the votes on the convention Rules Committee to block Jackson's initiatives, but decided they could afford to give ground here as the price for party harmony in 1988. Dukakis likely would be either the incumbent president in 1992 or on the political sidelines; in either case, he would not be seriously affected by changes in the rules that govern the nominating process.

Jackson won two important rules changes—one that in 1992 would tie more closely the selection of Democratic delegates to each candidate's share of the primary or caucus vote, and another to reduce sharply the number of superdelegates. Specifically, bonus-allocation systems like those in Florida, Illinois, New Jersey, New York, Ohio, and Pennsylvania in 1988 would be banned; such systems gave the primary winner an added advantage in delegates. As for the superdelegates, their numbers would be reduced from 644 to around 400 by removing most of the slots that were allocated to members of the Democratic National Committee (DNC). Although Jackson did not get every rules change he wanted (he had sought to eliminate the superdelegates' free-agent status, arguing that they should be required to reflect their state's primary or caucus results), his agents on the Rules Committee expressed satisfaction with the results, as did Dukakis's supporters.

The Dukakis camp was more concerned about holding the line on the party platform, which was the document their candidate would have to run on in the fall. Many party leaders, including DNC chair Paul G. Kirk, Jr., joined Dukakis to urge that the platform consist of a short statement of principles rather than a long litany of all the sometimes controversial policy positions that the party's interest group allies cherished. In contrast to their "bland is beautiful" approach, Jackson argued that the platform should include specific, clearly stated alternatives to the policies of the Reagan administration.

For the most part, Dukakis had his way on the platform. But unlike the rules compromise, which was hammered out in meetings several weeks before the July 18-21 convention in Atlanta, three of Jackson's proposed platform amendents went to the convention floor. Amendments calling for higher taxes on corporations and the rich and a commitment against the first use of nuclear weapons were defeated by margins of more than two to one. A third amendment that called for a territorial compromise between Israel and the Palestinians was withdrawn without a vote. But in exchange for Jackson's acceptance of a short platform, the Dukakis forces accepted modified versions of nine other Jackson planks. These included a denunciation of any aid to the Nicaraguan contras.

The vice-presidential nomination was Jackson's greatest disappointment. In the weeks before the convention, he had repeatedly emphasized his qualifications for the post and hinted that he might accept it if asked by Dukakis. But Jackson not only was not asked, but also he found out about Dukakis's decision to nominate Texas senator Lloyd Bentsen second hand, from a reporter for the *New Orleans Times Picayune.*

Dukakis's selection of Bentsen on July 12 ended weeks of speculation. The Bentsen nomination came as something of a surprise; other prospects had seemed to many observers to be more likely, particularly Ohio senator John Glenn. But the choice made sense politically. Dukakis believed that Bentsen's presence on the ticket not only would increase his chances to carry Texas but also would enhance his appeal in other southern states where he had run poorly during the primary season. Dukakis also hoped that the choice of the probusiness chair of the Senate Finance Committee would define him in the minds of the voters as a level-headed pragmatist rather than the tax-and-spend liberal that Republicans were making him out to be.

Because Jackson and many of his supporters felt that they had been snubbed in the vice-presidential selection process, the Bentsen nomination ensured that the media spotlight during the convention would be focused on Dukakis's efforts to mend fences. This effort turned out to be easier than some had anticipated. With conservative white voters in mind, Dukakis did not want to appear to capitulate to Jackson, but it was in Jackson's future political interest not to make the price of his support too high. What Dukakis ultimately offered his rival was not immediately clear, but Jackson played the role of team player once he had savored his moment in the spotlight. Following his stirring speech on the second night of the convention and the presidential roll call the following night, which Dukakis won, 2,876.25 to 1,218.50, Jackson left center stage.

As he had hoped, Dukakis had the final night of the convention to himself. Cheering an acceptance speech that emphasized that the fall campaign would be about "competence, not ideology," the Democrats concluded their most harmonious nominating process since they had last won the White House in 1976.

The August 15-18 Republican National Convention in New Orleans offered Bush and the Republicans a chance to react to what the Democrats had done. On nearly every point, they proceeded differently from the Democrats.

In contrast to the Democrats, the Republicans generally left their party rules unaltered. The Democrats had adopted a platform that was short (about four thousand words) and general, but Republicans wrote a document that was roughly ten times as long and loaded with specifics. Conservatives replicated their 1980 and 1984 platform triumphs on the issues of taxes, abortion, school prayer, defense spending, and strategic defense. Republican moderates were allowed a few carefully circumscribed sentences on issues such as AIDS, education, and child care.

The firestorm at the Republican convention was over the vice-presidential nomination, a matter the Democrats had resolved before their convention even began. Bush passed over well-known prospects like Dole, Kemp, and Wyoming senator Alan Simpson to select someone relatively unknown, Dan Quayle, the forty-one-year-old Indiana senator.

The Quayle nomination struck many as perplexing. Bush staffers claimed that Quayle was a "baby boomer" who was attuned to his generation; that he was more vital and vigorous than his sixty-seven-year-old Democratic counterpart, Bentsen; that with his good looks he would raise the ticket's appeal among women; and that he was acceptable to arch conservatives in the party who were still wary of Bush. But the main reason Bush picked Quayle may have been that after a career as an appointive official who had been beholden to others, Bush wanted someone who was clearly beholden to him and who would appreciate the opportunity to serve loyally in his administration. At the least, Bush did not want a prominent running mate like Dole or Kemp who might compete with him for headlines.

But almost immediately after Bush selected Quayle on August 16, the second day of the convention, critics and supporters second-guessed his decision. Some expressed doubts that Quayle was adequately prepared to succeed to the presidency should the need arise. But that concern was quickly overshadowed by questions about Quayle's service in the Indiana National Guard during the Vietnam War. By joining the guard, Quayle, a hawkish voice in Congress, had minimized his risk of being sent into combat. Moreover, newspaper accounts and even interviews with Quayle himself pointed to family connections that had won him preferential treatment. As the story grew, there was speculation that Quayle might be dropped from the ticket before he was formally nominated. Bush, however, reacted calmly to the criticism, sticking to his schedule and to his decision.

Republicans gradually turned Quayle's plight to their advantage by complaining of a "media feeding frenzy" and press overkill. On the final night of the convention, Bush, like Dukakis four weeks earlier, delivered a well-crafted acceptance speech. Soon after, he moved out to a clear lead in the polls, which he kept for the rest of the campaign.

Looking Ahead to 1992

If any dramatic changes occur in the nominating process for 1992, they are likely to be made by the same major players who have significantly influenced the process's evolution during the last twenty years—the national Democratic party, the states, and Congress.

In response to Jackson's initiatives, the Democrats already have approved changes in their nominating rules that will place even more emphasis on proportional representation in 1992 than there was in 1988. In winning these rules changes, Jackson's forces played their cards early and well. They had similar grievances in 1984, but agreed to let a postelection rules commission deal with their complaints. The so-called Fairness Commission, which was controlled by party insiders, lowered the threshold that a candidate needed to win delegates from 20 percent to 15 percent (where it will stay in 1992), but made none of the other significant changes that Jackson wanted.

In 1988 the Jackson forces made sure their proposed rule changes were incorporated into the party charter, not left to a commission. Either of the changes—namely, fewer superdelegates and an end to bonus primaries—could be removed from the charter by a two-thirds vote of the DNC. In the wake of Dukakis's defeat, some party leaders argued that they had only agreed to the changes to promote party unity for the fall campaign, and they urged review of the rules for 1992. But others indicated that to do so would be an act of bad faith.

The States

It is up to each state to decide how to elect its delegates—through a primary or a caucus—and to determine when its delegate-selection event will be held. Since 1980 national Democratic rules have required states to schedule their primary or first-round caucus within a three-month "window" that extends from the second Tuesday in March to the second Tuesday in June. Iowa, New Hampshire, and a handful of other states have been granted exemptions to choose their delegates earlier.

Although the Democrats' window did not slow the creation of more and more primaries on earlier and earlier dates, the nominating process in 1992 may not be as "front-loaded" as it was in 1988. Iowa and New Hampshire are likely to retain their positions near the beginning of the calendar, but candidates in 1992 probably will be able to devise strategies that do not go through Des Moines. The Iowa caucuses lost a bit of their luster in 1988 when the two winners, Dole and Gephardt, were knocked out of the race early.

It also seems likely that fewer states will participate in Super Tuesday in 1992. A number of Super Tuesday states felt that in 1988 the event was dominated by Texas and Florida and that they were ignored. Some, such as Maryland, are likely to return to their traditional late-spring primary date.

Congress

From time to time over the years, Congress has seemed poised to become involved in shaping the nominating process. The most extensive set of hearings in recent years was held by the House Administration Committee's Subcommittee on Elections in 1986. The subcommittee heard the concerns of witnesses about the possible effects of "front-loading" the process, but decided to see how it worked in 1988 before determining how to proceed. Since then, the subcommittee chair, Democrat Al Swift of Washington, has indicated that he may seek legislation that would establish a fixed starting date for primaries and caucuses that no state, including Iowa or New Hampshire, could violate.

But it is more likely that Congress will concentrate on campaign finance, the part of the presidential nominating process that it has played a major role in shaping. Discussions are likely to be held on eliminating the state-by-state spending limits, a facet of the public financing system that has been particularly bothersome to candidates in budgeting for the high-stakes events in Iowa and New Hampshire.

Beyond that, Swift sees little need for congressional tinkering with the nominating process. "Anyone can think up a system that's more orderly," he said. "But I don't see that this system was unfair to anyone." [11]

Notes

1. Interesting discussions of the presidential nominating process may be found in *Choosing the President,* ed. James David Barber (Englewood Cliffs, N.J.: Prentice-Hall, 1976); *The Elections of 1984,* ed. Michael Nelson (Washington, D.C.: CQ Press, 1985); John Aldrich, *Before the Convention: A Theory of Presidential Nominating Campaigns* (Chicago: University of Chicago Press, 1980); *Before Nomination: Our Primary Problems,* ed. George Grassmuck (Washington, D.C.: American Enterprise Institute, 1985); William Crotty and John S. Jackson III, *Presidential Primaries and Nominations* (Washington, D.C.: CQ Press, 1985); Byron E. Shafer, *Quiet Revolution: The Struggle for the*

Democratic Party and the Shaping of Post-Reform Politics (New York: Russell Sage Foundation, 1983); and Nelson Polsby, *Consequences of Party Reform* (New York: Oxford University Press, 1983).

2. Richard L. Berke, "For Dukakis Campaign, the Money Keeps Rolling In," *New York Times,* April 24, 1988.

3. Federal Election Commission, "FEC Releases Information on 1987 Presidential Spending," press release, February 11, 1988.

4. Even with the extensive media attention that Iowa's precinct caucuses received, only 11 percent of the state's voting-age population participated, and that figure was high for a caucus. The Minnesota caucuses held later in February drew only 5 percent of the state's voting-age population. By comparison, 34 percent of New Hampshire's voting-age population cast a Democratic or Republican primary ballot. *Congressional Quarterly Weekly Report,* March 5, 1988, 569.

5. Federal Election Commission, "FEC Announces Spending Limits for 1988 Presidential Race," press release, February 5, 1988. The national spending limit in 1988 was $23,050,000, plus an additional 20 percent for certain fund-raising costs that brought the overall limit to $27,660,000. Legal and accounting costs were exempt from the limit. State limits were set according to the voting-age population of each state, which ranged in 1988 from a low of $461,000 in New Hampshire to $7,509,505.60 in California; in Iowa, the spending limit was $775,217.60. Altogether, seven of the Democratic and Republican candidates reported spending at least $700,000 in Iowa; no candidate reported spending that much in California.

6. Federal Election Commission, "Presidential Primary Spending at $200 Million Mark," press release, August 18, 1988; and Rita Breamish, "Bush Spending," *Associated Press,* July 3, 1988.

7. *New York Times*/CBS News Poll, "Tuesday's Crossover Voters" and "Portrait of the Super Tuesday Voters," *New York Times,* March 10, 1988.

8. Rhodes Cook, "Race for the White House: Early Is the Norm," *Congressional Quarterly Weekly Report,* February 28, 1987, 380.

9. *New York Times*/CBS News Poll, "Portrait of Super Tuesday Voters."

10. E. J. Dionne, Jr., "Jackson Share of Votes by Whites Triples in '88," *New York Times,* June 13, 1988.

11. Rhodes Cook, "Was This Any Way to Nominate a President?" *Congressional Quarterly Weekly Report,* June 11, 1988, 1577.

3. THE ELECTION

Paul J. Quirk

Political campaigns are expected to fulfill two vital functions in a democracy. First, campaigns are the means by which candidates present themselves and their appeals to the voters. Second, campaigns provide the country with its best opportunity to consider where it is, where it is headed, and where it wants to go. In this respect, political campaigns are more than just contests between parties and personalities—they are vital to the health of democratic government.

Judged according to the first criterion, the 1988 presidential campaign was a success for George Bush and a failure for Michael Dukakis. As Paul Quirk shows, Bush communicated his themes effectively and stymied Dukakis's attempts to communicate his: the effects were clear, not just in the results on election day, but in the exit polls that explained the results. But, Quirk argues, the 1988 campaign failed dismally according to the second criterion; that is, it failed to bring important issues before the public in even a minimally serious way. In doing so, it was not unlike other recent presidential campaigns.

This chapter opens a discussion, joined in the next two chapters by Thomas Patterson and Jean Bethke Elshtain, respectively, about the quality of debate in modern election campaigns. Together, Quirk, Patterson, and Elshtain provide a range of perspectives and points of view.

The election of a president every four years is the central ritual of democratic government in the United States. The presidential election of 1988, however, did not give the American public an uplifting experience in self-government. Instead, it left many voters, politicians, and political commentators disgusted with a campaign that, in their view, was so superficial and negative that it represented a perversion of the electoral process. Even though George Bush and Michael Dukakis were both experienced, relatively moderate, and untainted by scandal, the campaign led many voters to wish they could choose someone else.

Quite likely, the campaign was also part of the reason an exceptional number of voters stayed away from the polls.

Yet, from the standpoint of the presidential candidates, especially Bush, the campaign accomplished much of what it was intended to do. The Bush campaign overcame a thirteen percentage point disadvantage in the polls in May to win by a solid eight-point margin in the popular vote in November.[1] The Dukakis campaign, although widely criticized as inept, at least avoided a landslide defeat on the scale suffered by the two preceding Democratic nominees, Jimmy Carter in 1980 and Walter Mondale in 1984. And it managed to narrow Bush's lead in the last few weeks before election day. If the two candidates had their campaigns to do over again, they probably would make few, if any, fundamental changes.

The apparent conflict between the citizens' and the candidates' perspectives on the campaign raises some important questions: How did the 1988 presidential election campaign serve the candidates' purposes and affect the outcome of the election? More broadly, how well did it perform the functions that a presidential campaign must perform to promote responsive and responsible democratic government? This essay argues that despite the unusual amount of dissatisfaction with the 1988 campaign, its main defects from the standpoint of democratic government were those of all recent presidential campaigns.

Presidential Campaigns and Democratic Government

At the root of the difficulty with presidential campaigns, there is a poor match between what a campaign must accomplish to strengthen democratic government and what a candidate must do to win the election.

The Requirements for Strengthening Democratic Government

Ideally, a presidential campaign should strengthen democratic government. A campaign should help the government respond to the public's considered values and priorities; it should facilitate (and not obstruct) the selection of policies that are likely to prove workable and effective; and it should increase the public's attachment to, and participation in, the democratic process. What is required of a campaign depends on how directly one believes the public should be involved in making policy decisions.[2] If a degree of popular control is desirable, a constructive presidential campaign must have four attributes.

First, the candidates must state their positions on the major issues facing the country. These statements permit voters to consider the positions, if they wish, in choosing between candidates. The positions need not be highly specific. Indeed, voters have no basis for judging detailed proposals; and a president who has campaigned on such proposals may lack needed flexibility after the election. At a minimum, however, the candidates must give the voters an accurate general sense of their policies. To make this information genuinely accessible to voters, the candidates must emphasize their policy positions in advertising and campaign appearances, and the media must call attention to them. It is not enough for candidates to put out position papers or make a few policy speeches that are relegated to the back pages of the newspapers.

Second, the candidates must confine their campaigns to responsible positions and essentially honest, even if debatable, claims. They must advocate policies that are affordable, have acceptable long-term consequences, and are considered workable by informed observers. They must refrain from exploiting superficially attractive proposals that would be harmful or impossible to implement. On occasions when unpopular policies, such as fiscal austerity, are necessary, responsible candidates may have no alternative to withholding information about their intentions. The candidates also must make claims that are at least sufficiently free of distortion and misrepresentation to be defensible before an informed audience. They should not base their campaigns on impossible promises or false claims about their opponents' failures or their own achievements.

Third, the candidates must conduct a wide-ranging debate throughout the campaign. It is not enough that they announce their policies without discussion; they must also confront each other on the merits of the issues. Without such confrontation, the campaign offers choices the voters may not understand and provides little opportunity for learning about them. The debate must address the candidates' records and qualifications for office as well as their policy proposals. To be most effective, it should not be wholly dominated by the candidates and their allies. There is an important role for unaffiliated participants, such as experts in various areas of policy, who can offer informed and relatively unbiased perspectives on the issues. The more penetrating and informative the campaign debate, the more honest and responsible the candidates will be and the more accurately the public will discern its interests.

Finally, the candidates should campaign primarily on rational appeals and issues relevant to the presidency. They must not distract attention from such discussion by relying heavily on emotional or symbolic appeals. Used in moderation, positive symbolic themes (in which, for example, a candidate is surrounded by family or wrapped in the flag) may increase the public's enthusiasm for the candidates and emotional attachment to the political system. But used to excess, they drown out rational discussion and cause cynicism among voters who recognize the manipulation. Negative symbolic themes (in which, for example, insignificant issues or episodes are used to link an opponent with crime, disloyalty, or class privilege) also are distracting and tend to undermine enthusiasm and attachment. In the long run, they may reduce participation in the political process.

Contrary to the assumption of many journalists, there is nothing objectionable about negative campaign appeals (those that involve criticism of an opponent's record or policies) as such. If negative appeals are as honest, responsible, and pertinent as positive appeals, they are just as helpful to voters. The difficulty with negative appeals is that they are especially prone to emotionalism and misrepresentation.

The Real World of Presidential Campaigns

The requirements that a campaign must meet to strengthen democratic government, unfortunately, bear little relation to how campaigns are actually conducted.[3] Under the prevailing circumstances of presidential electoral politics, the candidates lack the incentive to carry on anything resembling an ideal campaign. Nor do other participants, such as independent commentators and the media, play the roles they would need to play in such a campaign.

The shortcomings of presidential campaigns derive, fundamentally, from three sources. The most important is that most voters have only limited interest in the substantive issues of a political campaign. Although they may cast their votes on the basis of policy preferences, they invest little time in trying to understand the issues.[4] At least implicitly, they seem to recognize that, for an individual, to devote the effort needed to make a careful decision is unlikely to affect the outcome of an election or therefore the government's performance. A small minority of voters pay close attention to issues, often making politics an avocation. But the voters who are undecided during an election campaign and most central to the candidates' strategies are likely to be less engaged by politics than other voters.[5] For the most part, the voters direct their attention toward vivid, easily absorbed information.[6]

The news media, correctly perceiving what attracts a large audience, offer very limited information about a campaign.[7] In particular, television news broadcasts, from which most voters get the largest part of their information, emphasize short, colorful, dramatic segments. They concentrate on the so-called "horse-race" aspects of a campaign— the candidates' strategies and polls and other evidence of who is winning. They eagerly report gaffes and scandals. But the news media omit detailed coverage of the candidates' positions on the issues and provide virtually no discussion of the merits of those positions or the qualifications of the candidates. For example, they are less likely to consider whether a candidate's budget plan will work than whether it will attract voters.

Finally, there is a lack of independent commentary on the substantive issues of a campaign. The news media will correct a candidate on an unambiguous error of fact. On a point that is subject to even modest uncertainty, however, they will neither offer a judgment— undoubtedly a wise policy—nor try to report the prevailing judgment of knowledgeable persons. Whether from an exaggerated sense of the constraints of nonpartisanship or for fear of producing a boring story, they will cover such issues mainly by reporting the two sides in the debate. Campaign debate thus becomes a matter of one candidate's word against the other's, and both can say virtually anything they please without fear of being contradicted in a clear, credible, and embarrassing manner.

Presidential candidates design their strategies to fit the limitations of the media's coverage and the voters' attention. They formulate messages that can be presented in elaborately produced thirty-second television commercials and even shorter segments on network news broadcasts. These messages consist mostly of vague images, symbolism, and emotional appeals aimed at uninformed, undecided voters.[8] In Ronald Reagan's 1984 reelection campaign, for example, a strategy memorandum proposed a massive deployment of flags and other patriotic symbols to create the impression that a vote against Reagan was a vote against America.

The candidates discuss issues mainly by taking positions that have unambiguous political benefits. Candidates of each party respond to the strongest demands of the party faithful and, beyond that, exploit the party's areas of agreement with the typical independent voter. Democrats stress economic equity and promise new programs to solve social problems; Republicans stress traditional morality and promise to hold down or reduce taxes.[9] With respect to important problems that have no easy solutions—the issues that deserve extensive discussion in a campaign—the candidates usually content themselves with vague promises of achievement. Above all, they avoid giving the voters bad news. Mondale violated this last precept in 1984 by asserting that unless taxes were increased the budget deficit would remain unacceptably large, and the resulting political disaster taught a lesson to a generation of politicians. As a result, the candidates often neglect to address crucial issues facing the country.

Moreover, the candidates take advantage of the voters' low level of information and the lack of independent commentary on campaign debate to employ extremely relaxed standards of fairness, realism, and veracity. They ignore crucial issues. They make wildly exaggerated claims for their policies. Often using their vice-presidential running mates and other political allies to do the worst of the dirty work, they level harsh and sometimes misleading charges against their opponents.

The situation has been only marginally improved by formal televised debates between the candidates. Increasingly institutionalized in recent years, the debates have consisted of brief exchanges on a series of topics. Although they have displayed the candidates' differences, they have failed to explore any subject deeply enough to expose weaknesses in either candidate's position or improve public understanding of the issues.[10]

The Campaign of 1988

How did Dukakis and Bush campaign for president? What were the effects of the campaign on the election's outcome and on democratic government?

The Strategic Context

By the end of May, Dukakis and Bush were assured of first-ballot nominations by their respective parties. Between the two candidates, Dukakis seemed at the outset to have the advantage, but Bush had latent strengths that eventually proved crucial.

After overcoming seven opponents in the contest for the Democratic nomination, Dukakis had grounds to anticipate another victory in November. His moderate views on economic policy represented the new pragmatism in the Democratic party. Highly intelligent, Dukakis was considered a competent manager. He could point to a record of achievement as governor of Massachusetts: the state's long-depressed economy had grown so rapidly, boosted by an infusion of high-technology industries, that it became the leading model of what declining Rust Belt states aspired to achieve. Unlike Mondale in 1984, Dukakis had been able to win the party's nomination without making politically costly commitments to organized labor, civil rights organizations, or other Democratic interest groups. Finally, he had the advantage of the voters' normal tendency, after eight years with one party in the White House, to vote for a change.

To his disadvantage, Dukakis was from the Northeast, which is not where the Democrats most need the advantage of a regional favorite son on the ticket. His views on social issues like abortion and school prayer were those of the party's liberal wing. As a newcomer to national politics, Dukakis was relatively unknown to the public. And he was an indifferent speaker, rarely able to excite a crowd.

Bush's prospects for victory did not rest primarily on his personal attributes or appeal to voters. His outstanding personal trait was his experience in high-level political and governmental positions: member of the House of Representatives, ambassador to China and the United Nations, chairman of the Republican National Committee, director of the Central Intelligence Agency, and vice president of the United States. In all of these positions Bush had performed competently and without scandal—but also, as Sen. Robert Dole had pointed out during the primaries, without much of a record of achievement. Although he had essentially universal recognition, Bush also had difficulties with his image and weaknesses as a campaigner. He was seen by many as an effete member of the social elite—and, relatedly, as a "wimp." He was sometimes inarticulate. And he was prone to embarrassing gaffes—such as his claim, in an excess of competitive enthusiasm during the 1984 campaign, to have "kicked ass" in his debate with Democratic vice-presidential candidate Geraldine Ferraro.

During his career in politics, Bush had demonstrated ideological flexibility. After campaigning as a moderate for the presidential nomination in 1980 and attaining instead the vice presidency, he accommodated himself fully to Reagan's conservatism. Such flexibility denied Bush any highly enthusiastic constituency but allowed him to be a unifying figure among Republicans.

The main basis of Bush's support, apart from simple party loyalty, was his identification with Reagan. To the extent that the Reagan administration appeared successful, that Reagan remained popular, and that he embraced Bush, this identification promised to deliver votes in November. At a minimum, Bush was assured that the first of these conditions would obtain. Despite the accumulation of massive domestic and foreign debts, which most economists expected to burden the economy for a generation to come;[11] persistent social problems, such as homelessness, drug abuse, and the deterioration of public schools; and evidence of a steady decline in the competitiveness of American industry—the economy currently was performing splendidly, with high employment, low inflation, and one of the longest periods of sustained growth ever recorded. Most important, the nation was at peace.

As always, certain swing states and groups of voters were crucial to the candidates' strategies. A Republican candidate starts out with a strong base of relatively secure electoral votes—those of all the Rocky Mountain states; certain traditionally Republican midwestern states (Indiana, Kansas, and Nebraska); a handful of other Republican states (Alaska, New Hampshire, and Vermont); and, at least when a southerner does not head the Democratic ticket, most of the South,

including Florida. With 270 electoral votes required for election, this
bloc of about 150 electoral votes puts a Republican well on the way to
victory before the campaign has even begun. A Democrat has comparable security only in the District of Columbia, Massachusetts, and
Rhode Island, and a strong head start only in Hawaii, Minnesota, New
York, and West Virginia—for a total of 76 electoral votes.

Presidential elections are therefore won or lost in the remaining
twenty or so states, with around 300 electoral votes, and especially in a
handful of the most populous—California, Illinois, Michigan, New
Jersey, Ohio, Pennsylvania, and Texas, which by themselves have 184
electoral votes. To win the election, a Republican candidate must hold
the party's base and carry about two-fifths of the electoral votes of the
competitive states, whereas a Democrat must hold the party's smaller
base and take about three-fifths of the competitive votes. Contrary to
some views, neither the Republican party's larger base of electoral votes
nor its victories in four of the five presidential elections leading up to
1988 indicates a fundamental Republican advantage in presidential
elections such that, other things being equal, a Republican victory is
substantially more likely than a Democratic victory. Because the
independent vote is approximately one-third of the electorate, presidential elections are volatile. Large swings toward either party are possible,
and either party can readily win.[12]

In 1988 the crucial groups were those whose party preference or
turnout at the polls had varied significantly in recent elections. Blue-
collar workers, traditionally Democrats, had defected to Reagan in
large numbers. White southerners had been abandoning their traditional Democratic affiliation, especially in presidential elections, over
two decades. The Democrats wanted to bring both groups home, while
the Republicans wanted to make them permanent additions to their
coalition. Blacks were an additional target group for the Democrats
because, although they would vote around 90 percent Democratic, their
turnout rate was uncertain. Protestant evangelicals were a Republican
target for similar reasons. It proved highly significant for the campaign
that, except for blacks, all of these groups held generally conservative
views on social issues.

At the end of May, Dukakis enjoyed an advantage over Bush so
large, at ten to sixteen points in various polls, that it seemed to foretell a
Democratic landslide, making calculations about competitive states and
swing groups irrelevant. Bush's situation, however, was less desperate
than it looked. Much of Dukakis's support lacked a firm foundation. A
series of primary election victories over the extremely liberal Jesse
Jackson had made Dukakis appear to be both conservative and a
winner. These perceptions brought support that could not be expected

to hold up until November. Moreover, having emerged quite suddenly from the large field of Democrat candidates, Dukakis was still unknown to much of the public. He was subject to being, in campaign jargon, "redefined."

Formulating the Campaigns

Although the candidates had been directing their energies toward the November election since late spring, the first major events of the general election campaign occurred in the weeks surrounding the Democratic National Convention, which took place in mid-July in Atlanta, and the Republican National Convention, three weeks later in New Orleans. During this period, Bush and Dukakis assembled their organizations for the national campaign, selected their vice-presidential nominees, and explained their candidacies to the nation.

The Dukakis Campaign.   Dukakis's nomination campaign was praised as a model of organization and technical skill. His general election campaign was another story. It had several problems. In a departure from standard practice, Dukakis did not restructure and expand his nomination campaign staff, mostly recruited from Massachusetts, for the much larger undertaking of the general election campaign. As a result, he failed to exploit a great deal of the talent available in the Democratic party. Dukakis did not work well with the staff he had, often refusing to listen to them. "The campaign needs an ambassador to the candidate," a frustrated staff member remarked. Finally, the group responsible for Dukakis's advertising initially was disorganized, with no one clearly in charge, and later was directed by an advertising executive without experience in a presidential campaign. In all, the Dukakis organization was incapable of running an effective campaign.

In selecting a vice-presidential nominee, Dukakis sought to increase the ticket's appeal to moderate and conservative voters, especially white southerners. His choice of Sen. Lloyd Bentsen of Texas, however, was unconventional in two respects. Because the head of the Republican ticket was also from Texas (Bush had represented a Houston district in Congress), Bentsen could not be counted on to deliver his home state. And because Bentsen was one of the most conservative Senate Democrats, a supporter of Reagan's 1981 tax cuts and of military aid for the Nicaraguan contras, his presence gave the Democratic ticket a sharply divided ideological makeup. (Republicans said that the two Democrats should debate each other.) Ideology aside, Bentsen was a respected senior senator whose undeniable qualifications for high office became an important asset for Dukakis.

At the same time, Bentsen's selection increased the difficulty of securing enthusiastic black support. Late in the primary season, Jackson began to put himself forward as a potential vice-presidential nominee. Sincerely or not, Dukakis made a public display of considering Jackson. He also promised to inform Jackson privately if he decided to choose someone else. Apparently through an oversight, however, Dukakis failed to keep that promise, and Jackson got the bad news from a reporter asking for his reaction to it. The discourteous treatment was an embarrassment for Jackson, compounding the disappointment of his exclusion from the ticket. The Dukakis campaign had to work doubly hard to placate Jackson and his supporters at the convention. In fact, the convention became in large part a celebration of Jackson's candidacy. The extraordinary attention he received may have hurt the ticket with many white voters, but it helped secure his allegiance in the fall campaign.

The central themes of Dukakis's campaign were set forth in his speech accepting the nomination. Rising above his usual flat style of delivery to speak with assurance and feeling, Dukakis associated his candidacy with the American dream of opportunity for all—a point he personalized by recounting his origins as the son of poor Greek immigrants. Appealing to middle- and working-class concerns about economic fairness, he accused the Reagan administration of limiting opportunity to a privileged few and stated the central promise of his campaign: "good jobs at good wages for every citizen." He also blamed the administration for running up an unprecedented national debt, but in contrast with Mondale's heavy emphasis on the deficit in 1984, he discussed the problem perfunctorily, in a single sentence, and with no mention of higher taxes.

In a passage crucial to his strategy, he asserted, "This election isn't about ideology. It's about competence." As proof of his competence he claimed success at balancing budgets and creating jobs in Massachusetts. In so identifying the basic issue of the campaign, Dukakis hoped to keep the election from becoming a referendum on liberal positions on social issues or on liberalism as a political label.

Dukakis avoided any direct personal attack on the popular Ronald Reagan and even credited him with achievements in nuclear arms control. But he struck hard on the two main counts of his indictment against Bush: his failure to oppose the arms-for-hostages deal that led to the Iran-contra scandal and his cooperation with the "drug running" Panamanian dictator, Gen. Manuel Noriega. Dukakis did not discuss how he would avoid the budget deficits that he railed against or how he would create the good jobs that he promised.

As they had hoped, the Democrats got a good "bounce" from the convention. Before the convention, Dukakis's lead over Bush in the polls had been dwindling, but soon afterward it rose again to more than fifteen points.

The Bush Campaign. Benefiting from a seasoned staff and a candidate who was amenable to advice, Bush's organization was more effective than Dukakis's in the complex task of mounting a national campaign. Most of the leading personnel were veterans of Reagan's 1980 and 1984 campaigns or of the Reagan White House's sophisticated media operation. They included campaign chairman James A. Baker, who had headed Reagan's 1980 campaign and then served as White House chief of staff and secretary of the Treasury; campaign manager Lee Atwater, who had been Reagan's deputy campaign director in 1984; and director of polling Robert M. Teeter, who had performed the same role for the Reagan White House. The advertising team was made up of Madison Avenue professionals with prior experience in Reagan's campaigns and was coordinated by Bush's media adviser, Roger Ailes.

In Bush, the staff had a cooperative candidate. He worked to change his upper-class image—donning work clothes for campaign appearances and making conspicuous use of informal speech ("Read my lips"). He improved his debating style between the first and second encounter with Dukakis. Most important, Bush accepted the staff's judgment that Dukakis was vulnerable to a negative campaign and, although he was said to find such campaigning distasteful, he attacked Dukakis with a vengeance.

Bush's selection of a running mate, announced on the second day of the Republican convention, was less helpful. Most speculation about the second spot on the ticket had centered on Bush's primary rivals such as Sen. Bob Dole and Rep. Jack Kemp, and governors of important states such as George Deukmejian of California and James Thompson of Illinois. (Former secretary of transportation Elizabeth Dole was also mentioned, giving the Dole family two chances at the nomination.) In making the surprise choice of Dan Quayle, a second-term senator with very modest legislative credentials and no national reputation, Bush reportedly calculated that Quayle would appeal to the Midwest because he was from Indiana; to the Republican party's right wing because he had a strong conservative voting record in the Senate; to younger voters because, at the age of forty-three, he was of the "baby boom" generation; and to women because he was good looking.

Criticism of the Quayle nomination erupted immediately. Many Republicans were disconcerted by Quayle's inexperience and lack of distinction in the Senate. But attention soon shifted to the fact that

Quayle had performed his Vietnam-era military service, safe from combat, in the Indiana National Guard. The question was raised whether Quayle had improperly used the influence of his prominent Indiana family to get into the guard and escape the draft. After the convention, the press, seizing on a story that suited its taste for scandal, investigated thoroughly and learned that the guard had treated Quayle with considerable favoritism. Reporters also discovered that he had been admitted to Indiana University Law School, despite a weak undergraduate record, under a program designed for underprivileged students. Nothing in the national guard or law school stories demonstrated that Quayle had acted illegally or, by any commonly accepted standard, unethically. But the stories reinforced the image of Quayle as a person of slight accomplishment, someone whose success in life was largely the product of class privilege.

Despite the fuss over Quayle, Bush regained the nation's attention with his acceptance speech. He began by associating himself with President Reagan. He pointed proudly to the administration's accomplishments, citing economic growth, military strength, and peace, and he stated his determination to "complete the mission we started in 1980." He set a specific goal (later withdrawn as unrealistic) of creating 30 million new jobs in eight years. In a direct rebuttal to Dukakis's speech, Bush denied that the election was merely about competence, which he said "makes the trains run on time but doesn't know where they're going." He said the election was also about ideas and values. In a brief but pointed passage, Bush listed his differences with Dukakis on social issues: the mandatory Pledge of Allegiance in public schools, capital punishment, and school prayer, all of which Bush supported; and gun control, abortion, and the Massachusetts prison furlough program, which he opposed. He also promised emphatically not to raise taxes and criticized Dukakis's refusal to make the same promise. Of all these issues, only taxes and abortion have regularly occupied any president's attention.

More delicately, Bush also distinguished himself from Reagan. He spoke of the need to help struggling farmers, unemployed workers, the urban poor, and the homeless. More broadly, he called for racial tolerance, for making economic prosperity serve higher ideals, and for "a kinder, gentler nation." In short, Bush backed away from Reagan's hard-line conservatism on the welfare state. He also called for higher standards of ethics in the public service. Like Dukakis, Bush gave little specific information about his program. Unlike Dukakis, he did not promise to reduce the budget deficit. In fact, he made no mention of the deficit.

The public responded well. Just before the convention, Bush had pulled roughly even with Dukakis in the polls. Even with the embarrassment of Quayle, a few days after the convention the Republican ticket had a six-point lead.

Presenting the Message

Despite the folk wisdom that the public ignores a presidential election until after the World Series, the crucial phase of the 1988 campaign took place in late summer, while the champion-to-be Dodgers were still struggling to make the playoffs. In that period, Bush's performance was decisively superior to Dukakis's in the day-to-day competition of the campaign.

Although Bush continued to make the positive case for his own candidacy, he succeeded mainly because of his coordinated, daily attacks on Dukakis, defining the Democrat as a liberal outside the mainstream of American politics. Bush's staff used sophisticated market research to identify the specific charges likely to do the most damage. Bush described Dukakis as sympathetic to criminals and unconcerned about their victims. In particular, he criticized Dukakis for supporting a Massachusetts prison furlough program that allowed even first-degree murder convicts out for visits; he referred regularly to one such convict, Willie Horton, who had fled from Massachusetts and committed a rape in Maryland. Bush also derided Dukakis's membership in the American Civil Liberties Union (ACLU)—using an expression, "card-carrying member," that was reminiscent of the way Sen. Joseph McCarthy accused many Americans of being communists in the 1950s. Bush criticized Dukakis as inexperienced in foreign and defense policy and unappreciative of the need for a strong defense. He accused his rival of opposing "virtually every new weapons system that would insure our security." He even asserted that Dukakis rejected the strategy of nuclear deterrence.

Bush had other weapons in his arsenal of negative campaigning. He often charged that Dukakis had raised taxes in Massachusetts. Bush's most frequent complaint, however, was symbolic. He attacked Dukakis for having vetoed a Massachusetts bill that would have required public school teachers to lead their students in a daily recitation of the Pledge of Allegiance. Dukakis replied, correctly, that state and federal courts had found such bills unconstitutional, and he pointed out that both governors and presidents are sworn to uphold the Constitution. But Bush dismissed the objection, saying that he would have "found a way to sign the bill," and went on using the issue.[13]

The Bush campaign was proficient at keeping the voters' attention focused on these criticisms. It had the assistance of President Reagan, who seemed to view the election as a referendum on his presidency.

Reagan made appearances at thirty-five campaign events in sixteen states, showing warm support for Bush and characterizing Dukakis as "liberal, liberal, liberal." More important, the Bush organization carefully planned the day-to-day events of the campaign to have the maximum effect on the public. It made certain to have a single, dominant theme each day and to string that theme out for several days. It creatively scripted Bush's appearances to give the media a stream of interesting or entertaining stories. When Bush portrayed himself as saying to criminals, "Go ahead, make my day," and Dukakis as saying, "Go ahead, have a good weekend," the media had an irresistible story on Bush's criticism of the prison furlough program.

Dukakis and his campaign staff were unable to match the Bush organization's performance. A popular interpretation of Dukakis's failure is that he did not respond to Bush's negative campaign with a timely and aggressive counterattack. In fact, Dukakis spent several days in August touring Massachusetts when, by most accounts, he should have been campaigning around the country. According to one of his friends, Dukakis at first refused to answer Bush's attacks because he did not believe the public would take them seriously. Dukakis's staff reportedly had a hard time persuading the intellectual, policy-oriented Dukakis to come out as "Fighting Mike."

Such accounts, however, are overdrawn. Dukakis did a great deal of negative campaigning, probably not much less than Bush. He frequently attacked Bush on the Iran-contra scandal and the Noriega connection; he pronounced Bush a failure at keeping drugs out of the country and chastised him for refusing to promise that he would cut off foreign aid to countries that tolerate the drug trade; he asserted that Bush lacked the necessary skill to conduct foreign policy; and he attempted to link Bush with ethics scandals in the administration and even on Wall Street. What Dukakis was unable to do was conduct his negative campaign in the focused and compelling manner of the Bush organization.

To know exactly why Dukakis failed to present his message persuasively would require a detailed study of his campaign. The staff may have lacked the coordination or the creative talent to manage the daily events effectively. Certainly, the Dukakis advertising team was short of coordination and talent: when Bush aired a television commercial that blamed Dukakis for pollution in Boston Harbor, the disorganized Dukakis team took so long to produce a reply that California supporters took it upon themselves to do so. A major series of Dukakis advertisements depicting the "packaging" of Bush by a cynical group of handlers was so obscure that some people could not tell which candidate they were being urged to support. Beyond such matters of technical competence, the Dukakis campaign may have had less effective material to use; for some reason, Bush may have been less open to attack than Dukakis. Another possibility, however, is that Bush and his organization were more willing to use deceptive and inflammatory advertisements than was the Dukakis campaign.[14]

By the second week of September, Bush had eliminated the seventeen-point Dukakis lead from late July and assumed a solid ten-point lead of his own.[15] His approval ratings had risen since July by about twelve points, while Dukakis's ratings had fallen about seven points.[16]

The Televised Debates

The best hope for the Democratic ticket, at that point, was to get a boost from the televised debates. To do so would be difficult, however, because the schedule and format of the debates, worked out in negotiations between the two sides, limited their likely influence. The Bush campaign, which saw the encounters more as risks than opportunities, insisted on only two presidential debates and one vice-presidential debate, all squeezed into a short period in early fall. Each debate would consist of brief exchanges initiated by questions from a panel of journalists, who would have little opportunity to ask follow-up questions. By making it easy for the candidates to use set speeches and evade difficult issues, this format also limited what the voters were likely to learn.

The debates did not rescue the Democratic ticket. In the first presidential debate September 25, Dukakis outperformed Bush on debating points. He was generally more facile than Bush and put him on the spot in discussions of housing and health care. Bush, although opposed to legal abortion, could not say whether he believed a woman who received an illegal abortion should be subject to criminal penalties. On the other hand, Bush did well by repeatedly calling attention to Dukakis's liberalism on social issues. And Dukakis did nothing to overcome his public image as a passionless technocrat. Judging from the polls, the debate was a draw.

The remaining debates were not drawn but split. In the vice-presidential debate ten days later, Quayle had a chance to put to rest the widespread doubts about his qualifications; instead, he intensified them. He looked nervous. His memorized responses became painfully apparent when he recited the same answer, in almost identical language, three times. The decisive moment, however, occurred when Bentsen rebuked Quayle for allegedly comparing himself to President John F. Kennedy. Responding to a question about his qualifications, Quayle pointed out that he had served as long in Congress as Kennedy had when he was elected president. "I knew Jack Kennedy," Bentsen intoned. "Senator, you're no Jack Kennedy." It was arguable whether Quayle had implied that he was Kennedy's equal in all respects. In any case, the rebuke was a humiliation. Public response to the debate was overwhelmingly negative toward Quayle and positive toward Bentsen, who became the most highly approved of all four of the candidates. After the debate, the Republicans kept Quayle under wraps.

By the time of the second presidential debate, on October 13, Dukakis needed a decisive victory to have any real chance to win the election. Instead, he suffered a defeat almost on the scale of Quayle's. Overcoming his earlier nervousness and verbal hesitation, Bush gave a commanding performance. Dukakis, who was later reported to have been ill that day, was stiff and inarticulate. In what by many accounts was the crucial exchange, Dukakis missed an obvious opportunity to speak movingly of his personal feelings about crime when he was asked whether he would oppose capital punishment even if his wife Kitty were raped and murdered. The public, by a 49-33 margin, judged that Bush had won the debate.[17]

The campaign was for all practical purposes over. In the final three weeks before election day, Dukakis tried some new tactics— stressing a populist appeal with the new slogan, "I'm on your side"; admitting, at long last, that he was indeed a liberal; and objecting to the tone and tactics of Bush's campaign. He made some gains in the polls, mostly because the populist strains solidified the support of some wavering Democratic voters, but those gains were too little and too late.

The Decision

When the voters went to the polls November 8, they elected George Bush to become the forty-first president of the United States. Bush's victory was decisive: 48.9 million votes, or 53 percent of the popular vote, to Dukakis's 41.8 million, or 46 percent (see Table 3-1). The margin of victory was magnified as usual in the electoral college, with the Republicans winning 426 electoral votes to 111 for the Democrats. Bush's victory was narrower than Reagan's wins in the 1980 and 1984 elections. Moreover, Bush had no coattails; Republicans actually lost seats in Congress. Yet it was also one of the most one-sided victories in history by any candidate seeking his first presidential term.

Bush's success was national, extending to every region of the country. The modest decline in national support for the Republican ticket, compared with 1984, was approximately duplicated in each region.[18] Overall, midwestern and western voters divided their votes in roughly the same proportions as the entire country. Dukakis was strong in a handful of the more Democratic states in each region. In the

Table 3-1 Presidential Election Results by State

	Bush			Dukakis		
State	Percent	Popular	Electoral	Percent	Popular	Electoral
East						
Connecticut	52.0	750,241	8	46.9[a]	676,584	—
Delaware	55.9	139,639	3	43.5	108,647	—
D.C.	14.3	27,590	—	82.6	159,407	3
Maine	55.3	307,131	4	43.9	243,569	—
Maryland	51.1	876,167	10	48.2	826,304	—
Massachusetts	45.4	1,194,635	—	53.2	1,401,415	13
New Hampshire	62.5	281,537	4	36.3	163,696	—
New Jersey	56.2	1,740,604	16	42.6	1,317,541	—
New York	47.5	3,081,871	—	51.6	3,347,882	36
Pennsylvania	50.7	2,300,087	25	48.4	2,194,944	—
Rhode Island	43.9	177,761	—	55.7	225,123	4
Vermont	51.1	124,331	3	47.6	115,775	—
West Virginia	47.5	310,065	—	52.2	341,016	5[b]
Midwest						
Illinois	50.7	2,310,939	24	48.6	2,215,940	—
Indiana	59.8	1,297,763	12	39.7	860,643	—
Iowa	44.5	545,355	—	54.7	670,557	8
Kansas	55.8	554,049	7	42.5	442,636	—
Michigan	53.5	1,965,486	20	45.7	1,675,783	—
Minnesota	45.9	962,337	—	52.9	1,109,471	10
Missouri	51.8	1,084,953	11	47.9	1,001,619	—
Nebraska	60.1	398,447	5	39.2	259,646	—
North Dakota	56.0	166,559	3	43.0	127,739	—
Ohio	55.0	2,416,549	23	44.1	1,939,629	—
South Dakota	52.9	165,415	3	46.5	145,560	—
Wisconsin	47.8	1,047,499	—	51.4	1,126,794	11
South						
Alabama	59.2	815,576	9	39.9	549,506	—
Arkansas	56.4	466,578	6	42.2	349,237	—
Florida	60.9	2,616,597	21	38.5	1,655,851	—
Georgia	59.7	1,081,331	12	39.5	714,792	—
Kentucky	55.5	734,281	9	43.9	580,368	—
Louisiana	54.3	883,702	10	44.1	717,460	—
Mississippi	59.9	557,890	7	39.1	363,921	—
North Carolina	58.0	1,237,258	13	41.7	890,167	—
Oklahoma	57.9	678,367	8	41.3	483,423	—
South Carolina	61.5	606,443	8	37.6	370,554	—
Tennessee	57.9	947,223	11	41.5	679,794	—
Texas	56.0	3,036,829	29	43.3	2,352,748	—
Virginia	59.7	1,309,162	12	39.2	859,799	—

(continued)

Table 3-1   Continued

State	Bush			Dukakis		
	Percent	Popular	Electoral	Percent	Popular	Electoral
West						
Alaska	59.7	118,817	3	36.2	72,105	—
Arizona	60.0	702,541	7	38.8	454,029	—
California	51.1	5,054,917	47	47.6	4,702,233	—
Colorado	53.1	728,177	8	45.3	621,453	—
Hawaii	44.7	158,625	—	54.3	192,364	4
Idaho	62.1	253,881	4	36.0	147,272	—
Montana	52.1	190,412	4	46.2	168,956	—
Nevada	58.9	206,040	4	37.9	132,738	—
New Mexico	51.9	270,341	5	46.9	244,497	—
Oregon	46.6	560,126	—	51.3	616,206	7
Utah	66.2	428,442	5	32.0	207,352	—
Washington	48.5	903,835	—	50.0	933,516	10
Wyoming	60.5	106,867	3	38.0	67,113	—
Total	53.4	48,881,278	426	45.6	41,805,374	111

SOURCE: Adapted from "Official 1988 Presidential Election Results," *Congressional Quarterly Weekly Report,* January 21, 1989, 139.

[a] Vote percentages may not add to 100 percent due to vote for minor party candidates.

[b] One "faithless" elector voted for Lloyd Bentsen for president and Michael Dukakis for vice president.

Midwest, Dukakis carried Iowa, Minnesota, and Wisconsin, three Farm Belt states with reformist political traditions. Bush claimed narrow victories in Illinois and Missouri. In the West, Dukakis did well in the liberal Pacific states of Hawaii, Oregon, and Washington, which he won, and the relatively liberal California, which he barely lost to Bush. The other midwestern and western states went to Bush, mostly by very convincing margins.

Predictably, Bush had more difficulty in the East, Dukakis's home base and typically the most fertile ground for Democratic presidential candidates. Yet Bush still narrowly carried the region in both popular and electoral votes. Dukakis won his home state of Massachusetts, neighboring Rhode Island, West Virginia, and the District of Columbia—all Democratic strongholds. The two largest eastern swing states split in close elections—New York for Dukakis, Pennsylvania for Bush. The Republicans swept the rest of the East, taking New Jersey's sixteen electoral votes by an impressive 56-43 margin. Bush continued the party's domination of the South in presidential elections, with a win there almost as massive as Reagan's in 1984. Despite Dukakis's effort to court the South by campaigning as a moderate and choosing a southern conservative for vice president, Bush carried every southern state by at least a ten-point margin. His success in the region was part of the payoff for his decision to campaign as a conservative Reagan loyalist.

⌐ Traditionally Democratic groups returned to the party nationwide, but not in sufficient numbers to deliver the election. According to the *New York Times*/CBS News exit poll (see Table 3-2), blue-collar workers, who had given Reagan a nine-point margin over Mondale, preferred Dukakis over Bush—but only by one point. Families with moderately low incomes did much the same. Catholics increased their support for the Democratic ticket, compared with 1984, but still gave a majority of their votes to the Republicans. Those persons still willing to call themselves liberals, after a campaign in which the term was used as an epithet, voted 80 percent Democratic, compared with 70 percent in 1984.

Blacks were the principal exception to the trend among Democratic groups. A core component of the New Deal coalition, blacks moved against the stream and gave Dukakis 86 percent, slightly less support than they had given Mondale. Perhaps because Bush was not associated with Reagan's efforts to cut back civil rights enforcement, the 1988 election was less polarized along racial lines than the 1984 election. Some blacks probably remained alienated from the Democratic ticket because of the failure to nominate Jesse Jackson. The turnout rate among blacks fell by eleven points from 1984.

⌐ Traditional Republican groups supported Bush very strongly, although less than they had supported Reagan. Professionals and managers, white-collar workers, and families earning more than $50,000 all preferred the Republican ticket by at least a fifteen-point margin. White Protestants, whose conservative views on social issues Bush had made a central appeal of his campaign, responded with 2-1 support—among white fundamentalists and evangelicals, 4-1 support. In fact, following the trend of recent elections, a 59 percent majority of a'l whites voted Republican. Conservatives endorsed Bush as consistently as liberals supported Dukakis.

As in other elections during the 1980s, there was a sizable gender gap: men voted heavily Republican and women only narrowly so. Surprisingly, voters who came of age during the Reagan era supported the Republican ticket no more than older voters. Age was a significant influence mainly among voters older than sixty, whose greater support for Dukakis (49 percent) probably reflected concern about Medicare and Social Security.

The Republican ticket achieved its decisive victory because, on the

Table 3-2   Voting Choice by Demographic and Political Groups

	Vote in 1984		Vote in 1988	
	Reagan	Mondale	Bush	Dukakis
Total	59%	40%	53%	45%
Men (48%)	62	37	57	41
Women (52)	56	44	50	49
Whites (85)	64	35	59	40
Blacks (10)	9	89	12	86
Hispanics (3)	37	61	30	69
18-29 years old (20)	59	40	52	47
30-44 years old (35)	57	42	54	45
45-59 years old (22)	59	39	57	42
60 and older (22)	60	39	50	49
White Protestant (48)	72	27	66	33
Catholic (28)	54	45	52	47
Jewish (4)	31	67	35	64
White fundamentalist or evangelical Christian (9)	78	22	81	18
Family income under $12,500 (12)	45	54	37	62
$12,500-$24,999 (20)	57	42	49	50
$25,000-$34,999 (20)	59	40	56	44
$35,000-$49,999 (20)	66	33	56	42
$50,000 and over (24)	69	30	62	37
Republicans (35)	93	6	91	8
Democrats (37)	24	75	17	82
Independents (26)	63	35	55	43
Liberals (18)	28	70	18	81
Moderates (45)	53	47	49	50
Conservatives (33)	82	17	80	19
Professional or manager (31)	62	37	59	40
White-collar worker (11)	59	40	57	42
Blue-collar worker (13)	54	45	49	50
Full-time student (4)	54	45	49	50
Teacher (5)	51	48	47	51
Unemployed (5)	32	67	37	62
Homemaker (10)	—	—	55	44
Agricultural worker (2)	—	—	55	44
Retired (16)	60	40	50	49
1984 Reagan voters (56)	100	0	80	19
1984 Democratic Reagan voters (9)	100	0	48	51
1984 Mondale voters (28)	0	100	7	92

SOURCE: Adapted from the *New York Times*/CBS News exit poll, *New York Times*, November 10, 1988. The 1988 data is based on questionnaires completed by 11,645 voters leaving polling places in randomly selected precincts around the country. The 1984 data is based on questionnaires from 9,174 voters.

whole, the voters, and especially the undecided voters, saw Bush as the more qualified or personally appealing of the two candidates; they were more impressed by his campaign themes; and they felt more in agreement with his policy stands. The effects of Democratic and Republican party loyalties, another influence on many voters, almost precisely balanced out. In a series of surveys throughout the year, the Times Mirror news organization found that about two-thirds of the voters could say by January (well before the first caucus or primary) which party's candidate they would vote for in November and did not change their minds during the campaign. Of these strong partisans, half were Democrats and half Republicans.[19] So the election was fought out, in effect, among the other one-third of the electorate.

Judging from surveys and exit polls, the public responded to Bush's major campaign themes more strongly than to Dukakis's. A substantially larger proportion of Bush's supporters cited their candidate's political stands (as opposed to his party, personal ability, or running mate) as the major reason for their support.[20] Bush's most powerful themes were Dukakis's liberalism and his own conservatism, each cited as very important by nearly half of Bush's supporters, and his criticisms of Dukakis concerning the Pledge of Allegiance and the prison furlough program, each cited by almost 40 percent of them. Dukakis's most powerful themes, in descending order, were the Reagan administration's dealings with Noriega, Bush's role in the Iran-contra affair, and the selection of Dan Quayle.

As the Cable News Network/*Los Angeles Times* exit poll shows (see Table 3-3), Bush also had greater success than Dukakis with specific policy issues. The issue with the largest influence on voting decisions—the federal budget deficit—was more effective for Dukakis than for Bush, but evidently produced substantial support for both candidates. Of the 25 percent of voters who cited the deficit as among the most important issues shaping their decision, 60 percent preferred Dukakis and 40 percent Bush. National defense, cited as important by almost as many voters as the deficit (23 percent), worked in Bush's favor by more than a 5-1 margin. The next two issues in order of importance to voters—abortion and crime—were nearly as helpful to Bush as defense. Additional issues of lesser importance cut more or less evenly between the candidates—with Dukakis gaining some advantage on ethics in government, drugs, unemployment, and the environment, and Bush making gains on taxes and foreign trade.

The public was also more favorably impressed with Bush's abilities and personal attributes than it was with Dukakis's. As Table 3-3 shows, about one-third of the voters identified the candidates' experience as the most important consideration in their decision; not

Table 3-3   Reasons for Candidate Preference

	Percentage voting for	
	Bush	Dukakis
Why did you vote for your candidate?		
He has more experience (34%)	97	3
He's more competent (27)	73	26
He seems to care about people like me (24)	25	75
It's time for a change (18)	5	92
He has a clearer vision of the future (17)	52	46
He has a better vice president (13)	14	86
My party didn't nominate the best man (10)	50	44
He impressed me during the debates (7)	54	46
He will avoid a recession (4)	80	19
He's more likable (3)	52	46
What did you like least about his opponent?		
His views are too liberal (28%)	94	6
He ran a dirty campaign (28)	30	69
He has shown bad judgment (24)	46	53
He just leaves me cold (19)	55	43
He's too risky (15)	76	24
He's too close to the special interests (13)	26	72
He's too tied to the past (10)	10	88
He won't stand up for America (8)	65	33
He's too much of a wimp (7)	38	60
He isn't going to be elected (4)	63	34
Which issues were most important to your vote?		
The federal budget deficit (25%)	39	60
National defense (23)	84	15
Abortion (20)	63	36
Crime (18)	67	31
Ethics in government (17)	31	67
Taxes (15)	70	29
Drugs (14)	41	58
Unemployment (10)	35	64
Protecting the environment (11)	28	70
Foreign trade (5)	57	42
No issue, really (12)	52	45

SOURCE: Cable News Network/*Los Angeles Times* exit poll. Reported in *National Journal*, November 12, 1988, 2854.

surprisingly, in view of Bush's impressive resumé, they overwhelmingly preferred him. Considering that Dukakis sought to define the election as turning on the question of competence, it is striking that voters who decided on the basis of that criterion also preferred Bush—by a 3-1 margin. Dukakis's strong points were that he represented change and that he seemed to care about "people like me."

In part, the favorable response to Bush and his stands reflected the technical superiority of his campaign, which managed to focus the voters' attention on issues like capital punishment and the Pledge of Allegiance and make them pivotal in the election. The Dukakis campaign was less persistent in developing the one theme—"good jobs at good wages"—that the Times Mirror survey found to be his strongest appeal.[21] As much as anything, the voters' preference for Bush with respect to competence was probably a response to his manifestly more skillful campaign.

Even though the vice-presidential candidates normally have little effect on the voters' decisions, the difference in popular approval between Quayle and Bentsen clearly hurt the Republican ticket. Of the 13 percent of the voters who accorded central importance to the comparison between the running mates, nearly all voted for the Democrats. According to the Times Mirror survey, about 8 percent of Dukakis supporters said that Quayle was the main reason for their vote. Dislike of Quayle was cited as an important influence by 11 percent of Republicans who defected to Dukakis.[22]

Bush benefited massively, however, from his association with Reagan, a popular president at a time of peace and prosperity. Reagan's approval rating on election day, at 60 percent, was unusually high for a president at the end of his term; and 83 percent of the voters who approved of Reagan's performance as president supported Bush. More than two-fifths of the voters felt that their personal financial circumstances had improved during the past four years, compared with fewer than one-fifth who thought they were worse off; those who saw improvement favored Bush by a margin of more than two to one. Most of the nearly 80 percent of the voters who believed that the economy would stay the same or get better during the next four years also supported Bush. To a great extent, the election outcome was an endorsement of Reagan.[23]

The Consequences for Democratic Government

Beyond the consequences for the election outcome, did the 1988 campaign meet the requirements for strengthening democratic government? Taken as a whole, the campaign had some strengths as well as weaknesses.

Far from avoiding genuine issues, Bush and Dukakis stated clearly distinguishable positions in a number of areas. Bush was less willing than Dukakis to raise taxes, to permit abortion, or to protect industries from import competition. He was more willing to execute criminals and more eager to spend large sums for weapons systems.

While Dukakis's economic proposals often involved government subsidy or regulation, Bush's emphasized tax cuts or reduced regulation. Dukakis favored stronger environmental controls; Bush was more disposed to promote development. Dukakis suggested a new college loan program, which Bush criticized. Bush supported a constitutional amendment, opposed by Dukakis, to permit prayer in public schools.

Many voters were able to perceive some of these differences between the candidates and cast their votes according to their own concerns about issues. By October, 71 percent of the voters knew that Dukakis was opposed to the death penalty, and 65 percent knew he supported legal abortion.[24] Broadly speaking, the voters' choices corresponded to their views of which issues were important (Table 3-3). Bush's supporters were more likely to be concerned with issues that he stressed—especially national defense, crime, and taxes. Correspondingly, Dukakis's voters were more concerned with the budget deficit, ethics in government, unemployment, and the environment.

In some respects, however, the candidates' positions were distorted or simply concealed. Their agitated discussion of ideology did little to clarify their conceptions of the role of government. Dukakis tried to evade the question of ideology by claiming the election was about competence, as if presidents were charged with mere administrative tasks. Bush, on the other hand, called the pragmatic Dukakis a liberal so persistently that he in effect misrepresented him as an extremist. (The tactic also exploited the reflexive antipathy of many voters, apart from their views on issues, to the term *liberal* as a political label.)[25] Bush's ploy was the more successful. As a result, the electorate was ideologically polarized by a choice between two relatively moderate candidates.

While the candidates aired their views on some peripheral issues (gun control and the Pledge of Allegiance, among others), they failed to address other issues of great importance. Neither Bush nor Dukakis explained which programs he would cut or which taxes he would raise to reduce the budget deficit. They did not define strategies for peace in the Middle East, nor did they compare approaches for dealing with the historic changes under way in the Soviet Union. The distortions and omissions in the candidates' statements reduced the campaign's usefulness in promoting popular control of public policy. At the same time, they were hardly unique to the 1988 campaign.

Both Bush and Dukakis were willing at times to mislead the voters. Bush misrepresented Dukakis's fiscal record as governor of Massachusetts by suggesting that he had substantially increased state taxes and distorted his environmental record (far more activist than the Reagan administration's) by blaming him for the pollution of Boston

Harbor. In all likelihood, Dukakis misrepresented Bush's dealings with Noriega when he implied that Bush had simply ignored the general's involvement in smuggling drugs to the United States.[26]

But in the discussion of the policy problem most subject to lack of candor in recent elections—the budget deficit—the 1988 campaign was somewhat more grounded in reality than the two that preceded it. To be sure, neither Bush nor Dukakis laid out a credible plan to attack the deficit. While promising not to raise taxes, Bush proposed a "flexible" spending freeze that failed to convince most of his own economic advisers.[27] Dukakis claimed, implausibly, that he could eliminate the deficit largely by cutting waste and improving tax enforcement. Both candidates vowed not to cut Social Security.

But neither candidate promised to cure the deficit painlessly, as Reagan had in 1980 and 1984. One reason for the improvement was that Bush, while seeking the Republican presidential nomination in 1980, had strongly criticized Reagan's budget plans, coining the term "voodoo economics." He could not easily advocate similar plans in 1988. Another reason was that Dukakis, having learned the lessons of the 1984 Mondale campaign,[28] played his cards close to the vest regarding the possibility of a tax increase. The tax and deficit issues, therefore, were discussed with some realism. They had only modest salience in the campaign.

Much like other recent campaigns, the 1988 campaign offered hardly any serious debate about the merits of the candidates' positions. The candidates' speeches and television advertisements dealt with issues, for the most part, on the level of slogans and one-liners. The televised debates permitted such brief discussions of each topic, with such generous opportunity for evasion, that they amounted to side-by-side stump speeches. Instead of arguing about which new weapons systems were needed, Bush simply accused Dukakis of having opposed every recent weapons modernization program, and Dukakis retorted that Bush had never met a weapons system he did not like. As in a dispute between children ("No, I didn't!" "Yes, you did!"), the candidates contradicted each other on relatively straightforward matters of fact: whether Dukakis had raised taxes in Massachusetts and whether he had supported or abolished the prison furlough program.[29] In a debate with any depth or discipline, such factual disagreements would have been resolved decisively or would not have arisen in the first place. In all, the campaign provided voters with exceedingly little information upon which to judge the candidates' achievements or the merits of their positions on issues.

The use of symbolic and emotional themes was pervasive—from Dukakis stressing his immigrant origins to Bush's appearance at a flag factory. But these were of a piece with Carter's portrayal of rural virtue in 1976 and Reagan's proclaiming "morning in America" in 1984.

The one distinctive defect of the 1988 campaign was the prominence of misleading or inflammatory negative appeals by both candidates, especially Bush. Some of the attacks the candidates leveled against each other were entirely pertinent. Dukakis was right: Bush's performance in the Iran-contra episode was reason to question his judgment or courage. So was Bush, when he suggested that Dukakis's inexperience in foreign policy was a significant shortcoming; indeed, the governor had obvious difficulty articulating a responsible position on modernization of the strategic forces. Dukakis's willingness to grant furloughs to first-degree murders suggested a concern for criminals (or at least a strategy for their rehabilitation) that was unpopular in the country.

Some of the other charges, however, were more misleading than informative. Dukakis's attack on Bush for cooperating with General Noriega took no account of the circumstances in which he did so. Arguably, Bush's making the Pledge of Allegiance into an issue was much more irresponsible: he attacked Dukakis for upholding certain judicial rulings—intended to protect freedom of political opinion and the rights of religious minorities—that were essentially uncontroversial in constitutional law.

The unusually negative campaign seems to have alienated some voters. The public became relatively dissatisfied with their choice of candidates. By October, Bush had an approval rating (58 percent) as low as that of any winning candidate since 1960, while Dukakis had a rating (48 percent) lower than that of any other losing candidate.[30] A large minority of the respondents in a poll said that, given the chance, they would have voted "no confidence" instead of selecting either candidate.[31] Perhaps partly because they were disappointed with the candidates and the campaign, voters stayed away from the polls in record numbers. Just 50 percent of the eligible electorate turned out to vote, down from 53 percent in the less closely contested election of 1984, and the lowest participation rate since 1924.[32]

The campaign's main shortcomings, however, were the sketchy and somewhat distorted presentation of the candidates' positions, the considerable reliance on misleading or emotional appeals, and the lack of serious debate about the merits of the candidates' positions. Because of these limitations, it was impossible for the voters to make meaningful choices about some of the major issues facing the country. It was difficult for them to learn any more than they already knew about those issues. And it was harder than it would have been with a more disciplined campaign debate for the government to act effectively on some urgent issues, especially the budget deficit, after the election. Unfortunately, there is little to suggest that these common shortcomings of presidential campaigns were unusually pronounced in 1988.

Improving Presidential Campaign Debate

A presidential campaign cannot resemble a graduate seminar in public policy. The depth and seriousness of campaign debate is unavoidably limited by the fact that most voters devote very little time to following it.

Even so, a presidential campaign could offer the voters a great deal of information about the problems of the country, the plausible responses to those problems and their likely consequences, and the policy positions and other qualifications of the opposing candidates. Campaign debate could be held to reasonable standards of honesty and integrity. As the country becomes more educated and the means of communication expand, the underlying ability to conduct genuinely informative campaigns presumably increases. Furthermore, in an era when voters are not strongly attached to parties, and when economic and fiscal strains impose hard choices upon government, the need for such campaigns also increases.

Despite the inevitable limitations of presidential campaign debate, there may be ways to bring about some improvement. At a minimum, the televised debates should be institutionalized, perhaps with a requirement that the candidates participate as a condition for receiving federal campaign funds. The debates also should be made more useful. To cover the issues of the campaign with some thoroughness, at least three or four debates should be held. The debate format should be designed to keep the candidates from easily evading questions, obscuring issues, or getting away with inaccurate factual assertions. The more time devoted to a single topic, and the more authority an impartial moderator has to regulate the debate, the more easily such tactics can be exposed.

Another measure would be to place restrictions on the kinds of campaign advertisements that can be paid for with public funds. It is perverse that the public has been subsidizing presidential candidates (in the amount of $46 million each in 1988, of which more than half was used for advertising) to pay for thirty-second television commercials that influence the vote mainly through slogans and visual imagery. Congress could stipulate, for example, that subsidized advertisements must consist simply of a candidate talking, without distracting visual effects, and in blocks of time long enough to present an intelligible message.

The most important improvement in presidential campaigns,

however, would be for the print and broadcast media to provide the voters with considerably more information than they do now about the qualifications of the candidates, their past achievements, and the likely consequences of their policies. Such information would help the public to evaluate the candidates' claims. It also would impose some discipline upon those claims. The challenge for the media is to invent ways to provide interesting, nonpartisan coverage that is also substantive and critical.

Ultimately, it is uncertain how much presidential campaign debate can be improved. Nor is it certain how much even a substantial improvement would enhance either the federal government's ability to adopt workable, effective policies or the public's informed participation in choosing those policies. If nothing else, however, a more serious, responsible campaign debate would ensure a presidential selection process that could claim the public's respect.

Notes

1. ABC News/*Washington Post* poll, June 19-26, 1988. Unless otherwise noted, the source of poll data cited in this chapter is "Opinion Roundup: Ten Years of Public Opinion," *Public Opinion,* September/October 1988, 21-40. The principal sources on events of the campaign are the *New York Times,* national edition, and network television news broadcasts.
2. Some theories of democracy require a large and relatively direct role for the public in choosing policies. Others call for elected representatives to use broad discretion. For a discussion, see J. Roland Pennock, *Democratic Political Theory* (Princeton, N.J.: Princeton University Press, 1979).
3. For general treatments of presidential campaigns, see Nelson W. Polsby and Aaron Wildavsky, *Presidential Elections,* 7th ed. (New York: Free Press, 1988); Herbert B. Asher, *Presidential Elections and American Politics,* 4th ed. (Chicago: Dorsey Press, 1988); John H. Kessel, *Presidential Campaign Politics,* 3d ed. (Chicago: Dorsey Press, 1988); and Stephen J. Wayne, *The Road to the White House,* 3d ed. (New York: St. Martin's Press). For an evaluation of presidential campaigns similar to the one in this chapter, see Thomas E. Patterson, *The Mass Media Election: How Americans Choose Their President* (New York: Praeger, 1980).
4. On issue voting, see Asher, *Presidential Elections and American Politics,* chap. 4. For a useful perspective on the voters' efforts to acquire information, see Samuel Popkin et al., "Comment: What Have You Done for Me Lately? Toward an Investment Theory of Voting," *American Political Science Review* 70 (1976): 779-805.
5. See Asher, *Presidential Elections and American Politics,* 117-118.
6. Thomas E. Patterson, "Voter Control of Information," in *Political Persuasion in Presidential Campaigns,* ed. L. Patrick Devlin (New Brunswick, N.J.: Transaction Books, 1987), 175-184.

7. See Patterson, *The Mass Media Election;* and Doris A. Graber, "Press Freedom and the General Welfare," *Political Science Quarterly* 101:2 (1986): 257-275.

8. Kathleen Hall Jamieson, *Packaging the Presidency: A History and Criticism of Presidential Campaign Advertising* (New York: Oxford University Press, 1984).

9. Michael J. Robinson, "Can Values Save George Bush?" *Public Opinion,* July/August 1988, 11-13, 59-60.

10. For a balanced assessment of the presidential debates, see Sidney Kraus, *Televised Presidential Debates and Public Policy* (Hillsdale, N.J.: Lawrence Erlbaum Associates, 1988).

11. See, for example, Benjamin M. Friedman, *Day of Reckoning: The Consequences of American Economic Policy Under Reagan and After* (New York: Random House, 1989).

12. The difficulty in assessing the Republican advantage is that there are too few presidential elections within a few decades' time to isolate the idiosyncratic effects of particular candidates and elections. Much of the Republican party's recent success may reflect superior candidates and favorable national conditions over a period of several elections. For several perspectives, see James A. Barnes, "Democrats' Huge Electoral Hurdle," *National Journal Convention Preview,* June 20, 1988, 12; Stuart Rothenberg, "A New Look at the Lock: How the Republicans Can Lose," *Public Opinion,* March/April 1988, 41-54; Gerald S. Strom and Barry Fisk, "The Utility of Political Science: Forecasting Presidential Elections," *PS: Political Science* (forthcoming); and Nelson Polsby and Aaron Wildavsky, *Presidential Elections,* 186-187.

13. American constitutional doctrine is unclear about the degree to which executive and legislative officials should interpret the Constitution for themselves, as opposed to obeying decisions by the courts. But few argue, as Bush's position implied, that such officials may simply ignore firmly settled judicial rulings.

14. In a speech after the election, television commentator Walter Cronkite called the Bush effort the most sophisticated and cynical presidential campaign in history. Campaign manager Lee Atwater, whom some blamed for the tone of the Bush campaign, had run aggressive negative campaigns on behalf of several candidates in previous elections and had worked on a Ph.D. dissertation on negative campaigning.

15. *New York Times/*CBS News poll, *New York Times,* September 14, 1988.

16. For a chart tracing the changes in favorable and unfavorable ratings of the candidates, see *New York Times,* November 9, 1988.

17. ABC News instant poll reported in *New York Times,* October 15, 1988.

18. According to the *New York Times/*CBS News exit poll, in the East the Republican vote declined to 50 percent from 52 percent in 1984; in the Midwest to 52 percent from 58 percent; in the South to 58 percent from 64 percent; and in the West to 52 percent from 61 percent. *New York Times,* November 10, 1988.

19. "The People, the Press and Politics: Post-Election Typology Survey," Times Mirror, November 1988, mimeograph, 5.

20. Ibid., 24-25.

21. "The People, the Press and Politics: October Pre-Election Typology Survey," Times Mirror, October 1988, 5.

22. Times Mirror, "Post-Election Survey," 24-25.

23. William Schneider, "Solidarity's Not Enough," *National Journal,* November 12, 1988, 2853-2855. The data in this paragraph are from the Cable News Network/*Los Angeles Times* exit poll as reported by Schneider.

24. Times Mirror, "Pre-Election Survey," 23.

25. In polls, self-identified conservatives outnumber liberals by almost two to one (see Table 3-2). Yet liberal opinions are approximately as prevalent as conservative ones, and often much more prevalent, on a wide range of specific issues—including defense spending, support for welfare state programs, environmental regulation, gun control, abortion, aid to the contras, relations with the Soviets, and so on. For a sampling, see "Ten Years of Public Opinion." To avoid hostility to the liberal label, liberal politicians have been referring to themselves as *progressive.*
26. Bush claimed he was unaware of Noriega's involvement in drug trafficking at the time of his contacts with the general. In any case, other foreign policy objectives may have required working with him.
27. *New York Times,* December 14, 1988.
28. Paul J. Quirk, "The Economy: Economists, Electoral Politics, and Reagan Economics," in *The Elections of 1984,* ed. Michael Nelson (Washington, D.C.: CQ Press, 1985), 155-187.
29. Bush's charge that Dukakis had raised taxes was misleading. Tax revenues had increased because of economic growth (something Republicans would have been proud to accomplish), and there had been a rate increase, as in many other states, to adjust for an error in the original estimates of the effects of the federal Tax Reform Act of 1986. Dukakis's claim to have abolished the furlough program was equally misleading: after long defending the program, he eventually succumbed to pressure from the legislature and accepted a measure to abolish it.
30. Times Mirror, "Pre-Election Survey," 6.
31. Times Mirror, "Post-Election Survey," 47.
32. *New York Times,* December 18, 1988. A low level of interest in the election was already apparent in relatively small television audiences by the time of the conventions.

4. THE PRESS AND ITS MISSED ASSIGNMENT

Thomas E. Patterson

Every election is different, but in at least one way they are all the same: before and after the voting, candidates and the media invariably blame each other for the deficiencies of the campaign. Candidates charge that their speeches and position papers on important matters of public policy are neglected by the media; reporters and editors reply that the candidates and their advisers offer nothing but carefully packaged "media events" to cover. To the dispassionate listener, the likely lesson of this debate may be that both politicians and the media could do better if only they would try.

Thomas Patterson suggests that the very premises of the familiar argument are flawed. The candidates in a particular campaign cannot do much better than they actually do at framing the choice for the voters because politicians have allowed the political parties, which Patterson regards as the only sure foundation on which to build serious campaigns, to erode. As for the media, they are profit-making corporations whose business it is to sell newspapers and attract television viewers, not to try to take the place of the parties and candidates in defining the stakes for the voters. Patterson concludes that postelection finger-pointing by candidates and the media is largely beside the point: "The real weakness of the present system is that it is built upon the dismantling of the political party."

Many Americans are unhappy with the way we elect our president. Gallup trotted out the usual suspects in a June 1988 poll: too much money, too much time. The poll found that 70 percent of Americans feel that a shortened primary campaign would improve the process and 76 percent believe that reducing the amount of money candidates spend would help. But these problems, if they are problems, are largely derivative. The real flaw in the modern presidential campaign is that it asks its three principals—the voters, the candidates, and the news media—to exercise responsibilities they cannot exercise competently.

The voters are overwhelmed by their assignment. The nominating races attract large fields of contenders—a half-dozen or more self-starting candidates, most of whom are not nationally known before the election campaign. With their casual attention to politics, most voters have virtually no chance of acquiring a realistic understanding of what the various candidates represent. The voters must make their choices on the basis of shallow and unreliable information. Opinion polls in recent elections have shown that half or more of primary election voters cannot say with any accuracy where the candidates stand on issues of public policy.

Candidates also cannot fulfill their duty. They are cast adrift by the present system, forced to act on their own and to do whatever is necessary and credible to advance their candidacies. The structure of today's campaign denies them any realistic opportunity to exercise true leadership. The modern campaign is the very horror that the writers of the Constitution sought to avoid—an election process that hinges on what Alexander Hamilton called "the small arts of popularity."

The greatest flaw in the modern system of electing presidents, however, is its dependence on the news media. They are asked to organize public choice, a task for which they are not designed and are poorly suited. As Walter Lippmann, perhaps the foremost American journalist of his age, remarked: "Public opinions must be organized for the press if they are to be sound, not by the press as is the case today." [1]

The News Media's Role

As recently as the 1968 presidential election, the news media were an important but not decisive intermediary in presidential selection. Party leaders held the real power. In 1952, for example, Sen. Estes Kefauver defeated President Harry S Truman by a 55-45 margin in New Hampshire's opening primary. Kefauver then won all but one of the other twelve primaries he contested, and he was the clear preference of rank-and-file Democrats in the final Gallup poll before the national convention. Yet Democratic party leaders rejected Kefauver, choosing instead Illinois governor Adlai Stevenson, who, they felt, better represented the party's traditions.

The bitter Democratic campaign of 1968 brought an end to party-controlled nominations. Against the backdrop of opposition to the Vietnam War, Eugene McCarthy and then Robert Kennedy challenged President Lyndon Johnson's leadership, eventually driving him from the presidential race. The 1968 Democratic nominee, however, was not an antiwar candidate but was instead Johnson's vice president, Hubert Humphrey, who had not entered a single primary. When Richard Nixon beat Humphrey narrowly in the general election, disgruntled reform Democrats demanded changes in the nominating process. A 1970 Democratic party commission (the McGovern-Fraser commission) mandated that all national convention delegates be chosen in primaries or in open caucuses. (Previously, about two-thirds of the delegates had been chosen through more or less closed party processes.) To a substantial degree, the Republican party followed suit.

As a result of the party reforms, serious contenders for presidential nominations have no choice but to appeal directly to the voters. No amount of support from party leaders can take the place of votes from millions of ordinary citizens. One effect of forcing candidates to seek those votes has been to increase greatly the media's influence in the presidential selection process. The news media are the only effective route to the voters' consciousness.

The media have always been important in American elections, at times exceptionally so. Wendell Willkie was an obscure businessman until Henry Luce decided that Willkie would make a good Republican nominee in 1940 and used *Time* and *Life* magazines to bring him into prominence.[2] But the media's modern role in helping to establish the agenda of candidates and issues in presidential elections differs in degree from its role in the past. Once upon a time, as in Willkie's case, the press occasionally played a leading role in the nomination or election processes. Now it always does so.

The Issue of Capability

The media's political influence traditionally has provoked discussions about legitimacy. Stanley Baldwin's complaint in 1931 about British press lords Rothemere and Beaverbrook, that they were after "power without responsibility, the prerogative of the harlot through the ages," reflects one side of the legitimacy issue.[3] The idea of unchecked power is alien to liberal democracy. What is the mechanism of accountability for privately owned news organizations? The other side of the issue is the value of a free press. Who will guard the guardians if not free and untrammeled news media?

There is, however, another issue that needs to be raised about the press. It concerns not the press's legitimacy but rather its capability, not whether the press should be free to exercise power but whether it can exercise power competently.[4] Capability was the issue Lippmann addressed in concluding that public opinions must be organized for the press if they are to be sound.

The issue of capability is made especially compelling by developments that have made the press the principal intermediary between the presidential candidates and the voters. Although the press's new position is due largely to the default of the political parties, the reality of the modern presidential campaign is that the press is expected by its critics and apologists alike to organize election opinion and debate. Reporters often claim that they can do this job. But even if journalists did not want the responsibility, it is theirs by virtue of an electoral process that is built upon numerous primaries, self-generated candidacies, and weak parties.

Although the media have replaced the parties in many ways, what the media do now is not equivalent to what the parties once did. The press and the political party may both serve to link leaders with their publics, but the two intermediaries are very different in nature. The party has an incentive—the control of government—to organize in meaningful ways groups of voters that are demanding symbolic and policy representation in government. The press has no such incentive. Although the press plays a political role, it is by nature a business—the news business—and its organizational norms and imperatives are set by its basic character.

Thus, skepticism about the press's ability to be the chief intermediary between candidates and voters is justified. It came to this role by circumstance rather than by design. If the media were capable of organizing presidential selection in a meaningful way, it would be in spite of the fact that they were not developed for this purpose. As Donald Horowitz observes:

> Institutions are often a step behind the tasks they must perform. This is especially likely to be true if new tasks have been added to the old rather than displacing them, so that the problem is not simply one of transformation but of performing both tasks.[5]

Assessing Capability Through News Content Analysis

The media's capacity as an intermediary between candidates and voters is best evaluated by analyzing the content of the news. Although a study of, say, how news is gathered may be of some value, the main proof of the ability to organize public debate and opinion is the news agenda itself. Does the news provide the voters with a reliable, valid portrayal of their choices in an election?

To address this question, I conducted a content analysis of 1988 election news. The analysis was based on alternating issues of *Time* and *Newsweek* magazines from October 1987 to November 1988. For this study, the unit of analysis is the news paragraph. Each paragraph of each election news story in *Time* and *Newsweek* was classified according to its main subject, its main candidate (if any), and its favorability or unfavorability (if any) to that candidate.

In addition to the economy of analyzing a weekly rather than a daily news source, *Time* and *Newsweek* have the advantage of communicating a "purer" version of election news than do other sources. Daily news sources, whether print or broadcast, are compelled to pay attention to the candidates' travels each day; roughly 15 percent of daily election news is devoted to one aspect or another of the candidates' itineraries. *Time* and *Newsweek* can ignore such material and go straight to the core subjects of election news.

Another advantage of a study based on *Time* and *Newsweek* is that their election news bridges the gap between newspaper and television versions of the campaign. The similarity between *Time* and *Newsweek*'s coverage and that of the newspapers is obvious: each communicates through the medium of print. The similarity to television news lies in the form of news: like television, *Time* and *Newsweek* depend on the narrative style of reporting. Television's use of the narrative form derives from its need for tightly structured stories that can be understood readily by the viewers; television stories cannot be allowed to trail off with less important details as newspaper stories do. The news magazines rely on the narrative to compress related events and provide lively presentations.

"Winner-Take-All" News

Russell Baker of the *New York Times* aptly calls the press the "great mentioner." A candidate who receives heavy news coverage usually benefits from the attention; one who is largely ignored by the media is unlikely to have much success.

The media's ability to bring candidates into public view is most critical in the early phases of the nominating process. Except when an incumbent president is seeking reelection, the nominating races attract large fields of contenders. Most of them are not nationally known before the race begins. As a result, voters are asked to assess their choices quickly and to do so largely on the basis of what they can discover through the media. Yet the burden on the voters is made harder, not easier, by certain tendencies in election news.

Concentrating on the Race

The news media leave voters inadequately informed for two major reasons. First, election news is mainly about the strategic game played by the candidates and only secondarily about the policies and leadership at stake (see Table 4-1). In 1988 media coverage concentrated on the competition between the candidates. The election contest and the candidates' campaign styles and squabbles accounted for more than half of the news that was reported in *Time* and *Newsweek*. The press's tendency to concentrate on the strategic game was at its peak early in the election year, the time when the voters had their greatest need for information about the candidates' political positions. For the voter who

Table 4-1   Themes of 1988 Election News

	Proportion of news
Horse race (e.g., winning and losing, strategy and tactics, fund raising)	32%
"Campaign" issues (e.g., facts and rumors of scandals, allegations of dirty or low-level campaigning)	13
"Campaign" images (e.g., candidates' styles of campaigning, posturing, likability)	15
"Governing" images (e.g., leadership ability, trustworthiness)	7
Policy issues (e.g., foreign policy, domestic economy)	17
Candidates' orientation (e.g., personal and political backgrounds, ideology, group support)	16
	100%

was willing to dig deeply enough (including watching the televised debates on cable television), a fair amount of information about the candidates was available. But for the more typical voter, who "follows" the news rather than studying it, the early phase of the presidential campaign was mostly a story of horse race and strategy.

Second, election news does not provide the candidates with equal exposure. In 1988 five Republican candidates sought the press's attention but with vastly different results (see Figure 4-1). George Bush received substantially more coverage in the preliminary stage of the Republican race than did any of his opponents. He received twice as much coverage in *Time* and *Newsweek* as Sen. Robert Dole and more than ten times as much as another opponent, Rep. Jack Kemp.

One effect of this pattern of reporting was to keep the candidates' rankings more or less static until the Iowa caucuses and New Hampshire primary. As in earlier elections, the news coverage each of the candidates received closely paralleled his standing in the national polls. Bush had both a sizable lead in the polls and the most coverage, followed by Dole and, further down, the other Republican contenders.[6]

Even brief spurts in a candidate's news coverage often can be explained by indicators of electoral popularity. Democrat Bruce Babbitt got a flurry of attention from reporters when polls in Iowa suggested that he was gaining strength. Babbitt's surge with Iowa voters was either illusionary or short-lived, however, and he soon reverted to his media-poor position. In the four months preceding the Iowa caucuses, he received only 11 percent of *Time* and *Newsweek's* coverage of the Democratic contenders. Not surprisingly, when Babbitt dropped out of

Figure 4-1 News Coverage of the Republican Contenders in Early Stages of 1988 Nominating Contest

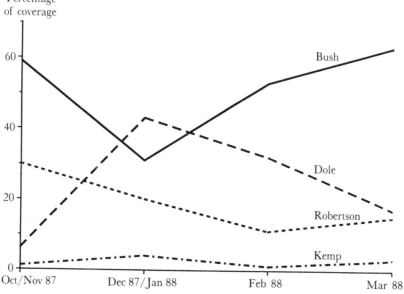

NOTE: Figure does not show coverage of Pierre duPont and other possible Republican nominees who, together, received 3 percent or less of the coverage in each of the time periods.

the campaign after Iowa, many Democratic voters claimed never to have heard of him.

The tendency for news coverage to concentrate on the leading candidates increases when the Iowa caucuses and the New Hampshire primary take place. Although Iowa and New Hampshire are low-population, unrepresentative states, reporters tend to project their outcomes onto the nation as a whole. An NBC correspondent declared, "Bush is dead," after Bush finished behind Dole and Pat Robertson in Iowa. With his Iowa win, Dole went ahead of Bush in news coverage for the first and only time in the Republican race. The allocation of news coverage to winners also was evident on the Democratic side. After Richard Gephardt won in Iowa and Michael Dukakis won in New Hampshire, each received a news bonanza.

In allocating coverage among the candidates on the basis of electoral success, the press is acting largely according to traditional news values. The function of news, Lippmann wrote, is to "signalize events." Winners are the real story—to downplay their victories would be to ignore the limited news space that newspapers, magazines, and broadcast media have available, the gravitation toward the "indisputable fact," and the need to capture what Lippmann called the "easy interest" of the news audience.[7]

Helping Out the Winners

The press's concentration on early primary and caucus winners is not designed to promote their candidacies, but it certainly has that effect. Paul Lazarsfeld and Robert Merton note that mass audiences subscribe to the circular belief: "If you really matter, you will be at the focus of mass attention and, if you are at the focus of mass attention, then you must really matter."[8] Support in the polls for George McGovern in 1972, Jimmy Carter in 1976, George Bush in 1980, and Walter Mondale (after Iowa) and Gary Hart (after New Hampshire) in 1984 rose substantially after the media spotlight focused on their candidacies early in the race.

This follow-the-winner pattern held true in 1988. Before the Iowa caucuses, a Gallup survey indicated that Hart led among Democratic voters in the South, which, with its Super Tuesday lineup of primaries, promised to be the crucial region in deciding the nomination. After Gephardt won in Iowa, a Cable News Network survey found that he had gone ahead in the South. Then, after Dukakis took New Hampshire, a Gallup poll showed Dukakis leading in the South. What is behind such surges? Certainly not information. Democratic voters did not know appreciably more about Dukakis a few days after the New Hampshire primary than they did before. But when the voters know very little about any of the candidates, and when one candidate suddenly is catapulted into the headlines, that candidate can pick up a lot of support. One or more candidates have done so in every recent presidential election.

Clearly, the press has the power to affect the outcome of nominating races. The significant issue, however, is not one of power alone but of power joined to purpose. What public goal is served? The answer is none. The press has no public purpose in dividing its coverage among contending candidates. The media's allocations are consequential, but are governed mainly by news values: the issue for the press is not which candidates would be good for a majority of the country but which are material for good news stories.

What a contrast to other democracies, or to the United States as recently as 1968, where the role of chief intermediary between the voters and potential nominees belongs to the political parties, which *are* concerned with the consequences of their actions. A party may misjudge its choices, but it at least weighs the effects on the political system of its alternatives before choosing. The press does not. By the standards of news, candidates are interchangeable: whether Dukakis or Gephardt or

Paul Simon or Al Gore breaks out from the pack in the early going is irrelevant. The news will always be about the winner, and the lucky candidate who wins early will always get a boost because of that.

Issue News

Journalistic norms also influence the choice of issues that are emphasized in election news coverage. The issues the candidates stress most heavily are not covered most prominently in the news. In the service of news values, the press promotes a political agenda of its own.

Candidates ground most of their appeals to voters in issues—society's problems and the government's attempts to deal with them. Because candidates have differing views on the nature of these problems and the solutions they prefer, they may take opposing positions. But it is society's recurrent problems to which their positions are a response. In his study of the speeches and statements of presidential candidates from Franklin Roosevelt to Jimmy Carter, Benjamin Page found that candidates, without exception, built their appeals around policy problems and proposed solutions:

> Challengers describe problems that need solving and condemn the incumbents' failure to deal with them. Candidates of the incumbent party point with pride to their real or imagined accomplishments. Both incumbents and challengers enunciate broad goals and conjure up visions of the glorious society which their future administrations will bring into being.[9]

News Values as a Barrier to Platform Presentation

The news media are not reliable transmitters of the candidates' platforms. In 1988, for example, Dukakis campaigned heavily on the themes of economic fairness and competent leadership. Bush's major theme was a promise to continue Ronald Reagan's agenda, although in "a kinder, gentler" way. Bush's and Dukakis's themes were not mentioned regularly in news coverage. Moreover, these themes were seldom the basis for an entire news story in *Time* or *Newsweek;* rather, they were mentioned in only a paragraph or two.

Bush and Dukakis were able to get the media to communicate their platforms with reasonable accuracy and thoroughness only twice: during the week of their respective nominating convention and during the campaign's closing week. These brief periods, less than a month in time, included more than a third of all such references in *Time* and *Newsweek* during the entire election. Most of the time, the candidates' policy stands made up a small fraction of election news. Before the party conventions, for example, Bush's policy positions accounted for only 9 percent of the coverage of his candidacy and Dukakis's positions accounted for only 8 percent of his coverage.

The news media, then, made no significant attempt to define Bush or Dukakis in the ways the candidates wanted to be seen. Although the messages of stump speeches are finely tuned by the candidates and their staffs to embody their positions and are repeated at nearly every campaign stop and before almost every audience, the media seem to think that these messages are largely meaningless, at least by journalistic standards. In the second presidential debate, George Bush became mildly angry when a questioner suggested that he was avoiding the issues. He noted that he had made several policy statements on a recent day, only to find that they were ignored in the news.

Why are the candidates' policy statements not regarded as very newsworthy by the media? Lippmann had an explanation: the underlying conditions of society, which give rise to the public's policy attitudes and the candidates' appeals, are not the basis of news. Instead, the news is an account of the overt phases of events. As Lippmann said, the news is "not a first hand report of the raw material [of society . . . but] a report of that material after it has been stylized." [10] Lippmann's example was a labor dispute; this kind of problem may fester for months or years, but it does not become news until it erupts in a strike or in violence.

The nature of news helps to explain why the most memorable policy phrase of the 1988 campaign was Bush's "Read my lips—no new taxes." Candidates' platforms become truly newsworthy only after assuming a stylized form. If Bush had chosen to express his opposition to new taxes in a conventional way, the press would have largely ignored his stand. Indeed, one could argue that a turning point in the 1988 campaign came when Bush recognized that serious policy discussion would not carry him as far in news coverage as sloganeering and posturing. As Colin Seymour-Ure has noted,[11] the press prefers clear-cut issues, those that neatly divide the candidates, provoke controversy, rest on principle rather than on complex relationships, and can be stated in simple terms, usually by reference to shorthand labels, such as "read my lips" or the "L-word" (liberal).

An Emphasis on "Campaign" Issues

In addition to its preference for clear-cut issues, the press has an affinity for "campaign" issues. [12] These are issues that arise out of the campaign itself, usually as the result of an error in judgment by a candidate. Examples from past campaigns include Carter's remark about lust in a *Playboy* interview in 1976 and vice-presidential nominee Geraldine Ferraro's decision in 1984 not to release her family's tax returns.

The degree to which campaign issues can dominate news coverage is evident from Michael Robinson's analysis of the 1984 campaign. Using a broad definition of what constitutes such issues, Robinson found that they accounted for nearly 40 percent of all election news. Included were Ferraro's taxes and her verbal battle over abortion with Archbishop John O'Connor; Mondale's criticized meeting with the Soviet foreign minister, Andrei Gromyko; and Reagan's inaccessibility to the press and his suggestion that the 1983 bombing of U.S. Marines in Lebanon was Carter's fault.[13]

The 1988 election also generated its share of campaign issues. In fact, until the Iowa caucuses, election news was dominated by two such issues: Hart's weekend fling with Donna Rice and Joseph Biden's plagiarizing a speech by British Labour party leader Neil Kinnock. No policy issue at any time during the campaign received headlines as bold as those that accompanied Hart's affair or Biden's blunder. Another 1988 campaign issue that dominated news coverage for several consecutive days was the revelation that Republican vice-presidential nominee Dan Quayle had pulled strings to avoid the Vietnam draft by enlisting in the Indiana National Guard. No candidate received more negative coverage in 1988 than Quayle, who, mainly by virtue of the newsworthiness of the military draft issue, was written about in *Time* and *Newsweek* almost four times as often as Democratic vice-presidential nominee Lloyd Bentsen (see Table 4-2).

Perhaps the most revealing instance of the press's preoccupation with campaign issues came shortly before the March 8 Super Tuesday round of primaries, which included twenty states for the Democrats and seventeen for the Republicans. Super Tuesday looked as if it would be the decisive encounter in the nominating races because of the great number of delegate seats at stake. Yet the media did little to assist the voters in their choice. Robert Lichter's content analysis of three networks' evening newscasts indicates that horse race news outpaced issue news twenty to one in the period just before Super Tuesday. The only candidate to break through this horse race barrage was a long-shot

Table 4-2   News Coverage of Dan Quayle and Lloyd Bentsen

	Total	Positive	Mixed	Negative	Neutral
		Amount of coverage (in paragraphs)			
Quayle	94	16 (17%)	30 (32%)	47 (50%)	1 (1%)
Bentsen	25	12 (48%)	7 (28%)	4 16%)	2 (6%)

contender, Republican televangelist Pat Robertson. He made news with a wild claim that Soviet missiles were entrenched in Cuba and an equally unfounded charge that Bush had masterminded the Jimmy Swaggart scandal to discredit all prominent fundamentalist ministers.[14] What gave Robertson's issues news value was that they were sensational, colorful, and unique—the stuff of headlines.

Stories about campaign issues often build upon themselves, creating suspense and heightened expectations as they unfold. They involve what James David Barber identifies as "action-reaction," the most common type of developing news story.[15] The Hart story, which ended with his dramatic departure from the race in May 1987, is an example. In contrast, ordinary policy issues are less compelling as potential news items.

News and Truth

In a noted essay, Lippmann distinguished news from truth, saying that the function of news is to bring an event into the open, while the function of truth is to create a picture of reality on which people can base their actions.[16]

The media turn clear-cut events and campaign issues into news; they do not seek the truth underlying these issues. Dukakis's alleged responsibility for pollution in Boston Harbor and the escape of prisoner Willie Horton became news because they were the heart of Bush's television ads. The press gave reasonably heavy coverage to these issues, but largely in terms of their effects on the voters. The news story was that Boston Harbor and Horton were contributing significantly to the surge of support for Bush in the early fall.

As a *Newsweek* reporter noted, the press made only a small effort to discover the truth underlying the issues. Was Dukakis a callused polluter and Bush a concerned environmentalist? Was Dukakis unconcerned about criminals and their victims? By and large, the press accepted the Boston Harbor and Willie Horton issues on the narrow grounds that were laid out in the Bush ads. Because the ads were not technically false, their claims went largely unchallenged by reporters. Toward the end of the campaign, after the damage to Dukakis's candidacy was complete, the press suggested that the Bush ads were mean and misleading. In no significant way, however, did the press seek the truth about Michael Dukakis.

News Images

Conventional wisdom holds that Truman stormed from behind to defeat Thomas Dewey in 1948 on the strength of a "give-'em-hell" speaking style and a barnstorming whistle-stop campaign across

America. News coverage of the final weeks of the 1948 campaign, however, did not convey this story. Instead, the Truman campaign was pictured as relatively ineffective and the candidate as mostly strident, turning off voters with harsh rhetoric rather than winning them to his side. The other Truman—he of give-'em-hell and whistle-stopping fame—became a prominent story line only retrospectively, in the days immediately following his November victory.[17]

The Truman example is revealing in that, until election day, reporters were working on the assumption that Truman would lose. The final Gallup poll, conducted several weeks before the election, showed Dewey with a seemingly insurmountable lead, a finding that confirmed the view of Washington insiders. News reports about the Truman and Dewey campaigns adopted a story line that fit the expected outcome: reporters wrote that Truman lacked appeal and that Dewey had touched a responsive chord among voters. As for whistle-stopping, reporters noted that both Truman and Dewey traveled by train.

Finding an Image that Fits

Reporters dressed Truman and Dewey in images that were consistent with the candidates' perceived standing in the race. These images were not complete fabrications: they were constructed from elements of the candidates' strategies and personalities. But they were highly selective images, tied to winning or losing. Truman-the-likely-loser was seen and reported differently by journalists than was Truman-the-surprise-winner: his rhetorical style was characterized as strident and offensive in the first instance and in the second instance as hard-hitting and appealing.

Compare 1988 and the media image of Michael Dukakis. A *Newsweek* reporter wrote after the election that Dukakis had lost largely because he failed to "de-ice his image." This observation was a persistent news theme during the fall campaign: reporters regularly said that Dukakis was finding it difficult to persuade voters that he was likable. Remarkably, the issue of Dukakis's likability was not a news theme before the fall campaign. Until then, Dukakis was portrayed in the media as highly competent. The difference was like night and day. The same candidate who earlier had been described by *Newsweek* as "relentless in his attack" and "a credible candidate" was later said by the same magazine to be "reluctant to attack" and "trying to present himself as a credible candidate."

The difference between the earlier and later portrayals was the difference between a candidate who was riding high and a candidate who had hit bottom. After the New Hampshire primary, Dukakis moved steadily toward the Democratic nomination. By late spring, he was ahead for the White House as well. He led Bush comfortably in the opinion polls, by as much as 15 percentage points after the Democratic convention. But the general election campaign was a different story. From mid-August to October, Dukakis trailed Bush badly in the polls. He narrowed the gap toward the end, but never drew much closer than seven to eight percentage points.

Bush's public support (and, consequently, his image) took a different course. In the early spring he carried the label of "wimp" and, although in command of the Republican race, he trailed far behind Dukakis in the polls. But Bush took the lead after the Republican convention and, as he did, he acquired a new image. Said *Newsweek* after Bush won in November, "Somehow, with his formal nomination at the August convention, [Bush] stepped out of Reagan's long shadow and became his own man." As for the wimp factor, *Newsweek* said it was "banished, as long as Bush is on the attack."

A fuller picture of how Bush and Dukakis were portrayed in the media is provided in Figure 4-2, which shows whether positive or negative news dominated the coverage of the candidates at each stage of the 1988 campaign. As the data indicate, a dramatic shift in the candidates' news coverage occurred after Bush overtook Dukakis in the polls. In the two preceding time periods, coverage of Dukakis was, on balance, positive; coverage of Bush was negative. In the two time periods after Bush took the lead, the tone of the coverage was dramatically reversed.

Images, Story Lines, and Votes

As the Truman-Dewey and Bush-Dukakis races suggest, the candidates' images, as described by the press, are highly malleable. Candidates who have trouble garnering public support usually are portrayed by the press as having a poor or weak image. On the other hand, strong contenders usually are pictured by reporters as having a commanding image.

This pattern raises the intriguing possibility that journalists' evaluations may be partially self-fulfilling. That is, by claiming that a candidate is weak or powerful, the press may actually influence the voters' perceptions. By November 1988 most voters thought that Dukakis was a pretty weak character and that Bush was a surprisingly strong one. Their view paralleled the portrayals of reporters, who claimed that they had drawn their conclusions about Bush and Dukakis from what the voters were saying. But it seems equally plausible that voters grounded their assessments of the candidates partly in the news they were getting.

Figure 4-2   Good Press, Bad Press: Bush and Dukakis

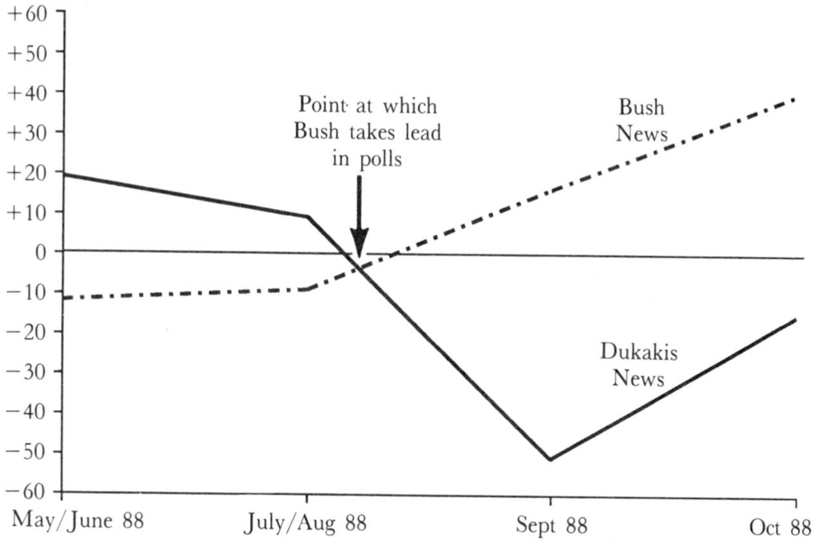

NOTE: "Bush News" and "Dukakis News" figures are the differences between the percentage of positive and percentage of negative news references to Bush and Dukakis respectively for time period indicated.

The Media as Effective Intermediary: A Forlorn Wish

For the past two decades, pundits and scholars have been offering advice about how the news media could better report on presidential elections. The assumption underlying most of this advice is that the media have the ability to bring reason to bear on the selection of presidents, if only they would do things differently. Reporters apparently accept this perspective. After each election, they vow to do better the next time.

How well the press does its job has a marginal influence on the quality of a presidential campaign. But the press cannot perform adequately as intermediary between the candidates and the voters no matter how conscientiously reporters approach the task. The media simply are not designed to fulfill this responsibility. They are in the news business, not the political business, and, as a result, their norms and imperatives are not those required for the effective organization of electoral coalitions and debate. The press's values produce a news agenda that bears little relationship to the choices at stake in an election.

The situation is a recipe for chaos. To a significant degree, the press introduces "random partisanship" into the selection of presidents.[18] Candidates are helped or hurt depending on how news values interact with campaign developments. A candidate who wins the right primary gets more than the victory should be worth, because the press blows it out of proportion. A candidate who makes a mistake loses big, because the news exaggerates the mistake. A candidate who is on a downslide gets saddled with a negative image, because it fits the media's need for a consistent story line.

Such realities expose the foolhardiness of the idea that the press, if it would only do things a little better, could make a presidential election into a sensible affair. By its nature, the press cannot do in U.S. elections what political parties do elsewhere. The press is not a political institution and has no good reason to act like one. Lippmann wrote:

> The press is no substitute for institutions. It is like the beam of a searchlight that moves restlessly about, bringing one episode and then another out of darkness into vision. Men cannot do the work of the world by this light alone. They cannot govern society by episodes, incidents, and interruptions.[19]

Even more illusory is the idea that the press can make up for defects in the political system. As Lippmann noted, the press inevitably magnifies the system's deficiencies.[20] The nominating process, for example, gives untoward influence to voters in Iowa and New Hampshire. But this bias is magnified by the press's buildup of these contests and its determination to cover the winners.

The problem of the modern political campaign thus lies deeper than the press. The real weakness of the present system is that it is built upon the dismantling of the political party, which, in Everett Carll Ladd's words, is "the one institution able to practice political planning." [21]

Other democracies understand that parties alone are designed for the purpose of representing majorities in election campaigns. Alone among democracies, the United States is willing to turn the task over to an institution, the press, that was designed for different purposes and lacks the incentives to do the job properly. In a basic sense, the present system of electing presidents is constitutionally flawed. No theory of democracy suggests, even remotely, that the news media should have or can fulfill the role they perform. Regrettably, however, America's media-based selection process is not going to go away, at least not until it produces an obviously disastrous outcome. All major electoral changes in U.S. history have come as a result of political upheaval, never because of plain reason.

Notes

1. Walter Lippmann, *Public Opinion* (New York: Free Press, 1965), 19. Original publication date was 1922.
2. James David Barber, *The Pulse of Politics* (New York: W. W. Norton, 1980), chap. 8.
3. Cited in Colin Seymour-Ure, *The Political Impact of Mass Media* (Beverly Hills, Calif.: Sage, 1974), 156.
4. Donald L. Horowitz, *The Courts and Social Policy* (Washington, D.C.: Brookings Institution, 1977). The author acknowledges his considerable debt to Horowitz's pioneering work on institutional capability, which has provided many general and specific ideas for this chapter.
5. Ibid., 23.
6. Writing on the 1984 preprimary period, William C. Adams noted that "those [candidates] who were 'poll poor' at the start stayed 'media poor' and went nowhere in the polls." The consequences, as Adams observes, are fairly predictable: "Prior visibility produces high poll standings, which ensures media coverage/legitimacy, which sustains poll standings, which ensure media coverage/legitimacy." William C. Adams, "As New Hampshire Goes..." in *Media and Momentum*, ed. Gary R. Orren and Nelson W. Polsby (Chatham, N.J.: Chatham House Publishers, 1987), 51-52.
7. Lippmann, *Public Opinion*, 221-226.
8. Cited in William C. Adams, "Media Coverage of Campaign '84: A Preliminary Report," *Public Opinion*, April-May, 1984. Reprinted in *The Mass Media in Campaign '84*, Michael Robinson and Austin Ranney, eds. (Washington, D.C.: American Enterprise Institute, 1985), 13.
9. Benjamin Page, *Choices and Echoes in Presidential Elections* (Chicago: University of Chicago Press, 1978), 192.
10. Lippmann, *Public Opinion*, 218-222.
11. Seymour-Ure, *Political Impact of Mass Media*, chap. 6.
12. Thomas E. Patterson, *The Mass Media Election* (New York: Praeger, 1980), chap. 5; Adams, "Media Coverage of Campaign '84," 12.
13. Michael Robinson, "The Media in Campaign '84, Part I," in Robinson and Ranney, *The Mass Media in Campaign '84*.
14. Robert Lichter, "Media Monitor" (Washington, D.C.: Center for Media and Public Affairs), mimeo.
15. James David Barber, "Characters in the Campaign: The Literary Problem," in *Race for the Presidency*, ed. James David Barber (Englewood Cliffs, N.J.: Prentice-Hall, 1978), 117.
16. Lippmann, *Public Opinion*, chap. 24.
17. Thomas E. Patterson, "Journalists' Images of Presidential Candidates" (Paper presented at the World Association for Public Opinion Research meeting, Montreaux, Switzerland, September 12-15, 1987).
18. Seymour-Ure, *Political Impact of Mass Media*, chap. 6.
19. Lippmann, *Public Opinion*, 222.
20. Ibid.
21. Everett Carll Ladd, *Where Have All the Voters Gone?* (New York: Norton, 1978), 72.

5. ISSUES AND THEMES IN THE 1988 CAMPAIGN

Jean Bethke Elshtain

If nothing else, the elections of 1988 provided an ongoing national seminar on the question: What constitutes a legitimate campaign issue? During the nominating contests, the "character issue" seemed to predominate. Gary Hart (tagged a "womanizer") and Joseph Biden (a "plagiarist") were forced to drop out of the Democratic race. George Bush had to overcome the "wimp factor" to defeat Robert ("Mean Bob") Dole for the Republican nomination. After the conventions, nominees Michael Dukakis and (especially) Bush were accused of campaigning on "hot-button," or symbolic, issues like abortion and patriotism. Commentators universally agreed that the voters were being shortchanged by the absence of a serious discussion of the federal budget deficit and other critical issues.

Jean Bethke Elshtain, in contrast to Paul Quirk and Thomas Patterson, the authors of the two preceding chapters, dissents strongly from the view that the elections of 1988 were issueless. In truth, she urges, issues are defined as what the voters care deeply about, not what political pundits think they should care about. Indeed, voters are "co-constructors" of issues—the candidate who speaks to their concerns will thrive politically, the opponent who talks past them will flounder. It is particularly wrong, Elshtain argues, to accuse Bush of neglecting "the issues" by concentrating on prison furloughs, the Pledge of Allegiance, and abortion. If those had not symbolized real concerns of the voters (that is, real issues), Bush would have lost.

The elections of 1988 puzzled and frustrated political analysts and, if we can trust the public opinion polls, many voters as well. Typical complaints went something like this: "The real issues are being ignored." As one letter writer to the *Los Angeles Times* put it: "Serious, substantive issues are not being addressed." Citizens frequently ex-

Thanks to Mark Kelso for his research assistance on this project.

pressed a lack of enthusiasm for the candidates of either party. Part of this disenchantment can be traced to the American tradition of mistrusting "politicians" no matter what their stripe. But, beyond that, many voters expressed their negative assessments in words that indicated deep disappointment that both presidential candidates seemed "packaged" and inauthentic.

Pundits had a field day trying to account for voter apathy or anger. Anthony Lewis, the distinguished columnist for the *New York Times,* traced lack of voter interest to the candidates' refusal to define or address the "real" issues. Lewis listed five such issues and indicted George Bush, in particular, for evading them in favor of insinuations about Michael Dukakis's patriotism that served only to "distract attention" from "many of those real issues." For Lewis, the real issues were economic uncertainty, U.S. competitiveness with other nations, education, drugs, and the environment. Charles Overby, vice president for news for Gannett, the nation's largest newspaper chain, declared in a speech in late September 1988 that the "campaign strategists have determined that campaign symbols play better with voters than issues." The *Washington Post* also entered the fray, editorializing that there were too many "fake issues in this campaign on both sides." Candidates, therefore, should "give up the confected issues and return to the real ones." Among the specific "non-issues" the *Post* noted was the controversy over the Pledge of Allegiance and whether it should or should not be a mandated activity in America's public schools.

The perception, then, which has continued in editorials and analyses in the campaign's aftermath, is that the candidates evaded and avoided *real* issues and that the news media aided and abetted them in this process. The media are charged with devoting too much attention to "symbolic" themes—such as abortion protest, fervor over prison furlough policies, heated debates about the Pledge of Allegiance, and other side shows—and not enough to "substantive" questions. Voter apathy can be traced directly to the evasions of the candidates and the manipulative chicanery of their "handlers," those men and women who package the candidates for public show.

Although such protestations are widespread and often angrily couched, they seem rather beside the point, even conveniently beside the point. Repeated indictments of media manipulation and candidate evasion fail to address the most salient questions. These include: What did the campaign of 1988 tell us about current American politics? What are our major preoccupations and concerns? Who gets to define these concerns, and in and through what symbolic and rhetorical devices? How are issues constructed? And why do so many people, experts and lay people alike, persist in presuming and evoking a cleavage between symbolic and real issues and themes?

This essay is divided into three parts. First, I will discuss would-be issues, those concerns that particular individuals or interest groups confidently predicted would become issues but which, in fact, did not—at least not in the way those individuals and groups anticipated. Second, I will explore the "issues" issue. In one of the ironies of the 1988 campaign, issues themselves became an issue, with each side claiming that the other was not dealing with real issues but was, instead, hiding behind a smoke screen of fraudulent or ideologically obfuscatory and inflammatory concerns. I will examine the construction of issues, offering several suggestions about the ways in which voters—average citizens—are "co-constructors" and help to set the broad thematic terms of a campaign. Finally, I will ponder briefly what 1988's issues and themes suggest about the future of political ideologies in the United States, including Americans' deeply ingrained but increasingly dubious categorizing of parties and candidates along a left-right or liberal-conservative spectrum. The essay aims to be exploratory and suggestive, encouraging readers to make further interpretations of their own.

Issues That Weren't

Preelection analysts were jaunty and self-assured in their forecasts about which issues were bound to emerge as salient in 1988. For example: two followers of the business press, using trend analysis, predicted in spring 1988 that "day care, parental leave, [and] elder leave" were "beginning to take off like a rocket" as dominant political issues. Taking their cues entirely from preoccupations in the business press, they concluded confidently that any politician who succeeded in weaving these issues together "in the same way the voters perceive them to be interconnected will strike electoral gold." [1] A second pair of analysts, in this case political scientists, pronounced that the issues affecting "key swing groups" would surely involve "the fairness of the Reagan policies" and that widespread "economic pessimism," said to be "the public's dominant mood," could be exploited by Democrats to their advantage. On foreign policy matters, the "main issue dividing the parties will be continued funding of the Nicaraguan rebels." [2]

In reality, neither day care nor Nicaragua emerged as major topics in the 1988 campaign, and economic optimism seems to have offset the pessimism used by many analysts as the baseline from which to launch their predictive sallies.

To be sure, each presidential candidate burdened reporters, allies, and opponents alike with fat position papers on "investing in our children" and future defense policy. But such overblown pronouncements are not the stuff campaigns are made of. Take the day care issue (or nonissue), for example. George Bush favored giving $2.2 billion in refundable tax credits to parents with children under age four so that mothers could afford to remain out of the work force. Michael Dukakis supported the goals of a proposal offered by congressional Democrats to use $2.5 billion, in the form of block grants to state and local governments, to pay for affordable child care programs for poor and moderate-income families. Yet child care failed to register as a high-voltage voter concern. The often baroque details of alternative schemes neither incited debate nor stayed in voters' minds.

Instead, attention quickly veered from block grants or tax credits to what is happening to American mothers, fathers, and children and what this has to do with the future of American society. The depth of commitment and fervor that surrounded the abortion issue, a phenomenon that experts rather consistently insisted either was not or should not be an issue at all, speaks to familial themes and anxieties; this is an argument I develop in the next section. The minimal point for now is simply this: even as many observers continued to chide candidates for not addressing the question of child care, the terrain shifted to a set of deeper, more evocative themes about the American family.

And what of pessimism or optimism about the economy? Bush claimed that the Reagan administration's economic policies had created 17 million new jobs during the previous five years and that these were good jobs. Dukakis insisted that the average weekly wage of the jobs that were lost in the country in the same five-year period was about $440 and that what replaced them were jobs paying one-third less. Somebody had it wrong. Or did he? That both candidates played fast and loose with statistics is clear but, again, rather beside the point. The more important question, for our purposes, is whether the details of economic policy took off as an issue in 1988. Did voters base their choice on whether Bush or Dukakis was more accurate? There is no evidence that they did. Indeed, if one moves to the deeper assumption that frequently guides the reflections of analysts (and many politicians)—namely, that voters invariably vote their own economic self-interest—one would go on to predict that poor and lower-middle-class persons (who were feeling an "economic squeeze," as candidate Dukakis put it) would vote en bloc for the candidate who claimed that things were bad but could be made better; hence Dukakis's pitch for "good jobs at good wages."

But voters seem not to behave as those who confidently define real economic concerns in terms of self-interest predict they will. This suggests that economic self-interest does not influence voting in the causal and predictive way many assume. Indeed, it turns out that there is no direct correlation between "how a person votes and how his or her economic standing has changed between elections." [3] Political analysts and candidates who cling to the unreliable indicator of economic self-interest are almost bound to get things wrong as they imbed "real" issues in a horizon framed by this assumption.

To some critics and frustrated candidates, the voters' failure to vote their pocketbooks indicates that they are muddled about the economy or, more precisely, about their own economic interests. But is this the case? As with child care, complex and contestable econometric discourse soon gave way in the public's mind to a set of diffuse assumptions and concerns about the nation's overall economic well-being. Thus political scientist Steven Kelman argues, contrary to the common wisdom, that the correlations that do appear between perceived economic concerns and voting are strong when one looks at how individual voters assess the overall economy rather than how they think they will be personally affected by one candidate's triumph over the other. Ironically, voters appear to focus more on the big picture, as they understand it, than on the pocketbook, as popular wisdom often defines it. [4]

Foreign affairs, as they are usually tagged, were another matter that did not surface as sharply defined issues or policy differences between the candidates. Whether to aid or to cut off the Nicaraguan opponents of the Sandinista regime died quickly as a salient issue and was scarcely talked about during the final weeks of the campaign. Nor did the candidates' differences on South Africa or the Middle East develop as important voter preoccupations. Rather, "defense" (as a general set of themes rather than a specific set of policies) and "experience" in "dealing with our adversaries" rose to prominence. Although the merest handful of voters, if called upon, could locate either Bush or Dukakis with reference to his support or rejection of particular weapons systems, evaluations of the overall position of the United States in a dangerous and rapidly changing world did figure in voters' minds as they sized up the two candidates. Try as he might, Dukakis was unable to launch either Nicaragua or Star Wars as a sharply defining issue that could draw voter support to his side. His promise to "stabilize" defense spending sent few pulses racing, perhaps because Bush also pledged to cut the waste out of the defense budget. But who was or was not capable of dealing effectively with Soviet leader Mikhail Gorbachev did matter. This question was one that voters answered based on their perceptions of the qualities and reliability of each man; it was not an issue open to calculations along narrow standards of rationality so much as a hunch arrived at through a complex series of informal but ultimately persuasive impressions.

One final example of "issues that weren't," at least not as the forecasts would have had them, in the 1988 campaign: throughout the spring and into the summer, a plethora of stories surfaced about the "gender gap," the assumed difference in how male and female voters assess and respond to candidates and policy initiatives. One early survey gave Dukakis a thirty percentage point lead over Bush among likely female voters, leading Jane Danowitz of the Women's Campaign Fund to proclaim: "We are going to deliver the next president!" [5]

But this lead disappeared as the campaign wound down. Final figures from the *New York Times*/CBS exit poll showed that a small majority of women voters favored Bush by 50 to 49 percent. Men, however, favored Bush by 57 to 41 percent. The gender gap that was *supposed* to make the difference—women going overwhelmingly for the Democratic ticket—did not materialize. What occurred instead, repeating the pattern of 1984, was a significant gender gap on the part of white male voters that worked to the benefit of the Republican ticket. Feminist leaders such as Betty Friedan claimed that Dukakis blew his early lead among female voters by failing to identify strongly with what they call women's issues. But there is little evidence to back that assertion. In fact, strong identification with the issues that national feminist lobbying groups have defined as central and nonnegotiable, particularly federal funding for abortions, would likely have increased rather than decreased Dukakis's "negatives." [6]

The gender gap *is* a question, a muddled one that requires much fine-tuned, sophisticated sorting out. Gender does not operate as a single, monolithic aggregation; hence, it was not an issue in the way many activists and analysts predicted early in the campaign of 1988 that it would surely prove to be.

Turning from presidential politics to the issues that determine the outcomes of congressional races, the picture is in some ways more focused on particular, local issues and questions. The decisive factor in the success or failure of most candidates for the House (especially) or Senate is incumbency itself. To attempt to trump the overwhelming advantages of incumbency, challengers search desperately for telling themes—sometimes linking themselves to the national ticket in a presidential election year, sometimes running from that ticket as fast as they can. Southern Democrats, for example, were sorely pressed in 1988 to maintain a discreet distance from Dukakis, not so much because of his stands on specific policy questions as because of the way volatile symbolic issues like prison furloughs and the pledge emerged as decisive.

Most studies, however, show "a diminishing connection between presidential and congressional voting." People not only vote for Congress largely on the basis of their assessments of the candidates with whom they are confronted, they evaluate those candidates "with little reference to national policies or personalities." [7] Members of Congress are increasingly at "the service of the organized," that is, of constituents for whom particular questions have become salient. Such issues may include preventing a toxic waste dump from being located in one's district or state, protecting a scenic shore line, keeping an army base open, or supporting policies for the elderly.

The Issues Issue

By early September, the editors of the *Washington Post* had had enough. "How did we get to this dreadful place so fast?" they asked. Although the *Post* concluded that "the two camps are assiduously avoiding real presidential issues," much of their editorial ire was reserved for the Bush campaign, which allegedly had become fixated with one nonissue after another, most importantly the flap over Dukakis and the Pledge of Allegiance. "It is, not to be too dainty about it, disgusting." [8] Dukakis, on the defensive, joined the chorus and declared, "The American people aren't interested in a debate over which one of us loves his country the most."

But clearly the American people were interested in such a debate, perhaps not over which candidate really loves his country so much as over the meaning of love of country, and what the country stands for. If this had not been the case, such heavily weighted symbolic issues as the pledge and, from Dukakis' side, fear of foreigners buying up America would not have played in Peoria, or anywhere else. For a complex set of reasons, analysts have relegated "value" issues such as these to a secondary and suspect status—seen as a way to draw attention away from "real" issues such as the budget deficit or whether to fund the Midgetman missile. But does this distinction, with its underlying assumption that symbolic and values questions are somehow less real than specific, limited policy matters, make sense?

I shall argue that it does not. For one thing, no handy criteria exist to allow either the voter or the political analyst to separate real from symbolic or rhetorical issues. Issues are what actually take root as preoccupations and themes. Thus, whether the symbolic meaning of the Pledge of Allegiance *is* an issue becomes the issue; the outcome of the 1988 election turned partly on who had best made his case. Voters and candidates are co-constructors of issues. Candidates speak and act in response to their perceptions of the concerns of the electorate. Their themes either soar or die depending upon whether a sufficient number of voters come to share their constructions. To claim, then, that candidates are trafficking in nonissues because they immerse themselves in weighty symbolism is to presume that which does not exist—a clear-cut division between the symbolic and the real, between issues and emotional appeals.

This point is worth belaboring because it speaks to a deeply rooted prejudice in Western political thought against political rhetoric, that is, against the hurly-burly of democratic politics itself. The prejudice emerged in its most powerful form in the writings of the great Greek philosopher Plato, himself an antidemocrat. Plato contrasted pure Truth, or the Forms (which are available only to a few wise philosophers, who in an ideal state would serve as its Guardians or rulers) to the "sophistry"—the rhetoric—of those he opposed. To Plato, rhetoric was an attempt to persuade through the use of "mere opinion," in contrast to absolute Truth. He carried his animus against rhetoric so far that he insisted that poets, those who traffic in volatile words and images, be ejected from the ideal republic.

The ancient suspicion of mere rhetoric, carried forward into modern times, goes hand in hand with disparagement of the unwieldiness and ambiguities of democratic politics. Yet democratic politics, without rhetoric, without attempts to persuade, is impossible. Consequently, it makes little sense to assume a cleavage between truth and rhetoric, or facts and opinions, or real and phony issues. Facts make sense only within a context that must be framed and articulated by somebody, whether a candidate, a media consultant, or a group of voters.

Thus, the speeches and symbols and rhetorical acts of our presidential candidates are co-authored by "we the people," depending upon how we receive their efforts. The appropriate questions to ask, of them and of us, are: What actions and reactions are evoked or provoked when a candidate frames an issue one way or another? What sort of relationship with voters does the candidate invite? Every speech, every symbol, every advertisement takes place within and helps to create a complex political universe. That is why frenzied polemical attempts, during the 1988 campaign, to sever style from substance failed. The two cannot be separated. They are each part of a larger way of thinking and acting—and that, finally, is what voters are called upon to judge and what they do judge. At least one influential analyst, E. J. Dionne, Jr., national political correspondent for the *New York Times,* arrived at this recognition in mid-September, when he wrote: "Mr. Bush and Mr. Dukakis have indeed quarreled over some issues, but it has been less an argument over the point of these proposals . . . in all their details, [as] in the more general sense they convey to the public." [9]

American presidents—and, in an election year, presidential candidates—are our foremost rhetorical figures. Citizens are engaged with them in a frustratingly complex series of actions and reactions. Thus, it was facile indeed for analysts to press the tired theme that there were real issues, known to them, that were being evaded by the candidates and ignored by the voters. Rather, wise analysts explored how issues and themes were constructed—for this itself was perhaps *the* issue. Voters are appropriately preoccupied with symbols and images as well as with statistics about the deficit and finely tuned proposals for day care or alternative defense strategies. What is at stake in an election is not just interests but identities, not just what we are to do but who we are and have become.

Take the abortion issue, for example. Dukakis, beset at campaign appearances by anti-abortion pickets and protests, attempted to define the matter out of the campaign by insisting that it had to do with an individual's private moral commitments. This construction did not work, however, because in the view of the anti-abortion movement, abortion was permanently politicized by the 1973 Supreme Court decision in *Roe v. Wade,* which in effect sanctioned abortion on demand at any time during the first six months of pregnancy. This ruling, by definition, made abortion both a public and a political matter—as prochoice people themselves acknowledged. But, having "won" in 1973 under the terms of the Court decision, defenders of "reproductive freedom" did not want the issue reopened in a way that might undermine the clear advantage they have had thus far with the courts. The anti-abortion forces, having "lost" in court, had an enormous stake in keeping the question before the public—in making certain that prochoice forces did not succeed in depoliticizing the matter.

Why should abortion be seen as a symbolic issue rather than something real, like a budget deficit? Perhaps because it taxes the limits of our political discourse, which has narrowed over the years to include only terms of self- or group interest. Abortion speaks to deep principles concerning the nature of the human being, the sanctity of human life, the rights and obligations of individuals, and so on. Because the question cannot be reduced to the by now standard political categories and responses, it gets tossed into a bin labeled "symbolic" or "emotional."

But the abortion issue refuses to stay in the political shadows. As with other divisive social, cultural, and moral issues, abortion got pushed to the forefront of public concern in the tumultuous years of the mid-1960s through the mid-1970s. Although some racial matters have been defused since that period, other volatile questions have not "gone away." Abortion is one. Handgun control is another. Crime, or the proper treatment of criminals, is a third. (Needless to say, the crime question carries with it certain racial undertones.) These subjects, to which the flap over the Pledge of Allegiance and its use or abuse in

America's public schools was added during the campaign, are so-called wedge issues. A wedge issue is one that can be exploited to the benefit of one side by separating potential voters from its opponent.

Wedge issues were conspicuous in the campaign of 1988. The Bush forces were able to make stick the perception that, although Dukakis might sound like a mainstream political leader in many of his policy proposals, on the level of values he was, in fact, at odds with the majority of Americans—including many who, by tradition and strict socioeconomic indicators, should be, and for decades were, solidly in the Democratic camp. This recognition prompted David S. Broder, the syndicated columnist for the *Washington Post,* to comment shortly before the election that "on some values questions, Dukakis is, in fact, outside the mainstream. The political culture of Massachusetts is as far left of center as the political culture of Reagan's circle of wealthy Californians is to the right. The difference is that Reagan always has known he had to defend his world view, while Dukakis seemed sublimely confident people would just accept his as correct." [10]

How could the Dukakis camp have felt such misplaced confidence in the soundness of its stance on value questions? Again, abortion politics is revealing. The national Democratic party has long been identified with the pro-choice, or the *Roe v. Wade,* position. This commitment stems from the party's deep immersion in the politics of various movements—the movement for women's liberation, for racial equality, and so on. With abortion having been identified as a litmus test by feminists, it has become nearly impossible for the Democratic party on the national level to moderate its position—a position not held by many of the party's traditional constituencies, especially white, working-class, urban voters and southerners and westerners who live in small to medium-sized towns, work in small businesses, or have average to below average incomes. Dukakis and his aides were willing to risk antagonizing those constituencies for two reasons. First, they were confident that traditional Democratic voters would not desert the ticket simply because they disagreed with the national party platform and the national candidate on abortion; and second, they could point confidently to public opinion polls that indicated that a substantial majority of Americans favored legal abortion in at least some circumstances.

But polls, in fact, tell us—and should tell policy analysts and campaign managers—very little. For as one digs deeper, one learns that the abortion controversy really involves a bitter clash between groups with different social backgrounds and value systems. The author of a definitive study of abortion politics discovered that, "Whereas one third of all prolife people made less than $20,000 a year, only one prochoice person in five made that little. . . . Conversely, whereas a little over a

third (35%) of prolife people made more than $30,000 a year, over half
of the prochoice people made that much. Prochoice income was, in fact,
clustered in the upper end of the income scale: Almost one prochoice
person in four . . . made $50,000 a year or more." [11]

Attitudes toward abortion do not exist in a bin sealed off from
other values, such as "beliefs and attitudes about motherhood; about
sexuality; about men and women; about the role of children; and, more
broadly, about such global things as morality and the role of rational
planning in human affairs. [A]ll are intricately related, and all shape
an individual's attitude toward abortion." [12] And because, as I have
already argued, most voters do not cast their ballots along narrow lines
of purely economic self-interest, a voter who some political analysts
might confidently expect on the basis of pocketbook issues alone to go
with the Democratic party could turn against the party on the basis of
value questions that cut deeper than marginal calculations of economic
self-interest.

Thus, a political scientist who has looked at abortion and
presidential elections found that abortion was, in fact, a polarizing issue
among white Democrats.[13] Indeed, the more voters learned about party
and candidate positions on abortion, the more polarized they became.
This polarization has had a disproportionate effect on Democratic
voters, driving a wedge between some traditional Democratic constituencies and their party: "The data suggest that the more informed the
electorate becomes the more the Republicans might stand to gain." [14]
The single most favored position among "white Republicans, indepen-
dents, and Democrats" is to allow abortion in cases of rape, incest, or
danger to the life of the mother but to restrict discretionary abortions.
The Republican national ticket in 1988 came closest to this position.
That, together with other values questions, worked to Bush's advantage
because Americans remain deeply divided about the social changes of
the last several decades. As party identification and loyalty continue to
decline, wedge issues are likely to continue to rise in importance. The
implications are great, even startling, suggesting nothing less than that
our usual political labels "like conservative and liberal, even Democrat and Republican, are of little use in describing the American
electorate." [15]

Before turning to the matter of conventional political labels and
whether they really label anything any more, consider briefly the issue
of media manipulation. The side that appears to be losing ground
during the course of a campaign invariably starts to bemoan trickery on
the part of advertisers, to cry foul, and to decry how voters are so
readily duped. In 1988 those laments came primarily from the Dukakis
camp. (In previous campaigns, Republicans could be heard telling a

similar tale: the media are out to get us, the voters are being gulled.) In fact, one of Dukakis's less successful advertising campaigns targeted the "packaging of George Bush," speaking directly to the theme of voter manipulation. The ads quickly backfired and were dropped. They failed because they suggested that American voters were being manipulated by the Bush campaign in order to cynically solicit emotional responses over the flag, prison furloughs, and so on. Unfortunately, as one critic put it and as television viewers "felt it," the ads were "dripping with contempt for the ordinary American whose votes, one would have thought, Dukakis is seeking. The voters, the ads make clear, are gullible and easily duped." [16]

A full discussion of the role of the media, and of advertising, in the 1988 campaign is beyond the scope of this essay. But a few words are in order. First, voters cannot be manipulated unless something real is there to be tapped. Clever ads and packagers cannot create concern and anxiety about crime, morality, and patriotism. These concerns can be directed and redirected and even misdirected. But that is different from straight manipulation. Second, our national elections do rely "heavily upon journalists to organize the choices facing the voters. . . . In the United States . . . [p]residential elections have become plebiscites in which candidates stand alone before the electorate and must depend upon the press to mediate their appeals." [17] Candidates, in fact, are forced to work through the media as their power and influence have grown and as clear-cut party and ideological loyalties have diminished. The media as an issue in presidential elections seems destined not to diminish as one considers the breakdown in perceived political categories and identities.

The Decline of Parties and Labels

What did the campaign of 1988 tell us about the shifting use of strongly evaluative political tags, especially liberal and conservative? The "liberal" candidate, Dukakis, claimed to be the true conservative and ran as fast as he could from the liberal label, which was reduced to the "L word" by his opponent, save in the waning weeks of the campaign when he attempted to turn a political liability into a last-ditch political hope. The conservative candidate, on the other hand, eschewed that label and, in the eyes of many who consider themselves true conservatives, remains suspect. What is at stake here? We are, and have been for the past several decades, in the midst of a situation in which conventional political categories are being dissolved but the need for a reconfiguring of political ideas has yet to be widely acknowledged. We are more and more frozen in a rhetorical and ideological deadlock that fails to illumine the real perils and possibilities of the present political moment.

Clearly this argument needs elaboration. Let's begin by taking a closer look at how voters actually divide. Party loyalty in the United States has consistently declined for decades, and abiding party identification is lower among the young than any other group. The first year that significant numbers of voters began to split their tickets was 1956. Now the ticket splitters make up as much as 45 percent of the electorate.[18] This decline in strict party loyalty and identification is not a phenomenon unique to the United States. The same can be observed in democracies everywhere.

The most persuasive explanation for this weakening connection between voters and parties is that people's lives are more and more diverse, with multiple overlapping loci of commitment and interest. At one time, being a union member, for example, virtually guaranteed Democratic party identification. No more. Unions are in a tailspin. Union members, having secured many important benefits over the years and no longer finding themselves in battles with management over clear-cut bread-and-butter issues, are increasingly animated by a plethora of concerns, including the value questions discussed above. When politics ceases to be dominated by the distribution of tangible economic benefits, problems of party identification and loyalty increase.

Thus, for example, environmental questions have driven a wedge between liberal ecologists in the Democratic party and traditional jobs-oriented working-class Democrats who fear that stricter controls on industrial production will force some companies out of business or provoke them to relocate, thus jeopardizing their jobs. As already noted, social issues, such as abortion, cut across traditional constituencies and party lines. Public opinion polls have indicated for a number of years that a solid majority of Americans favor national health insurance of some sort, job guarantees, and more protection of the environment. But equally solid majorities believe the federal government is too large, spends too much, and intrudes too directly into people's lives.[19]

From the beginning, the reform tradition in the United States—now embodied in the so-called progressive wing of the Democratic party—has presented what David Mayhew calls an ideologically confused profile, emphasizing at the same time both greater democracy and the streamlining of government through enhanced efficiency and professionalism. But the goal of efficiency and professionalism undercuts the other goal of more public involvement in politics.[20] Nor does the American conservative strand offer an ideologically pure vision. On the one hand, conservative libertarians insist that government should stay its hand at regulation, whether of economic or of moral matters. On the other, social traditionalists insist, with varying degrees of intensity, that the law as a moral force should be brought to bear to discourage or forbid practices they consider destructive, such as prostitution and pornography.

In early autumn 1987, a study conducted by the Gallup organization for the Times Mirror Company shed some light on the confused state of traditional political categories. The study offered "a remarkably detailed portrait of the political attitudes of the American people by employing a method of categorizing the electorate more precisely than the conventional party or ideological labels allow." [21] For any analyst or politician seeking to find, or to reconstruct, simple ideological thinking, the study is a quagmire. For example: although 68 percent of those surveyed thought too many children were being raised in day care centers, 66 percent rejected the idea that women should return to a traditional role in society.

Eschewing party or left-right categories, the Gallup analysts sorted voters into eleven distinct classifications: from "Upbeats" to "Disaffecteds"; from "Passive Poor" to "Partisan Poor"; and so on. All conventional labels dissolved as fine-grained differentiations emerged on a long list of measurements—economic, regional, demographic, male-female, race, religion, and social values. Unsurprisingly, those analyzing the responses discovered that Americans continue to express dual and not always easily reconcilable commitments to individual achievement and to equality, by which they mean a basic standard of fair play and simple justice. What emerges as the preeminent value varies not only from one voter classification to the next, but within individual voters, depending upon the issue at stake.

With ideological tents leaking and party identification fading, it seems clear that our standard terms of political discourse are ill suited to help us understand contemporary political realities. Those who seek absolute ideological clarity—neat divisions on "real" issues—are chasing a chimera. In the campaign of 1988, with the "issues issue" acting as a powerful magnet to force actions and reactions, one did not see forceful and entirely coherent conservative or liberal agendas emerge. This accurately reflected the public mood. We live in a complex time in which neither dramatic change nor determined restoration seems in the offing. The elections of 1988 should add further fuel to the fire of those social critics who have been arguing for years that a reorientation of American political ideas and commitments is needed. Yet candidates and voters remain trapped in conventional terms of debate.

The issues of 1988, together with the debate over issues, were construed as the avoidance of genuine discussion. Yet they may one day prove to have been the harbinger of as yet unrealized alterations in our political vocabulary. It would be too dramatic by far to suggest that

1988 was anything like a watershed. But perhaps it is not overstating the case to argue that the ways in which issue and themes are constructed have themselves become issues; that our reigning political vocabulary has reached the point of exhaustion; and, finally, that no separation between real and symbolic issues is either possible or desirable. Serious matters are at stake, and symbols are our markers on the road to whatever understanding and commitment we, as voters, ultimately reach.

Notes

1. Roger Craver and Jeffrey Hallett, "The Online Crystal Ball," *Campaigns and Elections* (March/April 1988): 49.
2. Edward G. Carmines and Michael B. Berkman, "The 1988 Presidential Election: A Strategic Analysis," *Political Science Teacher* (Summer 1988): 3-4.
3. Michael J. Himes and Kenneth R. Himes, "The Myth of Self-Interest," *Commonweal,* September 23, 1988, 493. The authors review recent political science and economic studies that question how much economic self-interest influences voting.
4. Additional support for this contention can be found in Gary C. Jacobson, *The Politics of Congressional Elections* (Boston: Little, Brown, 1983), 128. Jacobson argues that personal financial well-being is not a key variable in congressional races. I extend this finding to the presidential race.
5. Cited in "Closing the Gender Gap," *Newsweek,* October 24, 1988, 22.
6. Thus, Benjamin Ginsberg and Martin Shefter's conclusion from the 1984 elections remained apt for the elections of 1988: "The theory of the gender gap so often put forth since 1980 included more than a little wishful thinking both by Democrats and feminists anxious to portray themselves as a powerful force. The most persistant gender gap that developed during the 1984 presidential election resulted less from women's disavowal of Reagan and love for the Democrats than from the fact that . . . more male Democrats deserted than female Democrats." They note that orthodox Democratic—and, I would add, feminist—doctrine claimed in 1988 as in 1984 that women would be the key to a Democratic victory. "A Critical Realignment? The New Politics, the Constitutional Right, and the 1984 Election," in *The Elections of 1984,* ed. Michael Nelson (Washington, D.C.: CQ Press, 1985), 17.
7. Jacobson, *The Politics of Congressional Elections,* 132, 138.
8. "George Bush on the Pledge," *Washington Post National Weekly Edition,* September 5-11, 1988, 27.
9. E. J. Dionne, Jr., "Issues, or Their Lack, Reflect Voter Concern, or Its Lack," *New York Times,* September 18, 1988, 18.
10. David S. Broder, "Symbols and Substance," *Washington Post National Weekly Edition,* October 24-30, 1988, 4.
11. Kristen Luker, "Abortion and the Meaning of Life," in *Abortion: Understanding Differences,* ed. Sidney and Daniel Callahan (New York: Plenum, 1984), 27. Luker is the author of the superb *Abortion and the Politics of Motherhood* (Berkeley: University of California Press, 1984).

12. Luker, "Abortion and the Meaning of Life," 31.
13. Louis Bolce, "Abortion and Presidential Elections: The Impact of Public Perceptions of Party and Candidate Positions," *Presidential Studies Quarterly* 18 (Fall 1988): 815-829.
14. Ibid., 824.
15. E. J. Dionne, Jr., "Survey of Electorate Finds Weak Political Parties and Conflicts over Change," *New York Times,* October 1, 1987, D27.
16. Michael Barone, "These Dukakis Ads Just Don't Work," *Washington Post National Weekly Edition,* October 17-23, 1988, 29.
17. Thomas E. Patterson and Richard Davis, "The Media Campaign: Struggle for the Agenda," in *The Elections of 1984,* 111.
18. For example, in Texas a net 700,000 voters switched, casting Republican ballots for the presidency, Democratic for the Senate. In Virginia half who voted for Bush also voted for the Democratic candidate for the Senate. *New York Times,* November 10, 1988, 23.
19. Jacobson, *The Politics of Congressional Elections,* reviews this phenomenon.
20. David R. Mayhew, *Congress: The Electoral Connection* (New Haven, Conn.: Yale University Press, 1974), 168.
21. "Survey of Electorate," D27.

6. CONGRESS: A SINGULAR CONTINUITY

Gary C. Jacobson

Politics in the United States seems to have entered into an unprecedented era of "split-level realignment." Throughout almost all of American history, one political party or the other has tended to dominate both Congress and the presidency for stretches of approximately thirty to forty years at a time. Yet since 1968, the presidency almost always has been held by a Republican, while Congress has been dominated by the Democrats. This pattern of divided partisan control of the federal government reached its fullest expression in the elections of 1988, when Republican George Bush won a convincing victory in the presidential election even as the Democrats were adding seats to their already comfortable majorities in both houses of Congress.

Gary Jacobson describes the causes of the new alignment in American politics and its consequences for congressional elections. The House of Representatives is clearly a Democratic preserve, Jacobson shows, and the Senate somewhat less so. Incumbency and, in elections to the House, partisan redistricting may contribute in part to the Democratic ascendancy in Congress, but a more fundamental explanation is that the Democrats' supportive philosophy of government is better suited to the voters' expectations of their elected representatives in Congress than the Republicans' antigovernment stance. The theme of split-level realignment recurs in the following two chapters, by Erwin Hargrove and Michael Nelson.

The 1988 elections are open to a single, if superficial, interpretation: Americans voted for continuity. Voters elected Republican president Ronald Reagan's designated heir, Vice President George Bush, by a comfortable 54 to 46 percent margin over Michael Dukakis, the governor of Massachusetts. At the same time, they returned solid Democratic majorities to the House and Senate, leaving the partisan balance in Congress virtually unchanged.

This interpretation is not so much wrong as it is woefully incomplete, if only because the status quo the voters confirmed is so peculiar.

The continuity thesis obscures the two most striking features of contemporary electoral politics. First, presidential, Senate, and House elections have emerged as three distinct and, more important, nearly independent electoral arenas. Second, the legislative branch continues to be dominated by Democrats and the executive branch by Republicans. The immediate consequence of these two features is that Bush takes office with less partisan support in Congress than any newly elected or reelected president in U.S. history. This situation is "checks and balances" with a vengeance, and it is certain to have profound effects on the Bush presidency.

What happened in the 1988 congressional elections and why? On one level, the House and Senate elections produced very similar results: Democrats gained three House seats and one Senate seat. Yet these outcomes arose from two very different electoral contexts. The small net change in the House was the predictable consequence of a dearth of competition. The Senate results derive from a much more competitive set of elections and could have been sharply different with changes in only a handful of votes in a few states. In neither case, however, did the presidential election have much to do with the results.

The House Elections

The 1988 House elections, summarized in Table 6-1, produced astonishingly little change. Only nine seats switched party control, the fewest in American electoral history; 402 incumbents were returned to office, the most in history; and only 7.6 percent of the representatives elected to the 101st Congress were newcomers, the lowest proportion ever.[1] Although the average vote for House candidates was 0.6 percentage points more Republican than it had been in 1986, incumbents of both parties improved on their 1986 performance. The average Republican incumbent's vote was 2.2 percentage points higher than in 1986; the average Democratic incumbent's vote was 0.2 percentage points higher. Only 13 percent of House incumbents received less than 60 percent of the major party vote, another record low. Indeed, the average vote share of all House incumbents with major party opponents was 68.4 percent, a figure exceeded only in the 1986 election.[2] Five of the six incumbents who did lose were casualties of ethical rather than political lapses: they either were indicted or accused of wrongdoing. The number of open seats switching party control—three—was also the lowest on record. The triumph of the status quo was naturally bad news for Republicans, who entered the election forty-one seats shy of a majority and ended it forty-four seats shy.

The proximate reason why so few House seats changed hands is obvious: a dearth of qualified candidates, issues, and money to

Table 6-1 House Elections, 1988

	Democrats	*Republicans*
Net gain or loss	+3	−3
Freshmen	15	16
Incumbents reelected	243	159
Incumbents defeated	2	4
Open seats retained	11	13
Open seats lost	1	2

NOTE: Upon adjournment of the 100th Congress there were 257 Democrats and 178 Republicans in the House, with the three vacant seats allocated to the party that last held them. When the 101st Congress convened January 3, 1989, there were 260 Democrats and 175 Republicans.

challenge incumbents. All three ingredients are necessary for serious competition. Voters rarely desert an incumbent without an acceptable alternative, some good reasons, and some knowledge of both the alternative and the reasons. An effective challenge thus requires a qualified challenger with telling issues and enough money to inform the electorate about the qualifications and issues.[3]

Candidates, issues, and money are thoroughly interdependent. The shrewd, experienced career politicians who make the best candidates are more likely to run when the prospects of winning are greater. They are attracted to compete by a favorable political climate and potent issues that can be used to raise money, attack the incumbent, and win votes. Similarly, the people who control campaign funds favor challengers who have a plausible chance to succeed; they back promising candidates with exploitable issues. The actual damage an incumbent absorbs from unfavorable issues or contrary trends depends on how effectively they are exploited in the campaign, which depends in turn on the skills and resources of the challenger.

Without reason to believe that the incumbent is vulnerable to attack on some ground, the best potential candidates stay out of the race, leaving the field to inexperienced amateurs. Potential contributors write off unpromising challengers as hopeless causes. Incumbents who are assumed to be invulnerable thus escape the only kind of challenge that could prove the assumption wrong. Expectations become, if not self-fulfilling, at least self-confirming.[4]

National conditions and issues—the performance of the economy, the president's standing with the public, partisan trends—usually appear to favor one party. In a normal election, one party's challengers tend to be relatively strong, the other party's, relatively weak. One reason so few House incumbents were defeated in 1988 is that *both* parties had the weakest field of challengers on record. A simple but powerful measure of the overall quality of a party's challengers is the proportion who have ever held elective office.[5] In 1988, only 16.6 percent of the Democratic challengers and 9.8 percent of the Republican challengers had previously held elective office, all-time lows for both parties in any election since World War II. The proportion of experienced candidates among all 1988 challengers, 12.5 percent, was more than two standard deviations below the 1946 to 1986 mean of 21.3 percent. Seventy-nine incumbents had no major party opponent at all, the most since 1958, before Republicans had begun to contest seats in many parts of the South. Sixty Democratic incumbents were spared Republican challenges in 1988 compared with thirty-seven in 1980.

Providers of campaign money responded to unpromising challengers in the usual way. They ignored them. As of October 19, 1988, House incumbents had raised five times as much money as had House challengers—a record financial disadvantage. Spending by incumbents was 17 percent higher than for the same period in 1986; spending by nonincumbents was 16 percent lower. Political action committees (PACs) were particularly disdainful of Republican challengers and lavished most of their attention on incumbent Democrats, whom they understandably expected to remain in office and in the majority after the election.[6]

Experienced politicians and activists from both parties evidently concluded that 1988 was not a propitious year to take on House incumbents. Their thinking reflected the lessons of recent electoral history as well as a political climate devoid of clear partisan currents. Short-term national conditions and longer term electoral trends were not at all encouraging.

Neither party had reason to expect a particularly good year. The economy continued to expand, inflation remained relatively low, and unemployment steadily improved. But the experience of the October 1987 stock market crash, combined with gloomy speculations stirred by the United States' budget and trade deficits and weakened position in the international economy, left serious doubts about short- and long-term economic prospects. Americans enjoyed prosperity but worried about the economic future.[7]

Republicans could claim credit for presiding over peace as well as prosperity. Successful negotiations with the Soviet Union to rid Europe of intermediate-range nuclear missiles were followed by a new round of talks aimed at much broader arms reductions. Wars in Iran, Afghanistan, and Angola were winding down, and democracies had supplanted dictatorships in a number of countries. These successes of the Reagan administration were counterbalanced by revelations of its secret attempt to sell arms to Iran in exchange for American hostages and to use the profits to finance the contras in Nicaragua. Other trouble spots where the United States was active—El Salvador, the Middle East, the Persian Gulf—also held distinct risks, particularly after President Reagan's competence to manage foreign policy was called into question by the Iran-contra affair.

Reagan's approval rating dropped sharply when the affair was exposed, and it was slow to recover. The percentage of respondents in the *New York Times*/CBS News polls that approved of his job performance had remained in the mid- to high sixties through the first ten months of 1986. Then, between October and November, the approval rating plummeted twenty-one points. It rebounded only modestly thereafter, hovering close to the 50 percent mark throughout 1987 and the first half of 1988.[8] The Iran-contra revelations brought a lame-duck aura to the administration prematurely. Despite peace and prosperity, most presidential election polls put the Democrats ahead throughout the first half of 1988.[9]

In sum, nothing in the national political climate on the eve of the 1988 campaign suggested that either party's candidates could count on a particularly favorable partisan tide or could expect special help from national issues. Nor, of course, did either party have anything in particular to fear from national forces. But without exploitable issues or favorable trends, both parties' challengers could expect to have trouble raising money and persuading voters to desert incumbents. Such is the clear lesson of recent electoral history.

Trends in Competition for House Seats

The absence of short-term partisan trends underscored the relevance of longer term electoral patterns, which were not the least bit encouraging to House challengers. Figure 6-1 displays the nearly linear decline in the share of votes won by House challengers in postwar elections. The average challenger's share of votes dropped 0.4 percentage points from one election to the next between 1946 and 1988, falling from 40 percent to less than 32 percent.[10] The proportion of contests in which the incumbent received less than 60 percent of the major party vote has declined by two-thirds, from 39 percent to 13 percent. Figure 6-2 demonstrates this "vanishing marginals" phenomena, which excited so much analysis after it was first identified in the early 1970s.[11]

The trends identified in Figures 6-1 and 6-2 were initially taken by scholars to signify a decline in electoral competition in House elections. With more incumbents enjoying wide margins of safety, fewer should fail to win reelection. But as late as the 1970s, incumbents

Figure 6-1   Average House Challenger's Share of the Major Party
Vote, 1946-1988

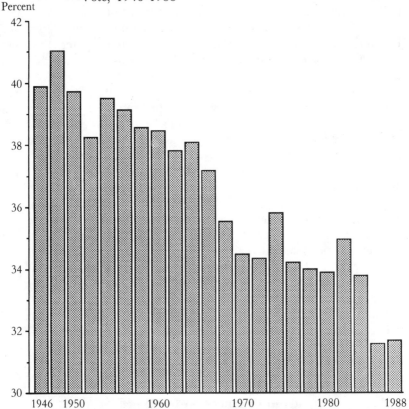

Percent

were no less vulnerable to defeat than they had been in the 1950s.
Their chances of losing did not fall because the voters in their districts
grew more fickle; a comfortable margin in one election became a
weaker guarantee of victory in the next election. Incumbents won by
wider margins, on average, when they won, but they were just as likely
as before to lose any given election.[12]

In the 1980s, however, incumbents really have become more
secure. Table 6-2 documents the significant decrease in the percentage
of successful challenges during this decade.[13] Taken together, Figures
6-1 and 6-2 and Table 6-2 demonstrate that competition for House
seats that were held by incumbents fell to distinctly lower levels in the
mid-1980s, extending the historical trend toward diminished competition into uncharted territory.

Because potential candidates and contributors behave strategically,

Figure 6-2   House Seats Won by Incumbents with Less Than 60
Percent   Percent of the Major Party Vote, 1946-1988

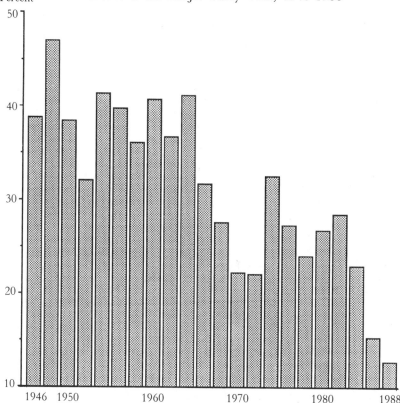

uncompetitiveness feeds on itself. The fewer the incumbents who are
defeated or even threatened with defeat, the more reluctant good
candidates are to run and contributors are to support challengers. The
cumulative lesson taught by recent elections is particularly discouraging
to Republicans.

The 1982 elections were especially critical in this regard. The
Republicans had made major gains in the 1980 House elections,
picking up an additional thirty-four seats to reach their highest total
since Watergate; twenty-six more seats would give them a majority. A
sense of momentum and the Reagan administration's successes in 1981
helped the Republicans to recruit a superior crop of challengers for
1982. But by election day, the economy was in its deepest postwar
recession, with unemployment in double digits, and popular dissatisfaction with Reagan was at the highest point of his entire presidency. As a

Table 6-2   Defeated Incumbent Candidates for the House,
1952-1988

Years	General elections		Primary and general elections	
	Percent	N	Percent	N
1952-1960	6.4	(1,979)	7.7	(2,008)
1962-1970	6.5	(1,978)	8.5	(2,020)
1972-1980	6.1	(1,911)	7.7	(1,945)
1982-1988	3.6	(1,588)	4.6	(1,604)

SOURCE: 1950-1986: computed from data in Norman J. Ornstein, Thomas E. Mann, and Michael J. Malbin, *Vital Statistics on Congress 1987-1988* (Washington, D.C.: Congressional Quarterly, 1987); 1988: compiled by author.
NOTE: The differences between 1982-1988 and each of the preceding three decades are significant at p<.001; differences among the other three decades are not significant.

result, only one Republican challenger was elected.[14]

The futility of Republican challenges in 1982 hampered the party's recruitment for 1984. Republicans had, in effect, used up some of their most promising talent in the wrong election. Thus, relatively few effective Republican challengers were poised to take advantage of Reagan's landslide reelection, and whatever opportunity it may have presented was largely missed.[15] Republicans gained only fourteen House seats, which made it more difficult for the party to attract strong challengers for 1986. In addition, Democratic incumbents who had survived the Reagan landslide would be tougher to defeat in 1986 without Reagan to head the Republican ticket, and the historic record for the president's party at the midterm election six years into an administration was dismal. The result was that, as a group, the 1986 Republican challengers were nearly as inexperienced and neglected by campaign contributors as the 1988 contingent would be two years later. Ironically, election day 1986 found the economy still growing nicely and Reagan's performance receiving widespread popular approval. Republicans might have done considerably better in 1986 had they fielded a group of challengers as talented as those who ran in 1982.[16]

Republican problems in recent elections have been exacerbated by conflicts with many of the corporate and business PACs that Republican party officials believe should be their natural allies. Business PAC support for Republican challengers has dropped dramatically since 1980.[17] Not only have PACs been turned off by Republicans' failure to advance in the House and to field promising challengers, but Democratic officials have vigorously solicited support for their party's challengers as well as incumbents by offering pointed reminders about who was going to run the House for the foreseeable future.[18] Business organizations have become steadily less willing to trade immediate access to powerful Democratic representatives for the dim hope of a Republican House majority. (Republicans last won control of the House in 1952.)

Although Democrats fielded fewer experienced challengers in 1988 than in any other postwar election, they were still well ahead of the Republicans in this regard. Democrats routinely can recruit a more seasoned crop of challengers because of their party's preponderance in state legislatures and other lower elective offices, and 1988 was no exception. In 1988 they also managed to mount a larger proportion of adequately financed challenges, at least according to preliminary data. As of October 19, Democratic challengers had out-raised Republican challengers by a margin of $21 million to $13 million, even though there were more of the latter than the former. PAC contributions to Democratic challengers—up 24 percent from 1986—were five times as great as PAC contributions to Republican challengers. In some cases, Democratic challengers were helped by incumbents of their party who were willing to redirect unneeded PAC contributions their way.[19] Although 1988 was by no measure a great year for congressional Democrats, they still managed to add to their large House majority while losing the presidency decisively.

With little in the immediate political setting or in longer term political trends to brighten the prospects of either party's challengers, both Democrats and Republicans mounted relatively few competitive House challenges in 1988. Their low expectations were readily met. It is hardly surprising that inexperienced challengers lacking adequate funds and profitable issues should fail to defeat incumbent members of Congress. But it would be a mistake to conclude from recent House elections that incumbents are now completely insulated from national tides. The true measure of an incumbent's strength is revealed only when it is tested under adverse conditions by a vigorous challenge. It is worth remembering that a comparable period of incumbent immunity—1968-1972, during which only thirty-four incumbents lost general elections compared with twenty-eight in 1984-1988—was followed by an election (1974) in which forty incumbents met defeat.

The Senate Elections

Although continuity also characterized the 1988 Senate elections, it was generated by a very different electoral process than in the House. In 1988, as in other recent years, Senate races were far more likely than House races to be vigorously contested. The state-by-state results are listed in Table 6-3. Democrats took four seats from Republicans, defeating three incumbents and taking one open seat. Republicans took three seats from Democrats, defeating one incumbent and taking two open seats. Twenty-one percent of the thirty-three Senate seats that were up for election changed party hands compared with 2 percent of the House seats. Forty-four percent of the incumbents won less than 60 percent of the vote compared with 13 percent of House incumbents. Four seats were won with less than 51 percent of the major party vote, three by Republicans. A shift of fewer than three percentage points in selected states could have elected three more Republicans or four more Democrats.

Close Senate elections have been common in recent years, with control of the Senate hinging on a small proportion of the total votes cast. In 1986, a switch of 55,000 votes, properly distributed, would have left the Senate in Republican hands. But with a similar redistribution of 42,000 votes in the other direction in 1980, Republicans never would have won a majority in the first place, and a shift of 35,000 votes in 1982 would have returned the Senate to the Democrats. For Republicans to have won effective control of the Senate in 1988 (fifty seats plus the vice presidency), it would have taken a switch of about 180,000 votes—about 0.3 percent of the more than 65 million votes that were cast in Senate elections.

Competition breeds competition. Senate contests are more often competitive than House elections because Senate challengers are more often experienced, high-quality candidates who are able to raise adequate funds. Superior candidates run in part because the record shows that Senate challengers have a decent chance of winning. The same dynamic that inhibits competition in House elections encourages it in Senate elections. At present, both parties are competitive in almost every state: twenty-two states are represented by one senator from each party; another nine have chosen senators from both parties in elections since 1978; and all but two of the nineteen remaining states—Hawaii and Massachusetts—have elected governors of the opposite party from their senators' during the past decade. The contrast with House elections could hardly be more stark.

To be sure, both parties' competitiveness in virtually every state does not mean that every Senate seat is hotly contested. Some Senate incumbents manage to entrench themselves as firmly as does the typical House incumbent, thereby discouraging formidable opponents and winning easily. But structural differences between the offices of senator and representative—salience to voters, constituency size, media market structure, and term of service, to name a few—make it considerably more difficult for senators to develop a reputation, deserved or not, for

Table 6-3 Senate Election Results by State, 1988

	Vote total	*Percent*
Arizona		
Dennis DeConcini (D)*	651,164	57.9
Keith DeGreen (R)	472,776	42.1
California		
Pete Wilson (R)*	4,835,014	54.4
Leo T. McCarthy (D)	4,060,259	45.6
Connecticut		
Joseph I. Lieberman (D)	686,018	50.4
Lowell P. Weicker, Jr. (R)*	675,225	49.6
Delaware		
William V. Roth, Jr. (R)*	140,827	63.4
S. B. Woo (D)	84,806	37.6
Florida		
Connie Mack (R)	2,204,575	50.4
Buddy MacKay (D)	2,014,924	49.6
Hawaii		
Spark M. Matsunaga (D)*	247,941	78.7
Maria M. Hustace (R)	66,987	21.3
Indiana		
Richard G. Lugar (R)*	1,411,945	67.7
Jack Wickes (D)	672,551	32.4
Maine		
George J. Mitchell (D)*	446,520	81.1
Jasper S. Wyman (R)	104,009	18.9
Maryland		
Paul S. Sarbanes (D)*	953,168	61.8
Alan L. Keyes (R)	588,519	38.2
Massachusetts		
Edward M. Kennedy (D)*	1,676,437	65.6
Joseph D. Malone (R)	877,643	34.4
Michigan		
Donald W. Riegle, Jr. (D)*	2,107,032	61.0
Jim Dunn (R)	1,346,103	39.0
Minnesota		
Dave Durenberger (R)*	1,171,678	57.9
Hubert H. Humphrey III (D)	853,004	42.1
Mississippi		
Trent Lott (R)	487,238	53.1
Wayne Dowdy (D)	431,048	46.9
Missouri		
John C. Danforth (R)*	1,412,146	68.1
Jay Nixon (D)	660,099	31.9

Table 6-3   Continued

	Vote total	Percent
Montana		
Conrad Burns (R)	189,074	51.9
John Melcher (D)*	175,003	48.1
Nebraska		
Robert Kerrey (D)	371,382	57.7
David K. Karnes (R)*	272,449	42.3
Nevada		
Richard H. Bryan (D)	175,508	52.1
Chic Hecht (R)*	161,273	47.9
New Jersey		
Frank R. Lautenberg (D)*	1,552,805	54.4
Pete Dawkins (R)	1,303,907	45.6
New Mexico		
Jeff Bingaman (D)*	309,819	63.2
Bill Valentine (R)	180,044	36.8
New York		
Daniel Patrick Moynihan (D)*	3,891,767	68.0
Robert R. McMillan (R)	1,828,291	32.0
North Dakota		
Quentin N. Burdick (D)*	171,557	60.5
Earl Strinden (R)	112,186	39.5
Ohio		
Howard M. Metzenbaum (D)*	2,473,816	56.9
George Voinovich (R)	1,870,359	43.1
Pennsylvania		
John Heinz (R)*	2,892,417	67.2
Joseph C. Vignola (D)	1,409,790	32.8
Rhode Island		
John H. Chafee (R)*	207,443	54.3
Richard H. Licht (D)	174,498	45.7
Tennessee		
Jim Sasser (D)*	1,021,080	65.6
Bill Anderson (R)	535,067	34.4
Texas		
Lloyd Bentsen (D)*	3,120,348	59.6
Beau Boulter (R)	2,111,765	40.4
Utah		
Orrin G. Hatch (R)*	428,001	67.8
Brian H. Moss (D)	202,873	32.2
Vermont		
James M. Jeffords (R)	162,265	69.4
William Gray (D)	71,511	30.6

Table 6-3 Continued

	Vote total	*Percent*
Virginia		
Charles S. Robb (D)	1,474,443	71.3
Maurice A. Dawkins (R)	594,252	28.7
Washington		
Slade Gorton (R)	840,017	50.8
Mike Lowry (D)	814,873	49.2
West Virginia		
Robert C. Byrd (D)*	408,693	64.8
M. Jay Wolfe (R)	221,911	35.2
Wisconsin		
Herbert Kohl (D)	1,122,019	52.2
Susan Engeleiter (R)	1,026,942	47.8
Wyoming		
Malcolm Wallop (R)*	91,053	50.3
John Vinich (D)	89,788	49.7

SOURCE: "Returns for Governor, Senate and House," *Congressional Quarterly Weekly Report,* November 12, 1988, 3301-3307.

* Indicates incumbents.

electoral invulnerability.[20] Thus, they are far more likely to be challenged by qualified, well-financed opponents.

This tendency was certainly true in 1988. Seventeen of the twenty-seven Senate challengers (63 percent) had previously held elective office; seven, all Democrats, had been elected to statewide offices. Nine of the twelve candidates for open Senate seats had held office, six of them in the House. All of the successful challengers, and five of the six open seat victors, were highly qualified candidates by this standard. The newly elected senators included three former governors (Robert Kerrey, D-Neb.; Richard H. Bryan, D-Nev.; Charles S. Robb, D-Va.), one former state attorney general (Joseph I. Lieberman, D-Conn.), a former U.S. senator (Slade Gorton, R-Wash.), three former U.S. representatives (Connie Mack, R-Fla.; Trent Lott, R-Miss.; James M. Jeffords, R-Vt.), and a county commissioner (Conrad Burns, R-Mont.). Only one was a political novice (Herbert Kohl, the millionaire owner of the Milwaukee Bucks basketball team). Campaign money followed quality; preliminary figures indicate that almost every Senate candidate with a plausible chance of winning raised an adequate war chest.

Not all Senate candidates had impressive political credentials, and about half the Senate winners had a fairly easy time of it. Local considerations largely determined the level of competition. Incumbents who for any reason seemed vulnerable invited stiff challenges, with national politics playing a decidedly minor role in such judgments. Because more of the Democratic incumbents appeared to be shoo-ins in 1988, Republicans failed to field strong candidates in more states than did Democrats, including four (Arizona, Virginia, Tennessee, and Maine) that Bush won handily.

Nothing suggests that potential candidates or contributors expected presidential politics to make much difference in the various Senate elections, and it did not. The statewide vote for senator was related only weakly to the statewide vote for president in 1988, as the regression equations in Table 6-4 demonstrate. With or without controls for incumbency, there is no statistically significant relationship between the share of votes won by Bush and the share won by the Republican Senate candidate. The tiny regression coefficient on the presidential vote in the second equation confirms the impression that, as Nelson Polsby put it, "the emperor [had] no coat." [21] Republican Senate candidates won in eleven of the twenty-five states (44 percent) that Bush won and in three of the eight states (38 percent) won by Dukakis, an insignificant difference. Mack, the Republican, won a close race for an open Senate seat in Florida, a state Bush won with more

Table 6-4   The Relationship Between the Vote for President and Senator in 1988

	Equation 1	*Equation 2*
Constant	27.16 (22.40)	46.51* (17.17)
Percentage of major party vote for Bush	.36 (.41)	.06 (.30)
Democrat is incumbent		−13.07* (4.73)
Republican is incumbent		7.46 (4.86)
$R^2 =$ N=33	.02	.52

NOTE: The dependent variable is the percentage of the major party vote won by the Republican Senate candidate; the standard errors of the coefficients are in parentheses; coefficients twice their standard errors and thus significant at $p < .05$ are marked by an asterisk (*).

than 60 percent of the vote; but Republican Gorton also won a close race for an open seat in Washington, which Bush lost. The most surprising Republican victory, Burns's defeat of Sen. John Melcher, took place in Montana, where Bush won only 53 percent of the vote.

Senate and House elections were as detached from each other as from the presidential election. Democrats took 61 percent of the House seats in states that were won by Democratic Senate candidates and 58 percent of the House seats in states won by Republican Senate candidates.

The National Campaigns

Dissociation between presidential and congressional elections is nothing new, but its extremity in 1988 is still remarkable. The national campaigns deserve some of the blame, with much the larger share going to the Bush campaign because it captured the agenda. In fairness to Bush, however, it is inherently difficult for a sitting vice president to mount a campaign that gives his party's congressional challengers much rhetorical ammunition. If the theme is affirmation and continuity—to maintain peace and prosperity—then it is hard for the vice president to make a case for "throwing the rascals out" of Congress. Incumbents of both parties can claim a share of the credit for good times.

In recent years, Republican House and Senate challengers have derived little benefit from their presidents' successes; elections that confirm Republican control of the presidency do not help the party much at the congressional level. Table 6-5 lists the House and Senate results in the four postwar elections in which Republicans retained the presidency. The party lost a Senate seat or two in every one of these elections and lost House seats in half of them. From this perspective, Bush's failure to carry more congressional Republicans into office with him was not the exception but the rule.

Still, the tactics adopted by the Bush campaign were singularly unhelpful to Republican congressional candidates, who could not easily

Table 6-5 House and Senate Seat Changes in Postwar Elections in Which Republicans Retained the Presidency

Year	Presidential winner	Vote	House	Senate
1956	Dwight D. Eisenhower	57.8	2 D	1 D
1972	Richard M. Nixon	61.8	12 R	2 D
1984	Ronald Reagan	59.2	14 R	2 D
1988	George Bush	53.9	3 D	1 D

NOTE: Vote is the percentage of major party votes won by the Republicans.

transfer attacks on Dukakis's patriotism, liberalism, and commitment to law and order to their Democratic opponents. Members of Congress who represent constituencies where such charges could have hurt have long since erected defenses against them. They have their own carefully considered positions on gun control, the death penalty, and other galvanizing social issues. As usual, congressional Democrats put whatever distance they deemed to be politically necessary between themselves and the top of their ticket. And in 1988 they enjoyed the option of running as Lloyd Bentsen Democrats.

The Bush campaign's positive themes—a "kinder, gentler nation" with a greater commitment to education, child care, and the environment—were scarcely calculated to give voters reasons to evict Democrats from Congress. Bush's decision to say nothing explicit about his plans to deal with the budget deficit was shrewd electoral politics; any detailed budget proposal would make more enemies than friends. But silence on the budget also meant that the only standard that Republican candidates for Congress could rally around was "no new taxes," which was not particularly effective at a time when majorities of the public favored tax increases to deal with a number of specific problems and were, in any case, skeptical about Bush's ability to keep his promise.[22]

Divided Government

The 1988 election repeats the pattern, by now familiar, of a decisive Republican presidential victory that leaves Democrats in firm control of Congress. However familiar, the pattern is still curious: Why divided government? Why, specifically, have Republicans not done better in congressional elections? The end of the Reagan era finds the Republican party no stronger in Congress than it was at the beginning. Republicans entered the 101st Congress in 1989 with 175 House seats; on average, they have won 179 House seats in the five elections in which Reagan was on the ticket or in the White House. Both numbers fall below their postwar average of 180 seats.

Republicans did do considerably better in Senate elections than in House elections during the Reagan era. After taking control of the Senate in 1980, they held on to it through two more elections. But they lost their majority in 1986 despite a healthy economy and a popular leader, and the forty-five seats they presently hold is only one more than their postwar mean. Despite the generally competitive nature of Senate elections, Republican prospects for retaking the Senate soon are not very bright.[23]

The Republicans' failure in congressional elections is all the more striking in light of other favorable developments during the Reagan era.

The electorate became significantly more Republican. The net Democratic advantage in party identifiers fell from about a margin of twenty percentage points over the Republicans before 1980 to about five percentage points in 1988; the largest Republican gains occurred immediately after the 1980 and 1984 elections.[24] Republicans also secured significant financial and organizational advantages over the Democrats. Their national House and Senate campaign committees leapt far ahead of the comparable Democratic committees in raising and spending money for candidates. From 1980 through 1986, the Republican committees raised a total of $418 million compared with the Democrats' $62 million.[25] The money was used to build technically sophisticated national organizations that can pursue an impressive range of party-building and electoral activities.[26] After a lag, the Democrats have begun to copy many of the Republican innovations, and the Republicans' financial and organizational lead has begun to dwindle—without having achieved any permanent gains.

Why have congressional Republicans taken so little advantage of favorable developments during Reagan's presidency? The standard answer—that the power of incumbency in Congress now swamps any other electoral force—is incomplete and insufficient. Undeniably, incumbency confers formidable advantages, but it cannot explain why Democrats defeated enough incumbent Republicans to regain control of the Senate (or why they lost it in the first place). It cannot explain why a larger proportion of Republican representatives (4.7 percent) than Democratic representatives (3.7 percent) have been defeated in the last five general elections. Nor can it explain why Republicans have not won more open seats. From 1980 through 1988, they took 28 percent of open Democratic seats but lost 20 percent of their own. Including new seats that were created by redistricting after the 1980 census, Republicans gained a net total of five open seats during this period. What is more, all of this gain occurred in 1980; since then, Republicans, on balance, have been losers in open seat contests. Over the three most recent elections, all held in a setting of continuing prosperity, peace, and popular approval of the president, Republicans made no net gains in contests for open seats.[27]

Disgruntled Republicans offer another explanation of their failures—namely, that Democratic gerrymandering after the 1980 census kept them from winning their fair share of seats in the House. But neither theoretical analysis nor empirical research offers any basis for believing that partisan redistricting cost Republicans more than a handful of seats, if any.[28] The continued Democratic domination of the House, then, is not merely the result of structural advantages produced by incumbency and gerrymandering.

One explanation that has attracted some recent scholarly support is that voters deliberately chose to divide control of the federal government between the two parties. Voters prefer Democratic Congresses *because* they prefer Republican presidents. Spatial logic provides the theoretical underpinning for this view: by offsetting Republican presidents with Democratic Congresses, moderate voters who find both parties' ideologies too extreme can induce policy compromises that are closer to their centrist position than either party would reach on its own. Empirical support for this proposition comes from polls showing that majorities endorse divided government.[29]

The voters' seeming contentment with divided control aside, there is little evidence that very many people consciously split their presidential and congressional votes between the parties in order to achieve ideological balance in government. Although presidential coattails seem paltry, no one has yet uncovered an anticoattail effect. It is doubtful, for example, that many voters who switched from Reagan in 1984 to Dukakis in 1988 changed their congressional vote from Democratic to Republican to maintain ideological balance. It also stretches the imagination to conjure many voters who, while vacillating between Bush and Dukakis in 1988, simultaneously vacillated in the opposite direction between Democratic and Republican House and Senate candidates. Still, some people probably did find it easier to vote for Reagan or Bush because they were confident that Democrats would retain control of Congress.

Another interpretation of pervasive ticket-splitting seems rather more persuasive. In this view, divided control of the presidency and Congress is more a byproduct of the electorate's self-contradictory preferences than the fulfillment of sophisticated ideological balancing.[30] Voters want different, often mutually exclusive things from presidents and members of Congress. At present, majorities believe that Republicans are more likely to deliver what they want from presidents and that Democrats are more likely to deliver what they want from members of Congress. Presidential and congressional votes thus express different, often contradictory preferences that pit the president against Congress as each tries to satisfy its constituents.

A variety of polling data show that Americans want mutually incompatible things from government: low taxes, balanced budgets, low inflation, a strong national defense, and a less intrusive bureaucracy but not cuts in social programs and services, greater exposure to market forces, or greater environmental risk. For example, large majorities favor a balanced budget, and even larger majorities want the balance to be achieved by cutting spending rather than raising taxes. But majorities also want to maintain or increase government spending for the poor, the elderly, farmers, the environment, education, and medical services. Indeed, despite their worries about deficits and their aversion to paying more taxes, more people than not are unwilling to see *any* program that they deem worthwhile cut to balance the budget. Americans clearly dislike intrusive, expensive "big government," but they also clearly appreciate most of the programs that comprise it. Similarly, majorities want a strong national defense but balk at paying for it through higher taxes or lower social spending.

During the 1980s partisan (Republican, Democratic) and institutional (president, Congress) differences combined to give voters the chance to express their contradictory preferences at the polls. They could vote for Republican presidential candidates who were committed to low taxes, low spending, deregulation, and a strong national defense. And they could vote for congressional Democrats who promised to protect their favorite domestic programs from the budget axe. Such a split vote is consistent with the public's view that Republicans are better at reducing deficits, ensuring prosperity, and defending the nation, while Democrats are better at protecting Social Security benefits, the poor, farmers, the unemployed, minorities, women, and the environment.

A split vote also is consistent with differences in the duties that voters assign to presidents and members of Congress. Presidents are expected to look after broad national interests and are held responsible for achieving collective goods such as peace and prosperity. Presidents can profit politically by imposing costs on specific groups and localities in return for greater, but more broadly diffused, national benefits. Members of Congress, in contrast, are expected to protect constituents from damaging government policies regardless of the broader benefits to the nation as a whole; they prosper by looking out for the particular. On election day, it is not so much that voters balance Democrats in one branch against Republicans in the other to get a government that is closer to their centrist views but that majorities prefer a president committed to a set of diffuse collective goods and congressional representatives who promise to minimize what voters have to give up to achieve them.

Congressional Democrats enjoy a further advantage over presidential Democrats. Democratic presidential candidates face the daunting task of trying to build a national coalition out of groups that are, in varying degrees, mutually antagonistic: blacks, Jews, working-class whites, southern traditionalists, and affluent college-educated and professionally educated liberals. It is not surprising that they often fail.

Democratic candidates for Congress are free to assemble local coalitions that may or may not include groups that are important to the party nationally. They can court organized labor, civil rights activists, feminists, and gun control advocates where this adds votes, or they can avoid such alliances where it does not. Similarly, the liberal tag that seems a liability in national elections can be an asset in many congressional districts; and where it is not, congressional Democrats have learned how to avoid it. Democratic presidential candidates may be hurt by the perception that their party is weak on defense; congressional Democrats are free to adopt any of a wide range of positions on this issue to fit local opinion.

Thus, a fragmented, decentralized electoral process allows congressional Democrats to turn a serious national problem—diversity and discord—to local advantage. Conversely, the advantage Republican presidential candidates enjoy because voters think their party is better at promoting diffuse collective goods like economic growth and a strong defense may not extend to Republican congressional candidates at all, especially if they can be portrayed as caring more about national interests than local needs.

The advantages of diversity and localism contribute to a final explanation of Democratic success in congressional elections: superior candidates. Although one would expect young politicians of ambition and talent to flock to an ascendant party, recruitment continues to be a major stumbling block for Republicans. Merely to note that Democrats predominate in the lower offices that serve as steppingstones to Congress only begs the question of why Republicans have not done better in contests for these offices, too.

The Republicans' problem may lie in an ideological view of government that, if taken seriously, undermines the foundation of most congressional careers. Members of Congress thrive on delivering particularized benefits to constituents, not on dismantling, in the name of efficiency or political philosophy, the programs that produce these benefits. They are elected to minimize the local cost of achieving national purposes, not to pursue visions of the national interest without regard for local effects. Thus, people who share Reagan's minimalist conception of government are unlikely to find a congressional career enticing or, once begun, very satisfying. If government is the problem, why embark on a career that can succeed only if you are willing to become part of the problem? The potential leaders who are most strongly attracted to the Republican goal of reducing the public sector are, by that very fact, ill suited to the politics of congressional elections.

The Democratic view of government is far more celebratory. Democrats believe that an active federal government is needed to cope with problems that are left unsolved, indeed created, by even the most vibrant private sector. Government service is an honorable vocation for

Democrats, who regard the activities that sustain a congressional career as worthwhile. With a broader talent pool to draw from, Democrats thus have far less difficulty finding attractive, experienced challengers who are comfortable with the demands of contemporary electoral politics.

Outlook for the Bush Presidency

The results of the 1988 congressional elections impose distinct constraints on the shape of the Bush presidency. Bush enters the White House with proportionately fewer copartisans in Congress than any previous president. As shown in Table 6-6, Bush takes office along with 175 Republican representatives, well below the 192 who were elected with Richard Nixon and Reagan in their initial victories, much less Dwight D. Eisenhower's 221, which gave Republicans their last House majority. Bush has a few more fellow Republicans in the Senate than did Nixon, but nothing like Reagan's majorities or Eisenhower's near majorities. This is divided government, indeed.

Furthermore, the Bush campaign did little to shape a "mandate" for the new president. Mandates are, of course, in the eye of the beholder. Winning presidential candidates routinely claim popular warrant for their policies; the question is whether anyone else in Washington concurs. Bush's claim to a mandate would be dubious on its face in the absence of discernible coattails; but the claim was left even more threadbare by a campaign that won by trumpeting Dukakis's shortcomings rather than Bush's plans.

The strategy of deliberate vagueness about solutions to budgetary problems was good electoral politics, but it left Bush with little ammunition to be used in the inevitable battles with the Democratic

Table 6-6 Republican Representation in Congress after Republican Presidential Victories, 1952-1988

Year	President	House	Senate
1952	Dwight D. Eisenhower	221	48[a]
1956	Dwight D. Eisenhower	201	47[a]
1968	Richard M. Nixon	192	42
1972	Richard M. Nixon	192	43
1980	Ronald Reagan	192	53
1984	Ronald Reagan	182	53
1988	George Bush	175	45

[a] The Senate had ninety-six members in 1952 and 1956.

Congress. Bush promised "no new taxes," but he also promised to reduce the deficit, to maintain defense spending, and to do more for education, child care, the environment, and the people who were left out of the Reagan prosperity. By refusing to say where the budget cuts that would pay for these programs should fall, Bush cannot claim popular backing for any particular cut. Nor is there much evidence of popular backing for any cut large enough to make an appreciable dent in the deficit. Bush's misty campaign promise to reduce the deficit through a "flexible freeze" showed that he had learned to appreciate the political magic in a little "voodoo economics."

If the campaign did little to define Bush's agenda, his record as vice president was even less informative. The very model of a loyal second, Bush carefully avoided any public expression of disagreement with his president. His own views remained obscure because they were so thoroughly subordinated to Reagan's. During the transition from election to inauguration, commentators of conflicting ideological persuasions were eager to fill the vacuum, presuming to tell Bush what voters had *really* elected him to do. But Bush was no more forthcoming about his plans than he had been during the campaign.

Continuing uncertainty about Bush's policy objectives makes predictions about his relations with Congress even more speculative than is usually the case with a new president. But the stark reality of a solidly Democratic Congress imposes clear constraints on what Bush can expect to achieve. If he were to pursue vigorously the goals dear to Republican conservatives—to cut social spending, begin deployment of the strategic defense initiative (SDI), re-equip the contras, enact the conservative social agenda—his prospects for success would be dim. A rancorous stalemate would be much more likely.

But the positive themes that Bush emphasized in his campaign suggest that he has other, less ideologically conservative priorities; so did his conciliatory meetings with former opponents after the election. If Bush really wants to cultivate a "kinder, gentler nation"—doing more for the poor, improving education, cleaning up the environment, helping working mothers—then a Democratic Congress will be more a help than a hindrance. Democrats share these goals, and their firm control of Congress gives Bush a perfect excuse to stiff the conservatives: "I'm with you, but we don't have the votes." Revenue constraints will keep the Democrats from becoming too activist.

A final possibility is that Bush has no considered domestic program and will shape his agenda by reacting to proposals that originate outside the White House. A political career spent carrying out others' policies may reflect an innate affinity for management rather than innovative leadership.

If Bush takes either the "kinder, gentler" or the managerial approach, the appropriate model for understanding his presidency may be the Eisenhower administration, not the administration in which Bush served as vice president. Bush's cabinet appointees—mainly pragmatic establishment Republicans with reputations for competence—are consistent with the Eisenhower model. Ironically, the real losers in an election won by trashing liberalism may be the Republican Right.

Any inclination Bush has to conduct a consensus presidency should be reinforced by the strong likelihood that Republican representation in Congress will not be appreciably greater after the 1990 midterm election. Only once in this century has the president's party gained House seats at the midterm.[31] In any case, Republican leaders seem to have given up on the House until 1992, after the next census redistributes seats to areas of presumed Republican strength in the South and West.[32] Barring a major disaster—a sharp recession, for example—Republicans are not likely to lose many House seats in 1990 either, if only because they hold so few already. The 1990 election is thus likely to demonstrate again the clear difference between the 1980s and the three previous decades in the extraordinary electoral safety of incumbents.

In the abstract, Republican Senate prospects for 1990 ought to be a good deal more promising. Republicans are potentially competitive in almost every state that has a Senate seat at stake, and the president's party has managed to add to its Senate strength in three of the last seven midterm elections. But Republicans already hold seventeen of the thirty-three seats that come up in 1990, and many more Republican than Democratic seats appear at this early stage to be vulnerable. Indeed, after reviewing individual cases, some observers speculate that the Democratic Senate majority could exceed sixty after the elections of 1992.[33]

The longer term outlook, then, is for divided government to persist. Republicans have all the advantages they need to maintain an edge in presidential elections, leaving Democrats' dreams of the White House prisoner to a Republican administration's failures and mistakes. But as long as voters continue to want different, mutually exclusive things from presidents and members of Congress, Republicans will find it difficult to make headway in Congress. Congressional Democrats have learned to survive successful Republican administrations; their main worry is another failed Democratic administration or a disastrously unpopular presidential ticket. Democrats actually do better in congressional elections when a Republican sits in the White House, especially, of course, at the midterm.[34] Ironically, George Bush's victory probably helped to seal the Republican party's minority status in Congress for the foreseeable future.

Notes

1. In addition to the six House incumbents who lost general elections, one, Ernie Konnyu, R-Calif., was defeated in the primary amid accusations of sexual harassment. The Republicans retained his seat.
2. These figures are calculated from "nearly complete, unofficial" vote returns reported in "Returns for Governor, Senate and House," *Congressional Quarterly Weekly Report*, November 12, 1988, 3301-3307.
3. Gary C. Jacobson, *The Politics of Congressional Elections*, 2d ed. (Boston: Little, Brown, 1987), 134-138; and Gary C. Jacobson and Samuel Kernell, "National Forces in the 1986 House Elections," *Legislative Studies Quarterly*, in press.
4. For the full exposition of this theory, see Gary C. Jacobson and Samuel Kernell, *Strategy and Choice in Congressional Elections*, 2d ed. (New Haven, Conn.: Yale University Press, 1983).
5. Gary C. Jacobson, "Strategic Politicians and the Dynamics of House Elections, 1946-1986" (Paper delivered at the annual meeting of the American Political Science Association, Washington, D.C., September 1-4, 1988).
6. David S. Cloud, "Big Bucks and Victory Often Go Hand in Hand," *Congressional Quarterly Weekly Report*, November 12, 1988, 3271-3272.
7. Samuel Popkin, "Outlook on the Future and Presidential Voting: The 1988 Election and Concerns for the Next Generation" (Paper presented at the annual meeting of the American Political Science Association, Washington, D.C., September 1-4, 1988); and "Optimism, Pessimism, and Policy," *Public Opinion* 11 (November/December 1988): 51-55.
8. *The New York Times/CBS News Poll August National Survey* (July 31-August 3, 1988), 10.
9. Popkin, "Outlook on the Future"; and "Opinion Roundup," *Public Opinion* 11 (November/December 1988), 36-37.
10. The regression of the average challenger's vote share on the election year (1946=1, 1948=2, ... 1988=22) gives

    $$\text{challenger's vote} = 41.1 - .41 \text{ election year}$$
    $$(0.36) \quad (.03)$$

    $R^2 = .91$, $N = 22$, $SER = 0.8$; standard errors are in parentheses.
11. The "marginals" are those House seats won by less than a specific margin; the usual standards are 60 percent and 55 percent of the two-party vote. The proportion of marginal seats has declined by either standard. See David R. Mayhew, "Congressional Elections: The Case of the Vanishing Marginals," *Polity* 6 (1974): 295-317; Albert D. Cover and David R. Mayhew, "Congressional Dynamics and the Decline of Competitive Congressional Elections," in *Congress Reconsidered*, 2d ed., ed. Lawrence C. Dodd and Bruce I. Oppenheimer (Washington, D.C.: CQ Press, 1981), 62-82; and Robert S. Erikson, "Malapportionment, Gerrymandering, and Party Fortunes in Congressional Elections," *American Political Science Review* 66 (1972): 1234-1245.
12. Gary C. Jacobson, "The Marginals Never Vanished: Incumbency and Competition in Elections to the U.S. House of Representatives, 1952-1982," *American Journal of Political Science* 31 (1987): 126-141.

13. Decades are defined by redistricting cycles.

14. Gary C. Jacobson, "Party Organization and Campaign Resources in 1982," *Political Science Quarterly* 100 (Winter 1985-86): 603-625. The threat of formidable Republican challenges did help to save some Republican incumbents by reducing the funds available to the strong crop of Democratic challengers.

15. Gary C. Jacobson, "Congress: Politics after a Landslide without Coattails," in *The Elections of 1984,* ed. Michael Nelson (Washington, D.C.: CQ Press, 1985), 215-237.

16. Jacobson and Kernell, "National Forces in the 1986 House Elections." Survey evidence suggests that approval of Reagan and optimism about the economy translated into votes for Republican House candidates—especially when combined with strong challenges.

17. Gary C. Jacobson, "Parties and PACs in Congressional Elections," in *Congress Reconsidered,* 4th ed., ed. Lawrence C. Dodd and Bruce I. Oppenheimer (Washington, D.C.: CQ Press, 1989).

18. David S. Cloud, "Feud Between GOP, PACs Stings Candidates," *Congressional Quarterly Weekly Report,* September 3, 1988, 2447-2450; and Brooks Jackson, *Honest Graft: Big Money and the American Political Process* (New York: Alfred A. Knopf, 1988), 82-94.

19. Cloud, "Feud Between GOP, PACs," 2450.

20. Jacobson, *Politics of Congressional Elections,* 93-95.

21. Ronald D. Elving, "Democrats Tighten Senate Hold by One Seat," *Congressional Quarterly Weekly Report,* November 12, 1988, 3251.

22. *The New York Times/CBS News Poll Post-Election Survey,* November 10-16, 1988, 14.

23. Elving, "Democrats Tighten Senate Hold," 3249-3250.

24. Michael B. MacKuen, Robert S. Erikson, and James A. Stimson, "Macropartisanship" (Revised version of paper presented at the annual meeting of the Midwest Political Science Association, Chicago, April 14-16, 1988), Figure 4; Gary C. Jacobson, "Meager Patrimony: Republican Representation in Congress after Reagan," in *The Reagan Legacy,* ed. Larry Berman (Baltimore: Johns Hopkins University Press, forthcoming).

25. Norman J. Ornstein, Thomas E. Mann, and Michael J. Malbin, *Vital Statistics on Congress 1987-1988* (Washington, D.C.: Congressional Quarterly, 1987), 99-100.

26. Frank J. Sorauf, *Money in American Elections* (Boston: Scott, Foresman/Little, Brown, 1988), chap. 5; and Paul S. Herrnson, *Party Campaigning in the 1980s* (Cambridge, Mass.: Harvard University Press, 1988).

27. In the 1985, 1986, and 1988 elections, Republicans took thirteen of fifty open seats from Democrats, and Democrats took thirteen of forty-six open seats from Republicans.

28. Alan I. Abramowitz, "Partisan Redistricting and the 1982 Congressional Elections," *Journal of Politics* 45 (1983): 767-770; Bruce E. Cain and Janet Campagna, "Predicting Partisan Redistricting Disputes," *Legislative Studies Quarterly* 12 (1987): 265-274; and Richard Born, "Partisan Intentions and Election Day Realities in the Congressional Redistricting Process," *American Political Science Review* 79 (1985): 305-319.

29. Morris P. Fiorina, "The Reagan Years: Turning to the Right or Groping Toward the Middle?" in *The Resurgence of Conservatism in Anglo-American Democracies,* ed. Barry Cooper, Allan Kornberg, and William Mishler (Durham: Duke

University Press, 1988).

30. For a more detailed and fully documented version of this section, see Jacobson, "Meager Patrimony."
31. Democrats added to their House majority in 1934 on a wave of popular enthusiasm for Franklin D. Roosevelt and his New Deal; during this period, the electorate was undergoing a major realignment, with the Democrats replacing the Republicans as the majority party nationally.
32. Phil Duncan, "Challengers Are Hungry for Winning Ideas," *Congressional Quarterly Weekly Report*, October 15, 1988, 2877.
33. Elving, "Democrats Tighten Senate Hold," 3250.
34. In the six postwar midterm elections during Republican administrations, Democrats have gained an average of twenty-six House seats and four Senate seats; in the five during Democratic administrations, Republicans have gained an average of thirty House seats and four Senate seats.

7. THE PRESIDENCY: GEORGE BUSH AND THE CYCLE OF POLITICS AND POLICY

Erwin C. Hargrove

As president, George Bush is the political heir to President Ronald Reagan in several ways. He was Reagan's choice to be vice president—the first incumbent vice president to be elected president since Martin Van Buren in 1836. He is a Republican—the only person to be elected to succeed a president of his own party since Herbert Hoover followed Calvin Coolidge in 1928. And he inherits as his legacy both the accomplishments and the remaining political problems of the eight-year Reagan presidency. In short, Bush seems likely to be a classic "president of consolidation," as defined and described by Erwin Hargrove in this essay.

As a president of consolidation, Bush's main challenge will be to deal with the side effects and aftershocks of President Reagan's major achievements, notably the mammoth federal budget deficit that resulted from the combination of substantial reductions in the federal income tax and unprecedentedly large increases in peacetime defense spending. Bush will be impeded in this task, Hargrove suggests, by the latest manifestation of the "split-level realignment" in the American political system—the Democratic Congress that was strengthened even as voters were choosing a Republican president in the elections of 1988. Yet Hargrove finds most of the qualities in Bush that a president of consolidation needs, including managerial experience in the federal government and an accommodating political style.

The Bush presidency will be a time of consolidation of the achievements and legacies of Ronald Reagan. Consolidation implies rationalizing, smoothing over, and correcting deficiencies uncovered by experience without rejecting the major achievements of the preceding president's administration. Five other presidents in this century have presided over periods of consolidation. They were the three Republicans of the 1920s who followed Woodrow Wilson—Warren Harding, Calvin Coolidge, and Herbert Hoover—and Dwight Eisenhower, after the long period of liberal reform of Franklin Roosevelt, and Richard Nixon, who accepted most of the policies of Lyndon Johnson's Great Society but reorganized many of them in the interests of better management and implementation.

In addition to presidents who consolidate reform, there are presidents who prepare for reform and those who achieve it. The cycle of politics and policy created by these three types of presidents is founded in the American ideology of liberalism, meaning commitment to individualism, equality of opportunity, and freedom of economic activity. Conservatives and progressives compete within this ideology. Both are optimistic about the possibilities of progress and the achievement of ideological goals, but each camp relies on different instruments. Conservatives prefer to have government play a minimal role and to rely on markets and private initiative to produce prosperity. Progressives accept the market but use government as a means of correcting market failures and fostering equality of opportunity. There is no place in this political universe for the reactionary or the radical.[1]

Reform themes are first expressed by presidents of preparation who articulate the directions of change but lack the congressional majorities necessary to enact reform. Consolidating presidents accept the reforms that are eventually enacted. For most of the twentieth century the presidents who have carried through large-scale programs—the presidents of achievement—have been progressives. But with the election of Ronald Reagan in 1980, the cycle shifted in a conservative direction, making Reagan the only conservative president of achievement in this century (see Table 7-1).

The election of George Bush brings us to the third stage of the fourth round of the cycle—a period of consolidation following a time of achievement. The question of whether and when the cycle of politics and policy might turn in a progressive direction is important for the Bush presidency because the ability or inability of progressive politicians to force such a turn will be, in large part, a consequence of Bush's effectiveness as a consolidating president.

Progressives, Conservatives, and Their Changing Constituencies

Mass publics incorporate the values of both conservative and progressive persuasions in their thinking. Americans are ideological conservatives and practical progressives, adhering to ideals of limited government while valuing the services and benefits that government provides.[2] This ambiguity is grounded in the essential character of American liberalism, which alternates in its emphasis between the primacy of the individual and the affirmation of community. And often

Table 7-1 Presidents of the Twentieth Century and Their Roles in the Cycle of Politics and Policy

| | *Stages of the Cycle* | |
Preparation	Achievement	Consolidation
Theodore Roosevelt/ William Howard Taft[a]	Woodrow Wilson	Warren Harding
		Calvin Coolidge
	Franklin Roosevelt/ Harry Truman[a]	Herbert Hoover
		Dwight Eisenhower
John Kennedy	Lyndon Johnson	Richard Nixon/ Gerald Ford[a]
Jimmy Carter	Ronald Reagan	George Bush

SOURCE: Adapted from Erwin C. Hargrove and Michael Nelson, *Presidents, Politics, and Policy* (Baltimore: Johns Hopkins University Press, 1984), 66-86.

[a] Presidents Taft, Truman, and Ford essentially continued the policies of the presidents they succeeded.

we are torn between conflicting ideals. Thus, people can easily endorse the principle of keeping taxes low and simultaneously call for government to do new things and oppose spending cuts in programs they value.[3] Our politics and policy therefore also shift back and forth.[4]

The character of these two strands within the American tradition helps explain the movement from one stage of the political cycle to the next. The high point in the cycle is the presidency of achievement, in which a decisive election victory gives a new president a greater than normal majority of his party in Congress, enabling him to achieve support for policies he advocates. The actual achievements occur within a brief period, usually during the first term. Wilson, Franklin Roosevelt, Johnson, and Reagan were most creative and effective in their early years in office. Partisan congressional majorities cannot be sustained for long, as the governing party runs out of ideas, implementation problems become visible, and a general desire for more orderly government brings a president of consolidation who rationalizes and scales back reform without rejecting it. But consolidating presidents are usually insensitive to emerging national problems. If their ideologies and programs are not formulated to embrace new issues, consolidation gives way to presidencies of preparation, in which reform themes to meet emerging problems are articulated and the cycle begins anew.

But the institutions of American government are obstacles to the easy creation of working majorities. Presidents of preparation articulate issues that their successors, the achieving presidents, are able to act upon only if extraordinarily electoral and legislative majorities can be created. John Kennedy was a conscious president of preparation; he introduced a legislative program knowing that little of it would be enacted, but hoping that a victory in the 1964 election would give him the necessary congressional support. After Kennedy's assassination, Lyndon Johnson effectively completed Kennedy's plan.

The pattern of the cycle cannot be predicted. Turns in the cycle are forced by critical elections in which the winning candidates articulate the themes that appeal to a majority of voters. Changes in the cycle's direction may be caused by extraordinary events, such as an economic depression. The Great Depression of the 1930s, for example, came so suddenly that there was no possibility of a president of preparation for FDR. In the 1988 campaign the dominant theme of the Republican party was continuity in a period of peace and prosperity. Michael Dukakis attempted to articulate emerging issues of social and economic discontent, but they were not strong enough public concerns to carry the day.

As evidence that the political cycle cannot be predicted, imagine some turning points that might have been. If Nixon had been elected in 1960, the period of consolidation might have continued. If Carter had been both more skillful and luckier, the Reagan era might never have occurred. But the historical context limits the possibilities. Although Hubert Humphrey almost won the 1968 election, it was clear that the period of domestic social reform was over, regardless of who became president. If Dukakis had won the 1988 election, he would have had to have been a president of consolidation despite his liberal ideology, at least until the budget deficit was reduced. Turns of the cycle are not necessarily partisan shifts. They are responses to widely felt historical imperatives. A brief examination of the Carter and Reagan presidencies should make this clear.

Jimmy Carter was a progressive president of preparation who tried to establish an agenda of new issues in the wake of the Great Society. He was not simply a consolidating, conservative Democrat as some have suggested.[5] Rather, he believed that the nation faced new problems that could be defined as "public goods" issues, such as energy conservation, tax reform, and welfare reform. He saw the need for a defense buildup after years of stable military budgets. He regarded inflation as the major economic problem (a position other Democrats had difficulty accepting, since their constituents suffered more from unemployment than from inflation).[6] He had great difficulty convincing Democratic members of Congress and Democratic interest groups, especially organized labor, of the merits of his views. Most politically active Democrats were still mired in the politics of the Great Society.

Carter's initiatives and failures—dealing with high inflation and the American hostages in Iran—paved the way for Ronald Reagan to take advantage of widespread dissatisfaction with government to assert the policy agenda that continues to dominate American politics. Reagan's electoral victory in 1980 was sufficient to elect a Republican Senate and to frighten many southern Democrats in the House into cooperating with Republicans for a working majority behind the new president. Reagan was thus able to pass a 25 percent cut in income taxes, a 15 percent increase in defense spending, and considerable budget cuts in domestic programs—although not enough to balance the federal budget. Reagan met the criteria of a president of achievement. His election victory gave him larger than normal support in Congress, and he was able to carry through a program of new ideas and to dominate the agenda of policy and politics. The 1984 and 1988 elections were fought in terms dictated by Reagan's agenda. In 1984 Walter Mondale, a liberal Democrat, accused the president of fiscal irresponsibility and promised to raise taxes to eliminate the budget deficit caused by the shortfall of government income after the tax cuts. Michael Dukakis learned from Mondale how politically fatal calls for taxes could be, but his promises for new programs were less than credible in light of the continuing high deficit. Reagan put the Democrats on the defensive, and President Bush will probably try to keep them there.

Reagan Legacies

In his 1980 campaign and in his first year as president, Reagan addressed the problems of "stagflation," slower economic growth, and lower productivity during the Ford and Carter administrations in a highly original way. His remedy for those problems was "supply-side" economics, which was an economic theory only in part.

Supply-Side Economics

The term was a symbolic code word for the presidential promise to the American people that it was possible to have deep income tax cuts, more modest budget cuts, and a massive defense buildup without inflation. The tax cut would so liberate entrepreneurial and investment energies among the business classes that the economy would begin to grow at a rate sufficient to close the deficit gap and to inhibit inflation. The Federal Reserve Board would cooperate by holding the money supply in check, to restrain inflation, without precipitating a recession.

This strategy was different from the old-fashioned Republican "trickle-down" appeals of the McKinley and Hoover eras. Those orthodox Republican presidents abhorred federal budget deficits, as did all right-thinking economists of the times. Reagan, like Democrats Kennedy and Johnson, promised that the nation could grow out of temporary deficits. And although his rhetoric and budget proposals attacked Great Society programs for the poor, he made no move to curb the entitlement programs of Medicare and Social Security, which benefit the middle classes and are far more expensive. He made it seem possible to eat one's cake and have it too.

The supply-side promises were a creative improvement over the stop-and-go economic policies of the Eisenhower, Nixon, and Ford administrations. Republican economics, since World War II and before Reagan, was cautiously Keynesian in its recognition that government might have to forestall economic downturn and possible recession by inflating the economy either through spending or by cutting taxes. But the emphasis of Republican economics was on fighting inflation, even if a mild dose of unemployment had to be tolerated in the process. Inflation ate away at a stable currency and at the foundations of economic stability as Republicans understood it.[7] But because this economic approach hurt the Republicans in presidential elections, Reagan turned to supply-side economics.

Reagan learned about supply-side economics from Republican representative Jack Kemp, who had developed a new repertoire of Republican appeals for his working-class Buffalo constituents. One of those appeals was the idea of tax reduction—not to increase purchasing power and recovery in recession, but to induce greater investment and economic growth for the benefit of all citizens. The gospel of wealth was to be hitched to populist politics. Reagan found this idea appealing, not only because of his well-known loathing of income taxes derived from his movie days, but because Reagan is a Democrat in his political style. Good orthodox Republican economists believe in pain: they cure recession with unemployment. But Reagan was able to use supply-side appeals to promise a bright economic future for working men and women, without pain. He disguised as economic theory what was essentially a political strategy.

Conservative Themes

Conservative parties in democracies often win elections by beating nationalistic drums, and Reagan was no exception. Nationalistic appeals are usually effective with blue-collar voters and proved to be so with traditionally Democratic working-class voters in 1980 and 1984. The addition of symbolically important and salient "moral" positions such as hostility to abortion, toughness on crime, and support for school prayer constituted a litany of Reagan appeals to religious conservatives, many of whom are southern Democrats. Traditional Republicans were persuaded by his attacks on government spending and regulation and praise for the free market. These economic, foreign policy, and moralistic appeals reinforced one another, especially in the increasingly Republican South.[8] This package of appeals was much richer than that used by previous Republican candidates for president, enabling Ronald Reagan to fulfill the 1964 dream of Barry Goldwater of creating a nascent Republican majority that ignored the Northeast and reached south and west to embrace the expanding nation. Nixon almost achieved the dream in 1972, only to be undone by Watergate. Reagan's achievement was to put Democrats and liberals on the defensive on both economic and moral issues by constructing a coalition in two presidential elections.

Much of Reaganite politics is inherently offensive. The typical Reaganite stakes out a purist position, identifies it as representing the beliefs of most Americans, and then puts liberalism on the defensive as clearly out of the mainstream. Hugh Heclo suggests that Reaganism, as an outlook on the world, will have staying power beyond Reagan: "Reaganism, like the headiest days of liberalism, offers a vision in which Americans can have it all: world leadership and economic growth without guilt or hard choices." [9]

But this is not to say that the voters have turned their backs on government in ways consistent with President Reagan's own philosophy. Public opinion surveys throughout the Reagan years consistently revealed that a majority of citizens like the social programs introduced by the Great Society—both middle-class entitlements and assistance for the poor—and do not want them scaled back.[10] Republican presidential landslides in 1984 and 1988 are best explained by peace and prosperity rather than by any mass public desire to diminish the role of government. In fact, the public has resisted major cutbacks in environmental and social programs. The Reagan administration promised to respect the "social safety net" in preserving government programs that help the poor. And Social Security and Medicare not only have been politically sacrosanct but have been expanded.

Nor did Reagan succeed in transforming the structure of American government. The nation's governors rejected his proposal for a return to a sharp division of labor between the federal and state governments, with the federal government taking most income maintenance programs, except welfare, and the states assuming authority for most education and social programs. Federal funds for social programs were cut drastically, but the programs still exist. Job training, occupational safety and health, and many regulatory programs have been restructured. But almost all of the programs that Reagan inherited were still intact after his eight years in office. There is apparently very little public disposition to cut them further. The outer limits of the Reagan revolution appear to have been reached.

The Budget Deficit

President Reagan thus leaves for his successor the legacy of the federal budget deficit. Although the political creativity of supply-side economics brought economic recovery after a severe recession in 1982 and 1983 that wiped out inflation, the gap between what the federal government spends and what it brings in was not closed, for two reasons. The American people want too much from government, more than the Reagan rhetoric will admit. And the promise of supply-side economics that deep tax cuts would bring increases in saving and investment sufficient to close the budget gap have not been realized. This is the flaw in the Reagan political formula that President Bush must face in economic policy.

Most of the damage to the budget was done in 1981 when the defense buildup was pushed through Congress without careful planning. Income taxes were cut 25 percent over a three-year period, and neither the president nor Congress had workable ideas about how to cut domestic programs sufficiently to make up the difference. Nor was there any political will to do so. David Stockman's account of administration budget planning in that first year makes clear that, when faced with the prospect of large budget deficits, the president and his top advisers chose to press their political advantage with Congress for the rest of the program, to maintain their mastery of the process and keep the momentum, and to worry about the deficits later.[11] The result has been large annual deficits, despite four tax increases between 1982 and 1986 and congressional cuts in the nondefense, discretionary side of the budget, which fell from 5.8 percent of GNP in 1980 to 4.1 percent by 1986. Increases in military spending also halted in 1986.[12] Still, the deficit in 1986 was almost $221 billion. The national debt doubled between 1981 and 1988 to $2.6 trillion. The annual deficits between 1983 and 1987 hovered around the $200 billion mark. More recently, under the constraint of the Gramm-Rudman-Hollings Act, the deficits have been coming down as a percentage of GNP. The deficit for fiscal year 1987 was in the $148 billion range, which is about 3 percent of GNP, down from the 6 percent of 1983.[13] But it was in the $155 billion range for fiscal year 1988, far higher than predicted by administration economists.

The Reagan revolution therefore was incomplete, just like the New Deal and the Great Society. Franklin Roosevelt was not able to carry the New Deal beyond the first wave of reforms after the "conservative coalition" of northern Republicans and southern Democrats coalesced against him in 1939. Lyndon Johnson's greatest successes were in programs for the middle classes, especially Medicare, and his antipoverty programs were palliatives with limited staying power. The limits to liberal reform are set by the difficulty of achieving long-term majorities for radical social and economic change. Liberalism preaches and practices the politics of equality of opportunity more than the politics of the equality of condition. By the same token, conservative reform is limited by the tenacious defense of entitlements created by liberal governments. The Reagan administration had hoped for a clean sweep in which most of the Great Society programs of the 1960s and the regulatory acts passed in the Nixon years would be swept from the books. But neither Congress nor a majority of citizens appears to have wanted such a revolution. Bush campaigned in 1988 with the promise to preserve the Reagan achievements but to address unintended side effects in other areas, such as the environment, civil rights, and military procurement. And he has made clear that the deficit must be reduced. He has thus presented himself as a president of consolidation.

Choices for the New President

The new president's strategy on deficit reduction will directly affect his latitude in other major policy areas. The trade deficit is in large part a result of the budget gap. The high dollar, necessary for attracting foreign purchasers of federal securities to finance the deficit, raises the prices of American exports. Domestic and foreign money that might go into capital investment in American industry is drawn into the unproductive purchase of Treasury notes and bonds to finance the budget deficit, thus inhibiting the development of American productive capacities. And the easy money in the hands of consumers made possible by low taxes and foreign financing of the deficit encourages excessive consumer spending, discourages saving, and reinforces the trade deficit.

George Bush will have to decide whether to modernize U.S. nuclear weapons systems—a choice that will be made more difficult by budget constraints. Newly urgent domestic problems also become more visible every day: the war on drugs, the need for environmental cleanup and repair of the American transportation infrastructure, and the growing awareness that large numbers of American children are living in poverty and not receiving adequate education and human services. The new president must also deal with the growing number of bankrupt savings and loans institutions with deposits insured by the federal government and with the recently discovered neglect of health and safety in the government plants that manufacture nuclear weapons. Attacks on these problems will require new money and resolution of the budget deficit impasse.

President Bush should have fewer problems in foreign policy. The creativity of Soviet President Mikhail Gorbachev has given the United States the opportunity to cooperate with the Soviets in the diminishment of the cold war, through arms reductions and resolution of regional conflicts. A bipartisan foreign policy consensus appears to be developing that favors continued negotiation with the Soviets without illusions. Regional conflicts in southern Africa, Afghanistan, and Cambodia appear to be on the wane. There are fewer target spots for the application of the Reagan Doctrine of rollback of communist encroachment and Soviet adventurism. The unresolved issue of communism in Central America is the most conspicuous problem, and Bush may have to choose between cooperation with Congress and confrontation on this issue.

President Bush will enter the White House with fewer serious domestic and foreign policy issues on his desk than any president since Eisenhower. One outstanding problem—the budget deficit—will provide the key to his presidency, and perhaps to its success or failure.

A Mandate?

George Bush's campaign for the presidency was a manifestation of the politics of the Reagan coalition. He made multiple appeals to the different core constituencies in that coalition. His so-called negative campaigning—attacks on the Dukakis positions on saluting the flag, school prayer, abortion, and crime—was aimed at winning over both religious fundamentalists and blue-collar Reagan Democrats. The policy of "no new taxes" was directed toward the entrepreneurial wing of the Republican party in the South and the West. And the promise of peace and prosperity was a general appeal to all voters. Bush also pledged that he would face new problems, like child care for working mothers and health care for people not covered by insurance, but made clear that such programs would be paid for with tax deductions and new forms of citizen contribution rather than through new federal funds. His promise to be "an education President" was to be fulfilled by exhortation rather than action.

Does Bush's victory mean that he has a mandate to act on the promises made in his appeals to his various constituencies? The religious Right can claim a mandate in behalf of school prayer, capital punishment, and reversal of the Supreme Court's decisions on abortion. But those issues are not directly in the purview of the president. Bush will be urged by conservatives to appoint administrators and nominate judges with "correct" views on these matters. One may assume that Bush will heed such urging to some extent but, like Reagan, he will not be willing to stage frontal asaults on these issues; he most likely realizes that majorities cannot be assembled to turn back the clock. Bush can fairly claim that he won a mandate to continue the Reagan policies that contributed to peace and prosperity, but such a mandate is not unlike that won by Reagan in 1984. It was a reward for work well done rather than a signal of approval for new policies. A president who wins a reward for past achievement is not thereby empowered to try new things. President Bush has not received a mandate to continue the Reagan revolution if that means scaling back government even further. The election of a Democratic Congress suggests just the opposite. He was elected because the voters like the present state of affairs and counseled "steady as you go."

Bush can rightly claim a mandate for no new taxes. He clearly sent a signal that was approved overwhelmingly. But in so doing the new president may have created a dilemma for his presidency. The promise of no new taxes may require an aggressive budget strategy of attack on programs that escaped the Reagan revolution. But is there a mandate for such an attack? An obvious alternative strategy—reaching a compromise with the Democrats in Congress to reduce the deficit by combining budget cuts with tax increases—would contradict what Bush regards as his mandate.

Michael Dukakis also campaigned as a president of consolidation. He attacked the deficit as a disgrace and promised to remove it, with new taxes only as a last resort. The Democrats called for a number of new spending programs, none of which would be possible without deficit reduction and economic growth, and these would necessarily have taken first priority over innovation. The political and economic constraints on policy development call for a consolidating president.

The Politics of Washington

George Bush is the fifth Republican to serve as president since the election of Dwight Eisenhower in 1952. Yet the Republicans have controlled both houses of Congress for only two years during that time, the first two years of the Eisenhower administration. Neither Nixon nor Ford worked with a Republican-controlled Congress. Reagan had a Republican Senate for six years, but the Democrats regained control in 1986. This pattern of divided control of the two principal branches of government—the Republicans dominating the presidency and the Democrats controlling Congress for the most part—is new in American history. For most of the rest of that history the president and the majority in Congress have been from the same party.

There are a number of explanations having to do with the power of incumbents to be reelected and the facility of Democrats at representing the interests of their constituencies. The Republicans have failed to achieve a partisan realignment comparable to that achieved by Roosevelt for the New Deal coalition. Instead we have a split-level realignment in which the Republicans are more than competitive for the White House and the Democrats have an advantage for Congress, leading to continuing partisan competition through institutional struggle.[14]

Republican presidents seek to enhance the powers of the executive branch by circumventing legislative restrictions on presidential conduct. Nixon pursued his rejected legislative goals through administrative rules and reorganization.[15] Reagan used National Security Council (NSC) staff members to implement foreign policy goals and thus avoid accountability to Congress. For their part, the Democrats have sought to strengthen Congress and its hand in policy making through the Congressional Budget Act, the War Powers Act, and legislative investigations like the Iran-contra hearings, and in appointment confirmation hearings, such as the dramatic hearings on the nomination by President Reagan of Robert Bork to the Supreme Court.

President Bush will be in a better position to overcome the politics of institutional stalemate than Reagan was or than Dukakis would have been. President Reagan effectively lost control of Congress after his first very successful year and for the rest of his term responded to congressional initiatives for much of the time. The one great exception was the successful passage of tax reform in 1986, a measure initiated by the president. But even that fundamental reform was able to pass only because of bipartisan support achieved after considerable bargaining and compromise across the aisle of each house. Since 1986 the Democratic leadership of Congress has dominated the legislative agenda with policies of its own on trade, health care, and Central America.[16] Dukakis would surely have faced a Democratic Congress hungry for legislative achievement and, if one can assume that a sternly responsible and moderate Dukakis would have insisted that the deficit be conquered before new spending programs were passed, there might have been the kind of conflict between a Democratic president and Congress seen in the Carter years.[17] As a president of consolidation, Bush will be in a good position to transcend the politics of institutional conflict. Because his goals will be to consolidate the Reagan gains rather than extend them, he will probably have the support of the Republicans in Congress and of a good many Democrats. The Republicans want to solve the deficit problem, and the Democrats will support modification of some of the least successful or popular Reagan social and economic policies. Congress as a whole will find it difficult to resist a centrist approach.

President Bush will, no doubt, receive advice from the more conservative Republicans to be a confrontational president who demands that Congress act in support of budget cuts without tax increases, aid to the contras, constitutional amendments to overturn Supreme Court decisions on school prayer and abortion, continuation of the strategic defense initiative (SDI), and the fight against communism in regions of the world where it has gained a foothold. From the perspective of the cyclical conception of politics and policy this is bad advice. The Democratic-controlled Congress would almost certainly rebuff such confrontational politics on the part of the new president. The history of presidential-congressional relations shows that the key to a president's legislative success is having a dependable following in Congress. Because his party will be a minority in both houses, Bush will have no such dependable following. He must create a working majority from the ranks of Republicans and Democrats who will support him fairly and regularly, particularly if he pursues centrist politics. There is no strong evidence that Bush would be able to rally public opinion against Congress in favor of a confrontationist strategy. Although the argument that Bush would do well to act as a president of consolidation is supported by the theory of cyclical politics and policy, it also seems to make sense politically.

The Politics of Economic Policy

It is an old insight of political scientists that Americans are ideological conservatives and operational liberals.[18] We pay lip service to the canons of limited government and individualism, but in practice we like government to provide for our Social Security and general economic well-being and to supply many tangible benefits, from student loans to agricultural subsidies. The American voice is frequently contradictory in its perpetual search for both individualism and community.[19] Thus it is possible for people to wish to help the poor but to resent welfare cheats, to want taxes to be low and at the same time want government to do good things for them. Contemporary public opinion polls reveal these ambivalencies that make it possible for voters to support Republican presidents and a Democratic Congress. A postelection national survey found that most respondents favor a crackdown on tax evaders and defense cuts to reduce the deficit. Most people strongly oppose new or higher taxes (except on cigarettes and alcohol) but also strongly oppose cuts in domestic programs or a freeze in Social Security benefits. Thirty-four percent believe reducing the deficit should be President Bush's top priority. No other issue drew double digit support.[20]

Dealing with the Deficit

Most economists and politicians also believe the federal budget deficit is a serious problem. The chief exceptions are true believers in the promise of supply-side economics, whose strategy would be to cut federal spending and stimulate the economy in order to grow out of the deficit. Martin Anderson, a Hoover Institution economist and Reagan White House adviser, argues that if the economy continues to grow at its current rate the United States will overcome the deficit in four or five years. He says capital gains taxes should be cut to stimulate business investment and job creation.[21] Paul Craig Roberts, an economist and Treasury official in the first Reagan administration, contends that the deficit issue is a red herring created by the Wall Street wing of the Republican party to discredit "entrepreneurial" Republican politicians who are still talking supply-side economics and politics.[22]

The majority of economists who write on the issue see the deficit as a serious long-term problem for the nation. Benjamin Friedman articulates the concern in his argument that we have been enjoying a "false prosperity" in the Reagan years by "borrowing from the future." [23] Friedman blames Ronald Reagan for the $1.1 trillion in deficits since 1981. The difference between the budgets he submitted to Congress and the final congressional decisions was only $90 billion. Reagan never submitted a balanced budget. The real cause of the deficit, according to Friedman, was the 1981 Kemp-Roth income tax cut of 25 percent over a three-year period without matching spending cuts, which neither the president nor Congress was willing to propose. The result has been a near tripling of the national debt, while the national income has increased by only half. The federal deficit has averaged 4.2 percent of U.S. national income since 1981. This is nearly three-fourths of the 5.7 percent of national income that individuals and business saved after spending to replace physical assets such as homes and machinery.

U.S. investment in new business plant and equipment has fallen to a smaller share of national income than in any previous period since World War II. The national infrastructure of highways, dams, and public buildings badly needs maintenance and repair. Economic productivity has flagged, with no significant increases in the 1980s in the amount of capital at the disposal of the average American worker. If productivity increases stay at the 1.1 percent level of recent years, the United States will be able to do no more than pay the interest on the national debt, leaving very little margin for increases in the standard of living. Friedman therefore sees the federal budget deficit as the symptom of a declining American economy. Too much domestic saving is going into paying back the debt and too little into productive investment. Government borrowing has absorbed nearly three-fourths of our private saving since 1980, and heightened competition among businesses and individual borrowers for the remainder has raised interest rates to record levels. The result is an expensive dollar that hurts U.S. exports. Increased imports at favorable prices have encouraged U.S. domestic consumption of foreign goods and caused a trade deficit for American industry. This problem is compounded by the fact that foreign investors have enabled the United States to finance its debt by purchasing U.S. securities. In addition, there has been a great increase of foreign investment in American real estate and other businesses. From 1981 to 1988 these changes contributed to the transformation of the United States from a creditor nation to the world's largest debtor nation. According to Friedman, the long-run economic consequence of the budget and trade deficits is a gradually diminished U.S. standard of living as we pay off the debt, see money leave the country, and fail to make sufficient productive investment at home.

Friedman raises two possible political consequences of these economic problems. First, an America that is not growing economically will become a stagnant society in which politics becomes a fight for pieces of a smaller pie. Second, a debtor nation will have less influence over its own economic life and over international economic issues than strong creditor nations like Japan and West Germany.[24] The right step, advocated by Friedman and most economists who address the deficit issue, is to begin reducing the federal budget deficit so that debt declines in relation to national income.[25] To do anything else is to move into slow erosion of the economy with incalculable consequences for politics.

Should a long-term deficit reduction plan be implemented, still other immediate dangers could complicate the careers of politicians and a long-term plan. The American economy is operating at such a high level of performance that inflation could again emerge as a problem. Efforts by the Federal Reserve Board to curb incipient inflation—by raising interest rates, for example—could produce recession, which would increase the deficit. But in such a situation the government would be unable to fight recession by deficit spending. Another possibility is that foreign holders of U.S. Treasury securities might sell them. The corresponding rise in interest rates could withdraw capital from more productive investment and damage the economy, perhaps triggering a recession. These kinds of shocks are far more likely if there is a widespread belief that the U.S. government is not implementing a long-term plan to reduce the deficit. Politicians therefore have both long- and short-term incentives to attack the deficit.

President, Congress, and the Deficit

George Bush campaigned on the importance of reducing the deficit. He did not take the optimistic view of the true supply siders that the deficit was not a problem. After the election he made a number of statements about the importance of deficit reduction and his willingness to work with the Democratic Congress on a plan. Bush is closer to traditional Republican economic orthodoxy, which sees a virtue in balanced budgets, than he is to the supply-side theory, which he described in his 1980 campaign for the presidency as "voodoo economics." He enthusiastically embraced the politics of supply-side appeals, however, in his campaign pledge not to introduce new taxes. He thus put himself on a potential collision course with the new Congress, whose leaders have been emphatic in their belief that deficit reduction will require a compromise package of budget cuts and tax increases.

The budget deficit for the 1988 fiscal year was approximately $155 billion. The Gramm-Rudman law, which calls for large reductions in that amount each year until the budget is in balance in 1992, will force the president and Congress to make some painful choices. Bush's plan for deficit reduction presented during the campaign was for a "flexible freeze" in which military budget increases would be held to the level of inflation, Social Security benefits would increase as expected, and the rest of the budget would be held in check for five years so that spending did not increase at a rate higher than inflation. The Bush proposal assumed that current rates of economic growth would continue and that it would be possible to cut interest rates on government securities, thus reducing government payments on the debt. According to this plan, in five years the deficit would wither away. The plan did not explain how to balance expected increases of 12 percent or so a year in Medicare payments with cuts in other programs, how to pay for pressing needs such as bailing out failing savings and loan institutions and nuclear cleanup, how to continue funding the war on drugs, AIDS research, and air safety improvements, or how to pay for new programs in child care, which Bush called for in his campaign.[26] Bush's budget team may suggest innovations such as taxing Medicare benefits as income to a greater extent in order that the middle class pay more of the cost, cutting Medicare payments to physicians, and making deep cuts in defense by more efficient planning and production of weapons systems or simply by freezing spending without regard to inflation.[27]

Roughly 70 percent of the budget is defense, Social Security in various forms, Medicare, and interest on the national debt. It will be difficult to make big reductions in those parts of the budget.[28] The remaining 30 percent of the budget is divided roughly equally between (1) routine maintenance of all the activities of the federal government from the president and the FBI to the Coast Guard and National Institutes of Health and (2) federal grants to the states in the form of social service and regulatory programs, most of which have been cut to the bone during the Reagan years. It does not appear to be politically possible to return the federal government to a pre-1961 role in which there were few such programs. Most experts believe that spending cuts can be found in both the 70 percent and 30 percent, but not enough to reduce the deficit gap for 1989 or subsequent years. New revenues will therefore be necessary. Possible sources of new revenue are so-called sin taxes on alcohol and tobacco and gasoline taxes; Congress might also close a few income tax loopholes. But Rudolph Penner, a former director of the Congressional Budget Office and a respected Republican economist, estimates that even such taxes will not be sufficient to close the budget deficit gap entirely by 1992, which is the Gramm-Rudman target year.[29] And there is no room in any of the estimates for any new programs, even with moderate revenue increases.

The Reagan strategy of budget reduction was to resist congressional tax increases and to push hard for program reductions. Now, however, there may be no way to reduce the budget significantly and avoid a tax increase without cutting defense and restricting entitlement programs like Social Security and Medicare. Reagan avoided such a confrontation because he was not willing to reduce defense spending and was not prepared to take on the middle class, the beneficiaries of entitlement programs.[30] White House pressure on Congress for spending cuts during the Reagan years cut most "pork barrel" programs to the bone. The poor are protected by presidential promises to respect the social safety net. The influence of the Office of Management and Budget on the spending plans of the departments and the dominance of the congressional budget process by the budget committees have squeezed at the "iron triangle" of spending collusion among the agencies, interest groups, and congressional subcommittees.[31]

Congressional Democrats would happily participate in a compromise package of cuts and revenue increases with the president, but they would not propose and enact such a program on their own because of the political risk of raising taxes. If the president refuses to accept tax increases, the deficit problem will continue to exist, with president and Congress each blaming the other. This is likely to be the situation for the first year or two of the Bush administration. If Congress will not give the president the cuts he requests, then he will have to accept taxes if he wishes to avoid the long-term economic costs of the deficit. But barring an economic shock, his political incentive to do so may be limited, because such long-term costs may not be fully visible for some time. And he will be constrained by his campaign promise of no new taxes.

The situation cries for education of the electorate by the president on the real economic issues facing the nation, but candidate Bush gave little sign that President Bush would undertake such a responsibility. The budget impasse creates a difficulty for politicians in that the economic benefits of budget reduction and the economic costs of failure to face the issue may not be apparent to voters except in the long run. But the short-term costs of deficit reduction, whether in program cuts or new taxes, will be apparent to voters immediately. Traditionally, politicians have dealt with such long-term problems by waiting for a shock, such as a recession, and then applying emergency measures in response to public demand for action. This time, however, the government may find that conventional responses to either inflation or recession may be less available should such a shock occur in the near future.

Domestic Policy

On November 21, 1988, the Comptroller General of the United States, who is also the head of the General Accounting Office (GAO), issued twenty-three reports on national domestic needs that should give pause to both president and Congress. The GAO is the accounting and evaluation arm of Congress, which continuously scrutinizes the implementation of federal programs. Its reports, which were intended to be nonpartisan, simply listed areas in which there was need for expenditure in order to meet the requirements of laws on the books. They were not a call for new programs.

The GAO reports identified a large number of national needs: new federal prisons; toxic and hazardous waste cleanup; more effective implementation of job safety laws; development of better data sources to permit federal executives to make informed decisions about the results of airline deregulation; the low supply of rental housing as construction built with federal subsidies is converted to condominiums; greater cost controls in Medicare and Medicaid; and better management of public lands, such as national parks, which are said to have suffered from federal budget cuts.[32] These problems will put additional pressure on the president to resolve the budget issue and to find new sources of revenues.

It is unlikely that Congress can hold the line against new spending forever; members of Congress are elected to do things for people. The

Reagan administration directly challenged that assumption, but it did not prevail. Programs of the past were not repealed, although they have been operating with reduced funding and with administrative management that has stressed spending as little as possible and reducing regulation as much as possible within the law.

Congress has had to change its ways in response to Reagan's challenges, neglecting new national problems in the process. Program evaluation by the GAO and other agencies has been used to cut the least effective programs in favor of programs that can pay for themselves. The discipline of the distributive impulses of congressional politicians has been great.[33] But any belief that the presidency can permanently muffle the congressional political incentive to get elected by doing good things for people flies in the face of the political logic of Congress and its genius as an institution for representation. A president of consolidation eventually will have to come to terms with such forces even if he has few domestic programs of his own.

Another domestic issue is the relation of government to moral and religious questions. Should government funds be used to pay for abortions under the Medicaid program? Should there be a constitutional amendment to overrule the Supreme Court on the legality of abortions? Is school prayer, also banned by the Court, constitutional? What should be done about gun control as a matter of national policy? Moral and religious fundamentalists are an important part of the Republican coalition, and the Bush campaign attempted to retain their loyalty by regularly raising the symbolic themes of flag, school prayer, abortion, and crime. The Republicans now have a strength they have not had, particularly in the South, and they will not let it go.[34]

But it is not clear how President Bush will satisfy the politically vocal leadership of this Republican flock. His cabinet appointments are centrists and moderates, people with a commitment to making government work, not antigovernment zealots, though he will surely make a few symbolic conservative subcabinet appointments in the departments of Education and Health and Human Services. The government will continue to oppose the use of foreign aid funds for abortion, and the attorney general will seek to overturn *Roe v. Wade,* the controversial abortion decision of the Supreme Court. But any Bush nominees to the Supreme Court will probably be moderates like his cabinet appointees, not ideological conservatives. The unanswered question is whether Bush so stimulated conservative political forces in his campaign for the presidency that he will have difficulty controlling and restraining such forces as he seeks to govern.

Foreign Policy

There is a direct correlation between expansionary foreign policies and assumptions that the American economy will pay for such policies. Expansionary, interventionist presidents have relied on growing economies and have articulated the mood of economic and foreign policy innovation. Thus, since 1961 the interventionist presidents have been those who believed the economic base would support such initiatives abroad: Kennedy, Johnson, and Reagan. The presidents who have presided over periods of economic stasis or contraction—Nixon, Ford, and Carter—have been less ambitious and more cautious about the U.S. role in the world. Bush is likely to join this group in history. John Lewis Gaddis points out that every one of the post-World War II shifts in foreign policy between global intervention and strategic defense grew out of a reassessment of economic resources at hand.[35] Truman believed that the economy could stand budget increases for defense, and fighting the Korean War, without inflation. Eisenhower tailored U.S. commitments abroad and defense levels to his estimate of what the domestic economy could support. Kennedy and Johnson linked an expanding economy with interventionist foreign policies. Nixon pulled back from global commitments, offering U.S. help to allies in defending themselves rather than U.S. forces. Part of that change was related to a faltering economy. Carter and Ford continued on the same course. But Reagan firmly believed that the economy would support a massive defense buildup and an actively interventionist foreign policy all over the world. Just as President Bush has come up against the outer limits of Reagan budget policies in economic policy, so he will necessarily pursue a cautious policy of commitments abroad.

Indeed the times call for consolidation. Gorbachev has taken bold initiatives, and the American role must be one of constructive response in which arms control and reduction agreements will be negotiated, regional conflicts may be defused, and issues of human rights are resolved. These will be the objectives of the new administration. If the Soviet Union cooperates, the easing of international tensions may allow a fresh start for a world facing enormous economic and environmental problems. By all accounts this is the policy area that most interests the new president. But he has shown little sign of foreign policy creativity in his career, much of which has been spent in foreign affairs. His appointments of a highly skilled and pragmatic lawyer and experienced government official, James Baker, as secretary of state and of Brent Scowcroft, once President Ford's national security adviser and also a pragmatist and seasoned government hand, once again to the post of national security adviser, reveals the president as a man who wishes to take maximum advantage of new opportunities without establishing any vision of his own.

The problems of communism in Nicaragua and El Salvador still fester, and Bush will have to find a way to resolve them, with the cooperation of other Latin American nations. It does not seem likely that either he or his secretary of state will risk political defeat in Congress on the issue of American aid to the Nicaraguan contras. By the same token, SDI will probably be put on the back burner, in part because it is expensive and also because it may be most useful as part of arms control bargaining with the Soviets.

Outstanding international economic problems, such as management of the large debts of Latin American nations to Western bankers and the instability of the international monetary system, are solvable and are issues with which Baker, as secretary of the Treasury under Reagan, is familiar. Virtually insoluble problems like peace in the Middle East and justice in South Africa will continue, and it is not clear that any American president will be able to do much, at least in the short run. The frustration for Bush may be that he will have to put foreign affairs aside because of the pressure of deficit politics. If he can succeed in resolving the deficit problems, there is a good chance he can play effectively to his strengths for negotiation and cautious consolidation on the world stage.

One identifying characteristic of a president of consolidation is an emphasis on resolving the administrative problems left by the president of achievement. In Bush's case the outstanding task will be to address issues of military budgeting and procurement. Increasing majorities in both Congress and the administration believe that military budgets should be approved for two-year periods, rather than one, in order to effectively plan the development of strategic weapon systems. The current process of one-year budgeting is too dependent on the fits and starts of short-term politics. But an emphasis on improved planning will require considerable change in the Pentagon's planning processes, under the purview of the secretary of defense and the president. Scandals of military procurement, which surfaced during the Reagan administration, centered on the illegal use of inside information by independent consultants to military contractors for the benefit of those contractors. The new administration will have to find ways to reduce corruption and strengthen the authority and continuity of Pentagon procurement personnel and procedures.

Bush: The Man and the President

George Bush is suited to be a president of consolidation by experience and temperament. He has had more administrative experience at the top of the national government than any president since Eisenhower: ambassador to the United Nations, head of the U.S. mission in China, director of the Central Intelligence Agency, and vice president. By temperament he is a conciliator and a pragmatic problem solver. The first task of a president is to fashion a rough unity among his goals, the politics of support for those goals, and the governmental processes of turning purpose and politics into programs.[36] Bush's style in this regard is apparent to some degree from the previous jobs he has held. He seldom articulates first principles or strong goals. Rather, his belief in addressing and solving problems as they present themselves requires a politics of ad hoc appeals rather than coalition building. His management of decision making has relied heavily on advisers and professionals, with Bush himself providing political cover. In short, his style is one that says, "Trust me and my friends, we know how to govern." Bush may have appropriated conservative ideological rhetoric from Reagan politics, but in his previous executive positions he has exhibited traditional East Coast Republican confidence in and commitment to intelligent governance.

Two profiles of Bush, in the *Washington Post* and *Newsweek*, present very similar pictures of the man and the politician. The *Post* study was based on two hundred interviews with people who have known and worked with Bush over the years. A central observation is that Bush is more at home with people than with ideas. He gives great emphasis to good personal relations with friend and foe. Rarely a planner, he responds to stimuli as they present themselves and has always been willing to trim his sails and compromise according to the prevailing political and policy winds. There is evidence that in executive jobs he has avoided difficult decisions and straddled conflicts. Former aides report that he did not dig deeply into the substance of problems or engage in intellectual debates, relying instead on advice from assistants and professionals he respected and giving his attention to managing the external politics or problems. He is willing to delegate and respects the expertise of others.[37]

Bush's flexibility has made him something of a political chameleon who takes coloration from the powerful figures he has cultivated in his rise to the top. Thus, the man who condemned Reagan supply-side ideas as voodoo economics in the 1980 presidential campaign is now its apostle to some degree. This change suggests that he may be willing to adopt doctrinaire positions expedient for his purposes. His espousal of Reagan conservatism, reflecting his flexibility, may conflict with his operational pragmatism and his desire to get along with everyone. According to *Newsweek*, his aides search in vain for a body of political beliefs. He has never liked campaigning, telling one election aide, "You know, if I were elected President, I wouldn't want people like you in government." [38] Government is for experts. This raises the question of Bush's inclination or ability to provide continuing public, political leadership for his policy goals.

George Bush has yet to demonstrate strong beliefs of his own in either politics or policy. The central strategies of the 1988 campaign appear to have been developed by his staff.[39] In selecting Dan Quayle as his running mate, he may have taken the course of least resistance; there were seemingly fewer liabilities with Quayle than with the other possibilities.[40] Such "flexibility" is somewhat different from the politics of compromise, in which the leader leads but sets realistic objectives. Bush combines both approaches in one rather unpredictable style. As he said in a postelection news conference, "I want to be on everybody's side." [41]

Bush's strength therefore would appear to be his genuine good will and open approach to others, his respect for good advice and high regard for professionals, and his willingness to be flexible. His weaknesses may be the opposites of those strengths: his political identity is uncertain, and he is perhaps too dependent on advisers. Joseph Papp, the New York theater impresario captured only the negative aspects of Bush's character in a discussion of how he would cast the candidate in a Shakespeare play: "Bush could portray Sir Andrew Aguecheek in *Twelfth Night*. He's passive, easily led. He's very little, nothing much. Trying to play a role out of his reach. . . . He carries a certain pain with him." [42]

By temperament, George Bush would seem to be an ideal president of consolidation, as long as he can avoid divisive issues. In managing such issues, he frequently appears to have straddled rather than confronted them. For example, during Bush's short tenure as head of the CIA, when conservatives were critical of CIA estimates of Soviet intentions, Bush created a second team of outside experts, led by a hard-liner (Professor Richard Pipes of Harvard) to second-guess the official estimates. Bush took no position himself.[43] Yet Bush has had a talent for building fences with people across the political spectrum and is, in his deepest responses, a conciliator and compromiser. His lack of intellectual certainty on issues can be a plus in reaching political compromises. The same lack could be a handicap in the face of an impasse because he may lack a reasoned position of his own. His strength is not likely to be in managing sudden crises, when he may very well give way to strong subordinates who have clear intentions to which he can subscribe.

It is easier to predict Bush's style as an executive and manager of policy making than it is to know how he will work with Congress and lead public opinion. He will likely be more active in shaping policy options and in doing his homework than Reagan. But Bush is not a John Kennedy or Jimmy Carter in his desire to understand the intricacies of issues. He will rely heavily on his staff to develop policy options. His selection of New Hampshire governor John Sununu as White House chief of staff suggests that Bush wants a strong hand managing the traffic of information in the White House. Sununu was a strong executive; he is an engineer by training and not given to political strategies of persuasion and compromise. Bush evidently expects his chief of staff to assist the president in developing policy options. Bush himself will deal with the public and congressional politics of issues, unlike Reagan, who assigned his chief of staff James Baker to work closely with Congress. In this sense Bush is more of a congressional politician than he is an executive. Others will manage the executive for him. This pattern would be consistent with his past style of management.

The president's policy assistants will be custodians more than advocates in the Bush White House, as Bush's selection of Brent Scowcroft to be national security adviser makes clear.[44] Scowcroft strongly believes that the job of the assistant for national security is to make the NSC system work by forcing all points of view onto the table. Policy analysis will be valued in the White House economic, national security, and domestic policy staffs to a degree that was not the case in the Reagan administration. If the White House staff plays the custodial role, no barriers would come between the president and his principal cabinet officers and department heads. We can expect that Bush will delegate most department business to the "outer cabinet" and use the secretaries of state, defense, and Treasury and the attorney general, the "inner cabinet," as staff to himself. The collegiality among top staff and cabinet officers in the policy areas of most interest to the president, foreign and economic policy, will be very high and informal, reflecting Bush's own informal style.

Because Bush respects the professionals in government, conflict between the White House and the department career staffs and between cabinet officers and their bureaucracies is likely to be minimal. During Reagan's years in office, career public servants filled many positions responsible for achieving his policy goals. Bush respects this "permanent government" made up of career personnel. As a result, responsiveness to the White House, organizational memory, and professional expertise are likely to be high for the next four years.

Politics and Policy of the Future

Two questions arise about a possible future turn of the cycle. First, under what conditions is a presidency of consolidation succeeded by a presidency of preparation? Second, must the cycle necessarily turn in a progressive direction after the Reagan and Bush years?

The cycle turns from consolidation to preparation when a skillful presidential candidate is able to convince a majority of voters that unresolved problems of the consolidating period must be addressed. The candidate draws on ideas, developed during the period of consolidation, which have come to form the intellectual capital that the new president of preparation will use as the basis for his programs. In the 1960 campaign, John Kennedy articulated most of the themes that were to guide his and Lyndon Johnson's presidencies. Jimmy Carter was less successful in moving his coalition in new directions in 1976. Michael Dukakis attempted, perhaps prematurely, to express such themes for the future in 1988. So we can expect a presidency of preparation when skill, ideas, and a widespread sense of dissatisfaction with the status quo meet in a presidential election. The skill of the candidate in bringing these elements together cannot be overemphasized.

But will the cycle move again in a progressive direction? The fact that Reagan and Bush are conservatives suggests that that is likely. Criticism of the Bush presidency will probably be directed toward the symptoms of conservative politics. But social and economic uncertainties could shake the foundations of the cycle and catapult us into altogether new patterns of politics and policy.

Future turns of the cycle of politics and policy will depend on long-term developments in the American economy. Resolution of the deficit problem will permit government to address long-term issues of economic productivity and growth. The competitiveness of the American economy, the productivity of labor, and the ability to manage growth in output without inflation are tasks ahead that will not be solved by balancing the budget.[45] Productivity in the United States began to decline in the Carter years, and there is no obvious way to increase it. A host of social, economic, and cultural factors are involved, and economists are not very good at knowing how to produce economic development.[46]

If the country resolves the budget deficit and attacks the trade deficit by investing more at home and selling more abroad, the era of consolidation could be prolonged. In due course a period of progressive reform politics could ensue as consciousness of unaddressed social problems becomes stronger. If progressives were to successfully raise quality-of-life issues requiring government action during periods of affluence, a new agenda of neglected social problems—poverty and the underclass, health care—would increasingly impinge on the middle class and make them responsive to reform ideas.

But if the deficit issue is not resolved, or if long-term economic growth is sluggish and accompanied by continual threats of both inflation and recession, the period of consolidation may be short. It is not clear, however, that progressive politics would be the beneficiary. Liberal politics works when the economic pie is growing—a rising tide lifts all boats. Turns of the cycle in a progressive direction in the past have reflected confidence that the money would be available to pay for new programs. American liberalism faced the problem of making the economy work to pay for social programs in 1964 by implementing the Keynesian remedy of a tax cut. But that was during a time of slack capacity and low inflation when a simple stimulus to the economy could be expected to work. It is not clear that this situation will appear again. Failure of the economy to grow may bring an increasingly quarrelsome politics very different from the vision of a constructive dialectic that informs this essay.

Notes

1. Erwin C. Hargrove and Michael Nelson, *Presidents, Politics, and Policy* (Baltimore: Johns Hopkins University Press, 1984), 66-86.
2. Lloyd A. Free and Hadley Cantril, *The Political Beliefs of Americans: A Study of Public Opinion* (New York: Simon and Schuster, 1968), 5-6; Sidney Verba and Gary R. Orren, *Equality in America: The View from the Top* (Cambridge, Mass.: Harvard University Press, 1985), 21-51.
3. Hugh Heclo, "General Welfare and Two American Political Traditions," *Political Science Quarterly* 2 (1986): 179-196.
4. Louis Hartz, *The Liberal Tradition in America* (New York: Harcourt, Brace and World, 1955).
5. Charles O. Jones, *The Trusteeship Presidency: Jimmy Carter and the United States Congress* (Baton Rouge: Louisiana State University Press, 1988): 211.
6. Erwin C. Hargrove, *Jimmy Carter as President: Leadership and the Politics of the Public Good* (Baton Rouge: Louisiana State University Press, 1988), chaps. 3, 4, and 5.
7. Erwin C. Hargrove and Samuel A. Morley, eds., *The President and the Council of Economic Advisers* (Boulder, Colo.: Westview Press, 1984), chaps. 2, 3, 7, 8, 9.
8. Norman Ornstein, Andrew Kuhnt and Larry McCarthy, *The People, the Press and Politics* (Reading, Mass.: Addison-Wesley, 1988).
9. Hugh Heclo, "Reaganism and the Search for a Public Philosophy," in *Perspectives on the Reagan Years*, ed. John L. Palmer (Washington: Urban Institute Press), 51.
10. Ibid., 56.
11. David A. Stockman, *The Triumph of Politics: Why the Reagan Revolution Failed* (New York: Harper and Row, 1986), chaps. 3, 4, 5, 9.
12. Joseph J. Minarik and Rudolph G. Penner, "Fiscal Choices," in *The Challenge to Leadership: Economic and Social Issues for the Next Decade*, ed. Isabel V. Sawhill (Washington: Urban Institute Press, 1988), 281-282.
13. Martin Tolchin, "Paradox of Reagan Budgets Hints Contradiction in Legacy," *New York Times*, February 16, 1988, 1, 12.

14. Benjamin Ginsberg and Martin Shefter, "Political Parties, Electoral Conflict, and Institutional Combat" (Paper delivered at the 1988 annual meeting of the American Political Science Association, Washington, D.C., September 1-4, 1988), 7-8.

15. Richard P. Nathan, *The Administrative Presidency* (New York: John Wiley and Sons, 1983).

16. Simon Lazarus, *New Republic,* November 28, 1988, 18-19.

17. Hargrove, *Jimmy Carter as President,* chaps. 3, 5.

18. Free and Cantril, *The Political Beliefs of Americans.*

19. Heclo, "General Welfare and Two American Political Traditions."

20. Media-Associated Press Survey, *The Nashville Tennessean,* November 28, 1988, 7-A.

21. Martin Anderson, "Streamlining Reaganomics for the 90s," *New York Times,* July 22, 1988, 23.

22. Sidney Blumenthal, "The GOP Approaches an Economic Fork," *Washington Post National Weekly Edition,* August 22-28, 1988, 22.

23. Benjamin M. Friedman, "The Campaign's Hidden Issues," *New York Review of Books,* October 13, 1988, 26-38.

24. Ibid., 27.

25. Ibid., 28.

26. Paul Bluestone, "Bush's Optimistic Illusion," *Washington Post National Weekly Edition,* June 20-26, 1988, 8.

27. Jack A. Meyer, "Social Programs and Social Policy," in Palmer, ed., *Perspectives on the Reagan Years,* 74-75; Rich Thomas, "Biting the Bullet," *Newsweek,* November 28, 1988, 30-31.

28. Minarik and Penner, "Fiscal Choices," 289-290.

29. Ibid., 306-313.

30. Meyer, "Social Programs and Social Policy," 73.

31. Paul E. Peterson and Mark Rom, "Lower Taxes, More Spending, and Budget Deficits," in *The Reagan Legacy: Promise and Performance,* ed. Charles O. Jones (Chatham, N.J.: Chatham House, 1988), 228-231, 232.

32. Robert Pear, "Reagan Is Leaving Many Costly Domestic Problems, the GAO Tells Bush," *New York Times,* November 22, 1988, A-20.

33. Lawrence J. Haas, "The Deficit Culture," *National Journal,* June 4, 1988, 1460-1467.

34. Nathan Glazer, "The 'Social Agenda,'" in Palmer, ed., *Perspectives on the Reagan Years,* 28.

35. John Lewis Gaddis, *Strategies of Containment: A Critical Appraisal of Postwar American National Security Policy* (New York: Oxford University Press, 1982), 354-356.

36. Hargrove, *Jimmy Carter as President,* preface and chap. 6.

37. Bob Woodward and Walter Pincus, "George Bush: Staying Close to His Past," *Washington Post Weekly Edition,* a five-part series in the editions of August 15-21, 22-28, August 29-September 4, September 5-11, and September 2-18.

38. *Newsweek,* November 21, 1988, 85-86.

39. Ibid., 146.

40. Fred Barnes, *New Republic,* November 28, 1988, 8-9.

41. *New York Times,* November 18, 1988, 8.

42. Joseph Papp, *New York Times,* September 27, 1988, B-8.

43. Woodward and Pincus, "George Bush," September 5-11, 15.

44. Alexander L. George, *Presidential Decisionmaking in Foreign Policy* (Boulder, Colo.: Westview Press, 1980), 195-200.
45. Isabel V. Sawhill, "Reaganomics in Retrospect," in Palmer, ed., *Perspectives on the Reagan Years,* 111.
46. Robert Samuelson, "Beyond the Budget Fuss," *Newsweek,* November 28, 1988, 33.

8. CONSTITUTIONAL ASPECTS OF THE ELECTIONS

Michael Nelson

Measured in words and clauses, the Constitution seems to be concerned mainly with the purposes of the federal government, the enumeration of its component parts, and the specification of the powers of the three branches. Less attention is given to how the officials of the government are chosen. Members of the House and, since the Seventeenth Amendment was enacted in 1913, members of the Senate are elected by the people of the various congressional districts and states. The president and vice president are chosen separately from Congress, by an electoral college. Supreme Court justices and other federal judges are appointed by the president, with the "Advice and Consent" of the Senate.

This chapter reviews some of the ways the electoral processes and other institutions created by the Constitution affected, and were affected by, the elections of 1988. Did the two-term limit on presidents, enacted by the Twenty-second Amendment in 1951, make a difference? How did being vice president help or harm George Bush's chances of becoming president, and what were the effects of Bush's selection of Dan Quayle as his running mate? How did the electoral college influence the conduct of the campaign? What are the causes and consequences of the "split-level realignment" that has produced divided partisan control of Congress and the presidency? How will divided control affect the politics of judicial selection?

The elections of 1988 occurred squarely in the middle of the three-year bicentennial celebration of the U.S. Constitution, which was written at the Constitutional Convention of 1787, ratified in 1788, and implemented in 1789. For this reason and one other, the elections provide a useful occasion to consider the Constitution's effects on the context, conduct, and consequences of the electoral process. The other reason is that in 1988, more than in most election years, the influence on the institutions of government of the constitutional design of

presidential, congressional, and—through the requirement in Article
IV, section 4, that each state have "a Republican Form of Government"—state elections seemed especially apparent.

To begin with, the Twenty-second Amendment's two-term limit
on presidents, as Francis Rourke and John Tierney point out in
chapter 1, defined much of the context for the presidential election. For
the first time since 1960, it was clear from the beginning of the
campaign that the election would be a contest between challengers:
Ronald Reagan, like Dwight D. Eisenhower before him, was constitutionally barred from running agin.

One of those challengers was the vice president, George Bush,
who occupied a constitutionally created office (Article I, section 3) that,
as Rhodes Cook observes in chapter 2, offered him certain distinct
advantages in winning his party's presidential nomination, but that also
seemed likely, in the view of many political observers, to cloud his
chances of being elected. Once nominated, Bush, like his Democratic
rival, Gov. Michael Dukakis of Massachusetts, was obliged to make his
first "presidential" decision: the selection of a vice-presidential running
mate. As Paul Quirk suggests in chapter 3, the perceived merits of the
two candidates' choices—Sen. Dan Quayle of Indiana by Bush and
Texas senator Lloyd Bentsen by Dukakis—may have influenced the
decisions of more voters than any other vice-presidential comparison in
history.

The campaign between the Bush-Quayle and Dukakis-Bentsen
tickets was both colored by and resolved in the electoral college, an
institution created by the Framers in Article II, section 1, and modified
in 1804 by the Twelfth Amendment. Electors received numerous letters
urging them not to vote for Quayle when they assembled in their state
capitals on December 19. Yet it was a Democratic elector in West
Virginia who voted "faithlessly," choosing Bentsen for president and
Dukakis for vice president.[1] More significant, 1988 gave birth to the
Republican "lock" theory, which holds that the electoral college's
distribution of votes among the states virtually guarantees the election
of a Republican president and vice president.

The merits of the lock theory aside, one constitutional aspect of the
electoral process strongly influenced the outcome of the elections and
their effects: the entirely separate conduct and status of presidential
elections and elections to Congress, the latter governed by Article I,
section 2, and by the Seventeenth Amendment, which was enacted in
1913 to empower voters, not state legislators, to elect senators. In 1988,
as in four of the five preceding elections, the voters chose a Republican
president but not a Republican Congress. The causes and consequences
of this "split-level realignment," [2] which, as a pattern rather than an

occasional aberration, is historically unprecedented, are profound. Gary Jacobson, in chapter 6, and Erwin Hargrove, in chapter 7, explore the ramifications of the new partisan arrangement for Congress and the presidency, respectively. For example, split-level realignment is likely to create a new, more divisive politics of judicial selection, a constitutionally shared responsibility of the Senate and the president under Article II, section 2.

The Constitution influenced the elections of 1988 in other, more subtle ways. In constructing the executive as a unitary office, the Framers made the president not just a political leader (the chief of government, comparable to the British prime minister) but also the anthropomorphic symbol of the nation and its deeply held values (the chief of state, resembling the British monarch).[3] Thus, it is not altogether surprising that Jean Bethke Elshtain, in chapter 5, finds merit in the highly symbolic nature of the presidential campaign, in which matters like the Pledge of Allegiance were more conspicuous than discussions of tangible public policies. (Quirk vigorously dissents.) The influence of the privately owned mass media, assessed by Thomas Patterson in chapter 4, is greater in the United States than in other nations partly because of the First Amendment to the Constitution, which ensures freedom of the press to the corporations that own newspapers, magazines, and television and radio stations.

Interestingly, since the enactment of the Bill of Rights in 1791, more constitutional amendments have dealt directly or indirectly with the presidency and vice presidency than with any other subject. In addition to the Twelfth and Twenty-second amendments, the Twenty-third Amendment (1961) empowers the District of Columbia to cast three electoral votes for president, thereby assuring the Democrats their only reliable base of support in the last six presidential elections. The Twenty-fifth Amendment (1967) acknowledges and contributes to the growing importance that voters attach to the vice presidency, both by providing a mechanism to fill vacancies in the office and by assigning to the vice president the central role in situations of presidential disability. The Twenty-sixth Amendment (1971) extends the franchise to eighteen to twenty-year-olds, a group that students of voting behavior have watched closely as a possible harbinger of a full-scale Republican realignment. Yet, having supported Reagan ardently in 1984, young voters were Bush's weakest age group in 1984.[4]

Even the obscure Twentieth Amendment (1933) earned the spotlight briefly in 1988. The first question put to Bush at the second presidential debate asked him to comment on the possibility that, under the terms of the amendment, "if you are elected and die before Inauguration Day, automatically, Dan Quayle would become the forty-first president of the United States."

In this essay, the more significant constitutional aspects of the elections of 1988 and their aftermath are discussed chronologically, in the order in which they arose during the campaign or will arise in the Bush administration and the 101st Congress. They are the two-term limit on presidents, the vice presidency, the electoral college, the split-level realignment, and the new politics of judicial nominations.

The Two-Term Limit

The original Constitution placed no limit on the number of times a president could seek reelection. Unrestricted eligibility was regarded by the Framers as an important principle of good government. To deny the president the opportunity for another term would tend, as Gouverneur Morris of Pennsylvania told his fellow delegates at the Constitutional Convention, "to destroy the great motive to good behavior, the hope of being rewarded by a reappointment." Stating the proposition more positively, Alexander Hamilton observed in *Federalist* No. 72 that "the desire of reward is one of the strongest incentives of human conduct ... the best security for the fidelity of mankind is to make their interest coincide with their duty." [5]

The Framers' intentions notwithstanding, a two-term tradition soon arose for presidents. This development was more the doing of Thomas Jefferson than George Washington, who stepped down after his second term, he said in his farewell address, mainly because he longed for "the shade of retirement." Jefferson was serving in Paris as ambassador to France while the Constitution was being written; from the start, he disliked intensely its omission of a term limit on presidents. As president, Jefferson proclaimed in 1807 (falsely invoking the "sound precedent" of the deceased Washington) that for anyone to serve more than two terms "will in fact become for life, and history shows how easily that degenerates into inheritance." [6] Future presidents, not always willingly, felt bound by this tradition until 1940. On the eve World War II, Democratic president Franklin D. Roosevelt ran for and won a third term and, in 1944, a fourth term. (He died in April 1945.)

When the Republicans, who had been frustrated by Roosevelt's long and politically successful presidency, regained control of Congress in 1947, they rapidly (ten weeks) and unanimously passed the Twenty-second Amendment, which provided that no person could be elected president more than twice. (Only one-third of congressional Democrats, mainly southern conservatives, supported the amendment.) With posthumous resentment of Roosevelt the main motive for enacting the two-term limit, little attention was given during the brief congressional debate to the Framers' rationale for imposing no limit at all.

Ironically, the constraints of the Twenty-second Amendment have been felt directly by only two presidents, both of them Republicans. Eisenhower was the first president to whom the amendment applied; he wanted to seek a third term in 1960, according to John Eisenhower, his son and deputy chief of staff.[7] Reagan was the second. Aware that he was barred from running again after his reelection in 1984, Reagan campaigned around the country to repeal the two-term limit, arguing that the voters should be free to elect whom they want for as long as they want. Although Reagan said that the limit should not be lifted for his sake, Republican representative Guy Vander Jagt of Michigan introduced a measure in Congress to repeal it in time for the 1988 election. Democrats in Congress did not treat the measure seriously, dismissing it as a partisan stunt.

In addition to hamstringing second-term presidents, the Twenty-second Amendment has had a wholly unintended consequence: it politically liberates their vice presidents. Knowing that the president cannot run again, the vice president is free to launch a campaign for the party's presidential nomination without unduly alienating the president. Richard Nixon, Eisenhower's vice president, was the first to do so and, partly as a consequence, he became the first incumbent vice president since 1836 to be nominated for president. As Cook indicates in chapter 2, one of the reasons Bush won the Republican nomination in 1988 is that he was able to spend the first three years of Reagan's second term building an extensive national campaign organization and raising large amounts of campaign funds.

Vice Presidency

The history of the vice presidency in this century, especially since 1945, has been one of steady progress toward greater visibility and responsibility. Yet the Constitutional Convention created the vice presidency as a weak office, and the Twelfth Amendment made it a despised one as well. The original Constitution empowered the vice president only to be "president of the Senate, but shall have no Vote, unless they be equally divided." Still, it at least awarded the office to the runner-up in the presidential election. The Twelfth Amendment, passed to accommodate the rise of political parties nominating complete tickets for each election, stripped the vice president of the status of being, presumably, the second most qualified person in the country to be president by separating the balloting for president and vice president in the electoral college. For many years, the vice presidency languished before undergoing its modern rebirth as a respected and politically significant institution.[8]

From the perspective of two centuries of U.S. history under the

Constitution, two aspects of the vice presidency's role in the 1988 presidential election seem especially noteworthy. First, the selection of Quayle as the Republican nominee for vice president ignited an extraordinarily widespread and hostile reaction among voters, paying backhanded tribute to the prestige the office now enjoys. Second, the incumbent vice president was elected president, laying to rest the fabled "Van Buren syndrome" that, some said, had prevented any sitting vice president from being elected president since Martin Van Buren in 1836.

The Evolution of the Vice Presidency

The nineteenth-century vice presidency was as weak and despised an office as its feeble constitutional status would have suggested. Yet improvements eventually took place extraconstitutionally: indeed, the contrast between the nineteenth- and twentieth-century vice presidents could hardly be more stark. No vice president was nominated for reelection by a party convention until 1912; since then every first-term vice president who has sought a second term has been renominated. None of the four nineteenth-century vice presidents who succeeded to the presidency—John Tyler, Millard Fillmore, Andrew Johnson, and Chester A. Arthur—was nominated by his party, much less elected, for a term as president in his own right; none is regarded by historians as a successful president.[9] In contrast, not only have all five twentieth-century successor presidents—Theodore Roosevelt, Calvin Coolidge, Harry S Truman, Lyndon B. Johnson, and Gerald R. Ford—been nominated, but all except Ford (who lost narrowly) were elected. As a group, they actually rank higher than the century's initially elected presidents.[10]

The record has been even more compelling since the end of World War II. In elections from 1948 to 1988, the vice-presidential candidate as often as not was the more experienced member of the ticket in high government office, including Walter F. Mondale in 1976, Bush in 1980, and Bentsen in 1988. Vice presidents have become the presumptive front-runners for their party's presidential nomination. Starting with Nixon in 1960, every vice president has led in a majority of the Gallup polls that measure the party rank-and-file's preconvention preferences for president.[11] Six of the eight most recent vice presidents (Nixon, Johnson, Hubert H. Humphrey, Ford, Mondale, and Bush) have been nominated for president, including (thanks in large part to the Twenty-second Amendment) the three who served presidents who could not or chose not to run for reelection.

The roles and resources of the vice presidency also have grown in recent years, to such an extent that the office has become virtually "institutionalized." [12] The vice presidency is significantly larger and more complex than in the past; it now enjoys a sizable and more professional staff, a White House office, a separate line item in the executive budget, and even an official residence. But the office also has become institutionalized in the broader sense that more vice-presidential activities now are virtually taken for granted. These include regular private meetings with the president, a wide-ranging role as presidential adviser, membership on the National Security Council, full intelligence briefings, public advocacy of the president's programs and leadership, diplomatic missions, attendance at cabinet meetings, and congressional and other liaison activities.

The reasons for the enhanced status of the vice presidency in government and electoral politics are several. At the turn of the century, the rise of national news media (mass circulation magazines and newspaper wire services) and a new style of active political campaigning in presidential elections enhanced the visibility and prestige of the vice president, which in turn made the office more appealing to a better class of political leaders. So did Franklin Roosevelt's successful claim at the 1940 Democratic convention that the presidential candidate has the right to name his own running mate. In the past, when party leaders had made that decision, they typically paired the nominee for president with a vice-presidential candidate from the opposite wing of the party, thereby discouraging the president from either trusting the vice president personally or entrusting him with useful responsibilities. Finally, after 1945, the combination of Truman's woefully unprepared succession to the presidency when Roosevelt died (Truman was unaware of the existence of the atomic bomb and postwar plans) and the proliferation of nuclear weapons heightened public concern that the vice president should be a leader who was ready and able to step into the presidency literally at a moment's notice.

The 1988 Vice-Presidential Candidates

As voters increasingly have come to judge vice-presidential nominees by their fitness to be president, most candidates for president have learned that, in filling the second slot on the ticket, they can do well politically by doing good governmentally. As Hamilton Jordan put it in a 1976 memo to his candidate, Jimmy Carter, "The best politics is to select a person who is accurately perceived by the American people as being qualified and able to serve as president if that should become necessary." [13]

Lessons of the Recent Past. Not much is purposely left to chance in modern vice-presidential selection, at least not when the presidential nomination is settled, as is now typical, well in advance of the convention.[14] The obvious lessons of Democratic presidential nominee George McGovern's hasty, casually screened, and, when evidence of undisclosed treatments for mental illness was uncovered by the press, politically disastrous selection of Missouri senator Thomas Eagleton in 1972 were instructive in this regard. In 1976 Carter set a precedent of sorts when he undertook a careful, organized, and unusually public preconvention search for a running mate; he chose Senator Mondale from a list of seven after conducting polls, long personal interviews, and detailed background investigations. Mondale followed a similar procedure as the Democratic nominee for president in 1984, erring mainly in the execution: he selected vice-presidential finalists whose competence to be president was less obvious than their symbolic representation of vocal interests within the party, notably blacks, women, and Hispanics. Mondale also neglected to evaluate adequately the financial records of his eventual choice, Rep. Geraldine A. Ferraro of New York.

Republicans, who suffered their own vice-presidential embarrassment when Spiro T. Agnew, the party's victorious nominee in 1968 and 1972, resigned in October 1973 as part of a plea bargain that enabled him to reduce prosecution on political corruption charges, also have adopted the new search process, albeit less publicly and, sometimes, less thoroughly than the Democrats. In 1976 Ford asked thousands of Republican leaders for their recommendations for vice president, assigned aides to request financial and other personal information from two dozen prospective nominees, and reviewed his options in several staff meetings before selecting Kansas senator Robert Dole. Four years later, Reagan confined his choice to three men—former ambassador Bush, Senate minority leader Howard Baker, and Ford—all of whom had long records in public life and already had undergone intense scrutiny as presidential candidates, thus obviating any need for detailed background examinations. Bush, Reagan's choice in 1980, was renominated in 1984.

Two conclusions can be drawn from the recent history of vice-presidential selection. First, modern candidates for president are sensitive to the public's desire that the vice president be of presidential caliber. In most of the recent instances in which a nominee had to be chosen, the presidential candidate undertook a search that was generally well designed to result in a reasoned, responsible selection. Second, candidates who do not choose wisely pay a price. A 1982 study (confirmed for the 1988 campaign by Patterson in chapter 4) indicates that in the general election campaign, vice-presidential nominees have been most likely to make the front page for problems such as scandals or blunders. To select a running mate whose competence is doubtful is to invite such coverage, thereby handing the other party a potent issue. Differences in the qualifications of the candidates also may become apparent in the vice-presidential debate, televised on all the networks, that has become a regular feature of the presidential campaign. Ultimately, the price of a poor selection is votes on election day.[15]

Bentsen and Quayle.   The 1988 vice-presidential nominations confirmed the lessons of recent history in every way. In early June, hours after the last primaries were over, Dukakis and his close friend and adviser Paul Brountas formally launched a search that was designed both to preserve the best of the Carter process and to avoid the mistakes made by Mondale. The goal was to find a vice-presidential nominee who had extensive Washington experience (starting with Eisenhower and Adlai Stevenson in 1952, all nine non-Washington-based presidential candidates have picked Washington politicians as running mates), a spotless personal and financial background, the respect of Dukakis, and a political base that would broaden the ticket's appeal in the general election. A week before the Democratic convention, Bentsen, whose manner, experience as a three-term senator, and strong support in Texas impressed Dukakis, was chosen at a late-night meeting of the governor and his closest aides.

The formal search for a Republican vice-presidential nominee began in July, when Bush appointed his close associate, Robert Kimmitt, to explore in detail the backgrounds of those being considered. Bush, offended by Dukakis's "marching arm-in-arm around" in public forums with prospective running mates and insisting "I know most of these people very, very well," designed a search procedure that was deliberately protective of the candidates' privacy. Among other things, he eschewed face-to-face interviews and told Kimmitt to report the results of the background investigations directly to him, without allowing his political staff to probe the findings for potential problems.

Bush pared down his long list of candidates to six names at a free-wheeling meeting with his staff on the Friday before the Republican convention. He was looking not just for electoral appeal in November but for a vice president much in his own image—personally compatible with the president, loyal, and grateful for the honor of serving. After concluding from his polls that no running mate could deliver a region or even an important state, Bush chose the agreeable Quayle, hoping that the young, handsome senator would broaden the ticket's appeal among women and young voters.

The results of the Bentsen and Quayle nominations were dramatic. Bentsen brought favorable publicity and votes to the Democratic ticket; indeed, by the end of the campaign, survey data showed that the Texas senator was the most highly regarded candidate of either party. Quayle, in contrast, was castigated in the press for using family connections to enter the Indiana National Guard rather than be drafted into the army during the Vietnam War and, more generally, for his undistinguished record in the Senate. His performance in the debate with Bentsen was so weak that postdebate polls found that not even Bush supporters thought Quayle had won. The Dukakis campaign ran frequent television commercials that raised the specter of "President Quayle." On election day, Quayle appears to have reduced Bush's margin of victory by four to eight percentage points.[16]

Bush won the election, obscuring the detrimental political effects of his selection of Quayle. But the voters' response to the vice-presidential candidates in 1988 underscores the political wisdom of choosing running mates with an eye to their competence, if needed, to be president. No prudent presidential nominee in the future will want to risk losing several million votes through the self-inflicted wound of a weak vice-presidential selection.[17]

Bush and the Van Buren Syndrome

Most modern vice presidents enjoy unique advantages when it comes to winning their party's nomination for president. If successful, they also suffer unique disadvantages in the fall campaign. In 1988 Bush made full use of the advantages and, with the help of President Reagan, was able to neutralize the disadvantages.

Getting Nominated. In addition to the opportunity the Twenty-second Amendment affords and the increased likelihood of being a political leader of some stature, vice presidents derive two other benefits from the office in their pursuit of a presidential nomination. The first is that their activities as party builder—campaigning during elections, raising funds at other times—and public advocate of the administration and its policies uniquely situate them to win friends among the political activists who influence presidential nominations. (Such campaigning also is good training for a national presidential campaign.) Second, the recent growth in the governmental responsibilities and resources of the vice presidency has made it a more prestigious position and thus a more plausible steppingstone to the presidency. Foreign travel and the trappings of the office—the airplane, mansion, seal, White House office, and so on—are physical symbols of prestige.

In sum, the modern vice president typically is an experienced and talented political leader who is loyal to the president and admired by the party—an ideal formula for securing a presidential nomination and one that Bush executed perfectly in 1988. Exit polls during the Republican primaries and caucuses showed Bush winning overwhelming support from voters who approved of Reagan's performance as president, even though all of Bush's opponents presented themselves as the true heirs to the Reagan mantle. Needless to say, such voters make up the vast majority of those who participate in Republican primaries and caucuses.[18] Bush's worst moment in the nominating campaign, his defeat in the Iowa caucuses, was the exception that demonstrated the rule. Because Reagan's farm policies had made him unusually unpopular in Iowa, Bush's association with the president was counterproductive in that state.

Getting Elected. For all their advantages in winning the party's nomination for president, vice presidents have had an unusually hard time getting elected. The Van Buren syndrome can be overstated—of the thirty-four vice presidents who served between Van Buren and Bush, only seven ran for president, and Nixon (1960) and Humphrey (1968) came close to winning.[19] But vice presidents carry certain burdens into the fall campaign that are as surely grounded in their office as the advantages they bring to a nominating contest.

Indeed, some of the activities of the modern vice presidency that are most appealing to party activists may repel many voters in the broader electorate that decides the election. Days and nights spent fertilizing the party's grass roots with fervent, sometimes slashing rhetoric can alienate voters who look to the presidency for unifying, not partisan, leadership. So can the vice president's role as advocate of the president's policies. Some administrations have relied on the vice president to defend their least popular actions and programs, freeing the president to dwell on more universally appealing proposals and accomplishments. Such a course is likely to win friendship and influence in the White House, but it may lead voters to associate the vice president with controversy.

Certain institutional qualities of the modern vice presidency also handicap the vice president-turned-presidential-candidate. The vice president cannot plausibly claim credit for the successes of the administration; that is a presidential prerogative. But the vice president can be attacked by the other party's presidential candidate for the administration's shortcomings. Such attacks allow no good response. A vice president who tries to stand apart from the administration will alienate the president and cause voters to wonder why the criticisms were not voiced earlier, when they might have made a difference. The vice president can say instead that loyalty to the president forecloses public disagreement, but that course is no less perilous. Strength, independence, vision, and integrity are the qualities voters seek most in a president, not loyalty.

Much of Bush's 1988 image as a "wimp" can be traced to the loyal subservience he displayed as Reagan's vice president. Bush also had to deal with Dukakis's charges about the Reagan administration's failures in drug enforcement and the Iran-contra affair. But more than any vice president since Van Buren, Bush benefited from a helpful and cooperative president in his efforts to overcome the political disadvantages of his office. In contrast to presidents Eisenhower and Johnson, Reagan put ego aside and publicly praised (even inflated) the vice president's contributions to what he began to call the "Reagan-Bush administration." The president not only proclaimed himself a "soldier" in the Bush campaign, but acted as one, campaigning wherever and whenever the vice president requested. As Rourke and Tierney note in chapter 1, Reagan even made certain popular decisions in advance of the election (such as appointing the first Hispanic to serve in the cabinet, Secretary of Education Lauro Cavazos, and signing a Democratically sponsored plant-closing bill). Conversely, he postponed the sending of farm foreclosure notices and the implementation of more stringent Social Security regulations until just after the election.

Reagan's most important service to Bush, however, was to become steadily more popular with the voters: his approval rating rose from 46 percent in November 1987 to 55 percent in November 1988, an unusually high figure among recent presidents.[20] On election day Bush won the support of at least 80 percent of the voters who approved Reagan's performance, while losing the votes of the 40 percent who disapproved Reagan by a margin of nine to one.[21]

What of the Van Buren syndrome? Bush appropriately cast it onto the political dustheap when he opened his first postelection press conference by quipping, "It's been a long time, Marty." But if the political handicaps of the vice president in a general election never were as strong as often was claimed, neither are they as meaningless as some suggested in the aftermath of the Bush victory. For a president leaving office, Reagan (like Andrew Jackson, the president with whom Van Buren served) was unusually helpful to his vice president, both in his actions and his popularity. Not all vice presidents can expect to be so fortunate.

Electoral College

The electoral college was a "jerry-rigged" improvisation of the Constitutional Convention, a last-minute compromise measure designed to enable the delegates to break their impasse on how the president should be elected.[22] The Framers' original scheme—to have

Congress choose the president—had carried with it a corollary that, in their minds, was ineluctable: the president must be restricted to a single term. (Otherwise, observed delegate George Mason of Virginia, there would be too strong a "temptation on the side of the Executive to intrigue with the Legislature for a reappointment," using political patronage and illegitimate favors to buy votes in Congress.) [23] Thus, the decision to allow the president to run again meant that some other method of selection would have to be devised.

In the absence of any agreed-upon alternative (election by the people was dismissed out of hand as being—Mason again—the equivalent of "refer[ring] a trial of colors to a blind man"),[24] a committee was charged to invent one. Its proposal, the electoral college, had the enormous political advantage of including something for everyone. According to the size of its delegation in Congress, each state was assigned a number of electors who, presumably, would be chosen by the people or their elected state legislators. If the electors failed to se-lect (by majority vote) a president, the House of Representatives would act in their stead.

Beginning soon after Reagan's landslide reelection in 1984, the electoral college was invoked frequently in discussions of the 1988 election. Indeed, long before the first vote was cast in the first primary or caucus of the presidential campaign, some political analysts declared that, barring catastrophe, the Republican nominee very likely would win. This prediction had less to do with political or economic analysis than with the purported lock that Republicans were said to have on the electoral college.[25] The lock theory simply took note that while Republican candidates for president had carried twenty-three states with 202 electoral votes in each of the five elections from 1968 to 1984, Democrats had consistently won only the District of Columbia, with its 3 electoral votes. Broadening the standard to include states that had gone for a party in four of these five elections only widened the disparity: 354 electoral votes (thirty-six states) for the Republicans, 13 electoral votes for the Democrats (D.C. and Minnesota). With 270 votes needed to win, the electoral college seemed to some to be so imbued with a Republican bias as to practically rig the election.

Evidence to counter the electoral college lock theory existed, but was mainly buried in the political science journals. Scholars argued that, rather than bias the outcome of the presidential election in any systematic partisan way (such that a candidate who received the most popular votes might lose the election), the electoral college almost invariably "magnifies" the margin of victory received by the popular vote winner.[26] The reason is that the unit, or winner-take-all, rule that every state but Maine follows translates even a modest popular vote plurality in a state into a sweep of the state's electoral votes. Prior to 1988 every electoral vote tally since the election of 1888 had magnified the national popular vote winner's margin. The 1984 election was an extreme example—Reagan's 59 percent of the popular vote became 98 percent of the electoral vote—but the average result for the last twenty-four elections was still impressive: 53 percent of the popular vote for the winner became 76 percent of the electoral vote.

The scholarly evidence further suggested that if there is a systematic bias in the electoral college, it is less to one party or the other than to the populous states and the groups of voters concentrated in them. Presidential candidates of both parties spend most of their time and resources in the twelve most populous states for the simple reason that, taken together, these states have a majority of electoral votes. (The heavily populated states also are more closely balanced between the two parties and are thus more competitive.) [27] Further, some of the groups whose members are most likely to live in these states (and whose views presidential candidates must consider seriously in planning their strategies for victory) are more liberal than the average voter: union members, urban blacks and Hispanics, Jews, and residents of metropolitan areas.[28] This concentration of voters helps to explain why liberal lobbyists were among the most effective opponents of abolishing the electoral college when the issue last came before Congress,[29] but it hardly supports the notion of a conservative Republican lock.

What did the presidential election of 1988 indicate about the electoral college lock theory? The superficial evidence could be interpreted in different ways. Bush carried all but two (Iowa and Oregon) of the twenty-three states that had supported the Republican nominee in every presidential election since 1968 and all but one (Washington) of the states that had gone Republican every time but once. Bush's 54 percent of the popular vote was magnified to 79 percent of the electoral vote, close to the historical average.

A fairer test for the presence of partisan bias in the electoral college would be to assume that Dukakis and Bush each had received 50 percent of the national two-party popular vote, then see which way the electoral votes would have gone. A reasonable way to impose this test, since Dukakis actually received 46 percent, would be to add four percentage points to his popular vote (and subtract four points from Bush's) in every state.[30] The result: a Democratic victory, by 279 to 259 electoral votes.

The electoral college's latent Democratic advantage in 1988 was no coincidence. Press reports suggest that Dukakis, giving up in mid-October on the idea that he could win a popular vote majority, deliberately adopted an eighteen-state strategy to amass a narrow electoral college victory, and that Bush's polls, toward the end of the campaign, briefly led him to fear that the strategy might work.[31] If the electoral college ever did select the popular vote loser as president, the new president, especially if winning the election in the face of public rejection was shown to have been a conscious strategy, almost certainly would have a tainted administration. The Twelfth Amendment could well be abolished. George Mason's warning notwithstanding, a strong majority of the voters already favor direct election of the president, and having their will thwarted in a particular election might stir them to action.[32]

More generally, the lesson of 1988 is not that there is an ingrained Democratic advantage in the electoral college, any more than there is a Republican advantage. (The two parties actually would have split the last four elections evenly if the popular votes had been tied.) [33] The lesson is, instead, that the source of the Democrats' failure in presidential elections is their inability to appeal to a sufficient number of voters.

Split-Level Realignment

The results of the elections of 1988 were singular in some ways. Never before has a president been elected (by a landslide, no less) while the other party gained ground in the House, the Senate, the state legislature, and the state governorships. Never before have voters given a newly elected president fewer fellow partisans in Congress than they gave Bush. Never has the Constitution's federal system—separate levels of government and separate branches within each level—been characterized by such partisan segmentation.

But 1988's singularities are best understood as extreme manifestations of the underlying pattern that has characterized American politics for two decades: Republican domination of the White House, Democratic ascendancy almost everywhere else. Republicans have won five of the last six presidential elections: Nixon in 1968 and 1972, Reagan in 1980 and 1984, and Bush in 1988. The last four Republican victories have been by landslides; in contrast, the Democrats' single victory (Carter in 1976, two years after the Watergate crisis drove Nixon from office in disgrace) was narrowly fought. From 1968 to 1988 Republican presidential candidates led their Democratic opponents in popular votes by 264 million to 215 million, by 2,501 to 679 in electoral votes, and by 251 to 54 in states (including the solidly Democratic District of Columbia). Indeed, Dukakis's 46 percent of the popular vote was easily the second best showing by a Democrat in recent presidential elections. (Compare 43 percent for Humphrey in 1968, 38 percent for McGovern in 1972, 50 percent for Carter in 1976, 41 percent for Carter in 1980, and 41 percent for Mondale in 1984.) Dukakis's 111 electoral votes almost doubled the Democratic tally in the two preceding elections combined (49 in 1980, 13 in 1984).

The Democrats, for their part, have dominated Congress and the states. The House has been a Democratic preserve since 1954; in 1988 the Democrats gained three seats to increase their majority over the Republicans to 260 to 175. The Democrats added one to their ranks in the Senate, a body they have controlled for all but six years since 1954. (The Democratic majority, after the 1988 elections, was fifty-five to forty-five.) At the state level, Democrats also maintained their long-standing hold on a majority of the governors' mansions, adding one in 1988 for a total of twenty-eight (of fifty). Their increase of 14 seats in the state legislatures gave them approximately 4,500 to the Republicans' 2,900. The Democrats control both legislative houses in twenty-eight states, the Republicans in eight.

Changing Patterns of Party Alignment

No historical precedent exists for the current political situation. Since 1968 different parties have controlled the presidency and Congress more often than not—twelve of twenty-two years—and in all cases, the president was Republican and Congress Democratic.[34] The party that did not occupy the White House controlled one house of Congress for another six years (the first six years of the Reagan administration, when Democrats had a majority in the House). Same-party control of the presidency and Congress prevailed just 18 percent of the time, during the four years that Carter, a Democrat, was president. In contrast, same-party control existed 79 percent of the time from 1900 to 1968.

Scholars and political analysts have offered a number of explanations of what has been happening recently in the political system. The most common theories—realignment and dealignment—seem less persuasive than a third: split-level realignment.

Realignment?   The normal historical situation in American politics has involved more than just same-party control of the presidency and Congress. For long periods of time, one party usually has exercised such control: in this century, the Republicans until the 1930s, then the Democrats. The Democratic majority came about through a party realignment that was led by Franklin Roosevelt in 1932 and solidified by his New Deal policies. The Roosevelt realignment was not unlike those that had occurred regularly (every thirty years or so) before then, around 1800, 1828, 1860, and 1896. Classic realignments such as these are marked by "a significant and enduring change in the party coalitions—that is, in the partisan loyalties of the electorate." [35]

New voters typically gravitate to the rising party during a classic realignment; some older voters change parties.[36] Political participation rises. Above all, classic realignments are top-to-bottom affairs: gains for the new majority party occur at all levels and in all the elected branches of the federal system.

The elections of 1980 seemed to some to augur a full-scale Republican realignment. Reagan's landslide was accompanied by substantial gains for his party, including 34 seats in the House, 12 in the Senate, 302 in the state legislatures, and 5 in the governors' mansions. Growing numbers of voters, especially the young, identified themselves as Republicans in national surveys.

But Republican hopes were diminished when the party lost seats in the 1982 and 1986 midterm elections and, perhaps most important, when it gained little ground from the Reagan reelection landslide in 1984. Young voters proved to be inconsistent, not reliably Republican; they voted Democratic in 1982 and 1986 and were Bush's weakest age group in 1988. Participation in elections declined, rather than increasing, as it had in previous realignments. The voter turnout rate in 1988 was 50 percent, the lowest since 1924.

Dealignment?   The elections of 1980 were not the first recent elections to prompt premature thoughts of realignment. The elections of 1968, coming as they did thirty-six years after the Roosevelt realignment and marked by substantial Democratic defections to third party candidate George Wallace, were described in one book as heralding the "emerging Republican majority." [37] But the 1970s witnessed not Republican gains among the voters, but losses for both parties. Fewer people identified themselves as either Republicans or Democrats, and those who did, when voting, were more inclined than ever to abandon their parties or to split their tickets.[38] The theory arose that the American political system was dealigning:[39] voters, with more years of education than in the past, were said to be relying less on partisan labels than on their own appraisals, derived largely from the now omnipresent mass media, of the candidates and issues in each election.

But the dealignment theory was as surely undermined by political developments in the 1980s as the classic realignment theory. Dealignment implies a virtual randomness of partisan election outcomes over time—a dealigned electorate presumably would swing back and forth erratically between Republican and Democratic candidates. Instead, voters have settled into a discernible partisan pattern: Republican presidents, Democratic Congresses and state governments. What is more, the direction of change in the main statistical indicator of dealignment has been reversed: more voters, not fewer, recently have been identifying themselves as party loyalists.[40]

A New Kind of Alignment. Because neither realignment nor dealignment describes the modern political situation, a new term has to be employed: split-level realignment. Presidential politics, for its part, clearly bears some of the hallmarks of a classic realignment. The New Deal coalition of blue-collar ethnics, liberals, Catholics, Jews, blacks, and southern whites crumbled when blacks made civil rights and minority progress central issues of American politics during the 1960s, thereby antagonizing many southern whites and, eventually, northern ethnic workers. By 1988 Democrats no longer could win the presidency by, as Dukakis did, better than any Democratic nominee in the history of polling, uniting the party's base of voters; the base simply had become too small.[41] Republicans not only have added many disaffected Democratic voters to their coalition in presidential elections, they also have taken command of the rhetorical high ground in policy debates. Like Republicans in the 1940s and 1950s, when the Democratic New Deal coalition was dominant, modern Democrats have become the "me-too" party, accepting Republican definitions of most foreign and economic policies and promising mainly to pursue them more fairly and efficiently. Their current political posture confines Democratic presidential candidates almost entirely to winning elections that are marked by special circumstances, such as a scandal or a severe economic recession during a Republican administration.

But the realignment in presidential politics has not carried over into other arenas of political competition, in the top-to-bottom manner of past party realignments. Democratic control of Congress is as solid as ever. Some of the Democrats' success in congressional elections can be attributed to partisan redistricting by Democratically controlled state legislatures, but not much, as Jacobson notes in chapter 6. As Jacobson also argues, although incumbency is a powerful inertial force in congressional elections, the power of incumbents to maintain their positions in the House and, to a lesser but still impressive degree, in the Senate, does not explain why Republicans have not done better at winning open seats.[42] Nor does incumbency account for either the Republicans' success in capturing the Senate in 1980 or their loss of it to the Democrats in 1986.

The Basis of Split-Level Realignment

A number of theories have been advanced to uncover the basis of split-level realignment. Some voters may prefer to reinforce the constitutional checks and balances between Congress and the presidency by placing different parties in charge of each branch.[43] Others may regard Democratic control of Congress as the best safeguard of their desire for an active federal government and a Republican president as insurance against their corresponding fear of high taxes.[44] But, more than in either of these explanations, split-level realignment is grounded in the voters' expectations of presidents and of individual members of Congress and in the nature of the Republican and Democratic parties.

Voters' Expectations.   Other than the vice president, the president is the only nationally elected official in the United States. Not surprisingly, most voters have national criteria in mind when they decide whom to support in presidential elections; that is why "peace and prosperity" is the standard formula for victory for the presidential candidate whose party can make the best case that it will provide them.

If Congress were a nationally elected branch of government, voters might well employ national criteria in choosing it as well. But Congress is a locally elected branch. Each member represents one state or congressional district; correspondingly, each voter has a say in the selection of just 1 of 435 representatives and, over a period of six years, two of one hundred senators. Predictably, most voters base their choices in congressional elections less on the consequences for the nation (neither they nor the few members of Congress they each help to elect is likely to have much leverage over national policy) than on the consequences for their own state or district.[45] Not national, but local prosperity forms voters' standard of judgment in congressional elections; not the federal budget, but the share of the budget that is spent on them; not national defense, but the local defense installations and contracts that generate jobs and income for their communities.

Different expectations of presidents and individual members of Congress help to explain the modern pattern of divided partisan control of the two branches. In recent years, voters usually have regarded Republican presidential candidates—more confident of their political ideology, more nationalistic in their view of foreign affairs, and less associated in the public mind with the "special interests" stereotype—as their best guarantors of national well-being. But, because most voters have their states and districts in mind when judging candidates for Congress, it is pragmatism, not ideology, they look for; localism, not nationalism, that preoccupies them; and their particular special interests, not special interests in general, that are at stake. The Democratic party, with its more sympathetic view of government, comes out ahead on all counts according to most voters' criteria for congressional elections. The Democrats enjoy the same advantage, and for the same reasons, in other state and local elections, whether for governor or state legislature.

The Nature of the Parties.   The nature of the Republican and Democratic parties also helps to explain their varying success in congressional and presidential elections. The Republicans, despite some differences between their evangelical "moralist" and economically motivated "enterpriser" wings on social issues like school prayer and abortion,[46] are a fairly homogeneous party—white, middle-class or higher, Protestant, and conservative. The Democrats, in contrast, are raucously diverse—white, black, and Hispanic; liberal and conservative; Catholic, Protestant, and Jewish; uneducated and professionally educated.

In fielding candidates for Congress, the Democrats' diversity is politically beneficial. It corresponds well to the nation's geographic diversity. Depending on the character of each state or congressional district, the Democrats usually have little trouble fielding a candidate who is ideologically, ethnically, and personally suitable. In elections to Congress or to other state and local offices, the Democratic party is, in one place or another, virtually all things to all people: liberal in the North, conservative in the South; pro-gun control in the city, anti-gun control in the country; environmentalist in most parts of the nation, development-oriented in the industrial areas; and so on. The candidates of the more homogeneous Republican party, not surprisingly, seem almost everywhere to have been cast in similar molds.

But heterogeneity haunts the Democrats in presidential elections. Ideologically and otherwise, the Republicans do not have to worry about defining their party's identity when writing their platform or choosing the candidate who will represent them to the nation. They have little problem projecting a confident, united front at their presidential nominating conventions. The 1988 Republican convention put Bush into the lead against Dukakis for the first time, a lead Bush never relinquished. In contrast, the Democrats, who thrive on being many different parties in local elections, face the challenge of deciding which one party they will be in nominating a candidate for president. Almost invariably, either the decision is contentious, producing unhappy losers and a divided party and projecting to the voters an image of vacillation and incompetence, or, as in the last two elections, the presidential nominee achieves temporary unity by making such sweeping concessions to the most vocal constituencies in the party (the vice-presidential nomination to feminists in 1984, a remarkable share of the spotlight for Jesse Jackson to blacks in 1988) as to alienate substantial numbers of voters.

The Consequences of Split-Level Realignment

For many years students of American politics have remarked upon the persistence of conflict between the president and Congress. In 1940 Edward S. Corwin traced the main source of contention to the Constitution, which designed the two branches in such a way as to create "an invitation to struggle." A quarter-century later, James MacGregor Burns argued that internal divisions in the Republican and Democratic parties created a "deadlock of democracy" by limiting the parties' ability to bridge the constitutional gulf between White House and Capitol.[47] Yet neither constitutional design nor intraparty divisions seem nearly as potent a force for interbranch conflict as the split-level realignment that now typically places the presidency in Republican hands and Congress under the control of the Democrats.

The period of split-level realignment—1968 to the present— already has been marked not just by differences between the president and Congress over policy, but by each branch's efforts to weaken the other. As Benjamin Ginsberg and Martin Shefter note, through unilateral military actions, efforts to reduce spending on federal grant programs to states and congressional districts, and other assertions of presidential authority, "Republicans have reacted to their inability to win control of Congress . . . by seeking to enhance the powers of the executive branch and to circumvent legislative restrictions on presidential conduct. The Democrats, in turn, have responded to the Republican presidential advantage through legislative investigations . . . as well as through the imposition of statutory limits on executive power," including the War Powers Resolution, the Budget and Impoundment Control Act, and the Ethics in Government Act.[48]

In one area of constitutional responsibility, split-level realignment seems especially likely to heighten conflict between the president and Congress: appointments to the third branch of government, the federal judiciary.

Courts

Article II, section 2, says that the president "shall nominate and by and with the Advice and Consent of the Senate, shall appoint . . . judges of the supreme Court" and, by implication, other federal judges. By involving both the president and the Senate, the Constitution assures that a split-level realignment almost certainly will affect the politics of judicial appointments.

Judicial Appointments, 1900-1968

The pattern of Supreme Court nominations through most of the twentieth century was simple: the president nominates, the Senate readily confirms.[49] From 1900 to 1968, forty-two of forty-five, or 93 percent, of all Supreme Court nominations were confirmed by the Senate. Twenty-nine of the confirmations came by voice votes, most of them unanimous or nearly so.[50] The average vote of approval for the other thirteen confirmed nominees was a comfortable sixty to fourteen.

The patterns of nominations to the district federal courts and the federal courts of appeals (or circuit courts) in this period were different but, if anything, even more consensual. Since the 1840s, district court nominations (there are ninety-five districts, with at least one in each state) have been governed by the norm of senatorial courtesy, under which the Senate customarily refuses to confirm a judicial nomination that is opposed by a senator of the president's party who is from the nominee's home state. To forestall the embarrassment of rejected appointments, presidents typically have solicited suggestions from the appropriate senators before nominating district judges. The working arrangement was well described by former senator and attorney general Robert F. Kennedy: "Basically, it's senatorial appointment with the advice and consent of the president." [51]

The politics that governs nominations to the thirteen circuit courts, which, except for the District of Columbia circuit, have jurisdiction over several states and mainly hear cases that are appealed from the district courts, embodies some of the conventions of Supreme Court and district court nominations. Presidents have more discretion in making appointments to the circuit courts than to the district courts, but senators are more likely to be consulted on circuit court than on Supreme Court nominations. Hardly any district or circuit court nominations were rejected between 1900 and 1968.

Judicial Appointments and Split-Level Realignment

As we have seen, 1900-1968 was a period in which the same party usually controlled the presidency and the Senate. Cooperation on judicial appointments is what one would expect in a political setting of this sort.[52] In contrast, the era of split-level realignment has produced its own, more conflictual politics of judicial selection.

Conflict between the president and the Senate has been most visible in appointments to the Supreme Court. All thirteen Supreme Court nominations since 1968 have been made by Republican presidents, all but three of them to a Democratic Senate. The rejection rate for Supreme Court nominations since 1968 is four of thirteen—31 percent—compared with 7 percent during the earlier years of the century.[53] (The rejection rate for Republican presidential nominations by a Democratic Senate is four of ten, or 40 percent.) No Supreme Court nominee has been confirmed by voice vote since 1968, compared with 65 percent (twenty-nine of forty-five) who were confirmed *viva voce* before then.

The main explanation for the new level of conflict over Supreme Court nominations is not surprising: Senate Democrats have realized that to continue the tradition of customarily deferring to the president on appointments is to cede control of the Court to the Republicans. When Reagan nominated the brilliant, experienced, but ultraconservative Robert Bork to the Court in 1987, Democrats made that point publicly, then defeated the nomination, 58-42, the widest margin of rejection in history. Fueling Senate resistance has been the liberals' success from the 1930s to the 1970s at stacking the federal judiciary with sympathetic judges and at broadening the rules and procedures of the courts in ways that serve the causes of blacks, feminists, environmentalists, and other Democratic constituency groups.[54]

Conflict of a different sort has been brewing in the realm of lower court nominations, where the Senate's influence traditionally has been greater. Here President Reagan, not the Senate, found the norms of the pre-1968 period confining and became more assertive than presidents previously had been. To be sure, senatorial courtesy continues to limit the president's ability to impose unwelcome nominations on the Senate. But the president also has a ploy, which Reagan used, namely, to withhold a nomination to a vacant judgeship until the Senate can be persuaded to confirm someone acceptable to the president.[55] The arrangement that Reagan and the Senate eventually worked out on district court nominations was for the Republican senator from each state with a vacancy to submit the names of several acceptable nominees to the Justice Department's Office of Legal Policy. Prospective judges then were screened and interviewed thoroughly to test their conformance to the administration's conservative legal philosophy before a decision about whom to nominate was reached by a White House committee. Not surprisingly, Democrats eventually began to rebel, especially after they regained control of the Senate in the 1986 elections.[56]

A "Bush Court"?

Reagan's landslide election victories and, for his first six years, a Republican Senate made him an unusually powerful president. For that reason, Bush's first term may provide a more typical view of the new politics of judicial appointments. At the start of the Bush administration the three oldest Supreme Court justices are also the three most liberal: Harry Blackmun (who turns eighty-one in 1989), William Brennan (eighty-three), and Thurgood Marshall (eighty-one). The Supreme Court is so evenly balanced on many issues that to replace even one of them with a conservative could tip the Court to the right. Many Democratic senators fervently expressed their commitment not to let this happen during the Bork controversy.

Bush has several strategies, none of which is guaranteed to succeed, to choose from if one of the three liberal justices should leave the Court.[57] First, he could nominate a moderate who would be palatable to Democrats. Such a nominee almost certainly would be confirmed by the Senate, but at considerable cost to Bush among conservatives in his own party. The Republican Right was disappointed with its hero, Reagan, on many matters of legislative policy on social issues like abortion and school prayer; what mollified them to some degree were his conservative judicial appointments. Bush, whose conservative bona fides always have been doubted by the right, could deliver no less without risking an angrily divided party.

Bush's other strategies involve nominating conservative justices whom Senate Democrats would find it hard to reject regardless of their objections on grounds of ideology. He could nominate a senator. By tradition, notes Henry Abraham, "the Senate almost invariably treats as a *cas d'honneur* the presidential designation of a sitting member and normally also, although not so predictably, of a past colleague in good standing." [58] Or Bush could choose someone, albeit conservative, from a Democratic constituency group, such as a woman, a black, a Hispanic, or a Jew. The idea would be to disarm the opposition, as Reagan did when he nominated Sandra Day O'Connor to the Court in 1981.

Either the constituency or the Senate strategy runs the risk of being too clever by half. The norm of Senate deference to its members was last tested in 1945, when Truman nominated Republican senator Harold Burton; it may well have eroded in the modern era of split-level realignment. (It cannot help matters that the three most recent senators named to the Court—Burton, James Byrnes, and Sherman Minton— were rated among the eight "failures" in a scholarly ranking of ninety-six justices.) [59] As for confining his selection to conservatives from Democratic constituencies, that not only would limit severely Bush's range of choice but also would run the risk of being seen as politically craven. Reagan's unsuccessful nomination of Douglas Ginsburg, a politically conservative Jew, was so regarded in 1987.

During the campaign, Bush promised that he would appoint "moderate people of conservative views" to the judiciary. As a political formula, that ideal is on a par with promising low inflation and low unemployment or law and order with justice. But whether Bush or any other Republican president in the era of split-level realignment can make the formula work in practice is uncertain. Also uncertain is his ability to secure Reagan-style cooperation from the Senate in district and circuit court nominations.

Appointments to the federal judiciary aside, split-level realignment has affected the courts in another way. Democratic party dominance extends not just to Congress, but to most of the state governments as well. For this reason, many state courts recently have become more liberal than the federal courts. In numerous areas of law, they have found broader justifications in state constitutions for civil rights, civil liberties, and other liberal legal causes than the U.S. Supreme Court has found in the U.S. Constitution. Studies by Ronald Collins, Peter Gailie, and John Kincaid have documented the recent rise of this new-style "judicial federalism"—the legal equivalent of a split-level realignment.[60]

Conclusion

Discussions of the Constitution pervade the electoral process in a variety of forms. During the 1980s one or both political parties endorsed numerous proposed constitutional amendments in their platforms, including two that were passed by Congress but not ratified by the states (the Equal Rights Amendment and an amendment to give the District of Columbia voting representation in Congress) and several others that have remained at the discussion stage, on topics ranging from school prayer to a line-item veto. Recent Republican platforms also have pledged the party to appoint federal judges who will interpret the Constitution strictly and, on the abortion issue, with respect for "the sanctity of human life"; Democrats have lambasted the Republicans regularly for concocting ultraconservative constitutional litmus tests. For their part, voters have endorsed proposals to replace the electoral college with direct election of the president and to impose a twelve-year limit on representatives and senators.[61] Commentators have suggested other constitutional amendments, including one to restrict the president to a single six-year term and another to require voters to cast a straight party ballot for president and Congress.

None of these suggestions to alter the Constitution has been adopted. Yet the frequency with which they are discussed is one indication of how thoroughly the electoral process is imbued with constitutional influences. Some of these influences—the two-term limit on presidents, the vice presidency, the electoral college, the separate election of president and Congress, and judicial appointments—were thrown into sharp relief by the elections of 1988. Other constitutional issues have been prominent in the past: one thinks of states' rights in 1964, the war-making power in 1968, impoundment in 1972, impeachment and the pardon power in 1976, and the numerous constitutional issues that the parties raised in 1980 and 1984. Still others, no doubt, will emerge in future elections.

Notes

1. B. Drummond Ayres, Jr., "Electoral College's Stately Landslide Sends Bush and Quayle into History," *New York Times,* December 20, 1988, 13.
2. The term was invented by political analyst Kevin Phillips. Other terms for this phenomenon have circulated, including "hollow realignment" and "incomplete realignment."
3. Erwin C. Hargrove and Michael Nelson, *Presidents, Politics, and Policy* (Baltimore: Johns Hopkins University Press, 1984), 20-24.
4. According to the ABC News exit poll on election day, Bush barely outpolled Dukakis among eighteen- to twenty-four-year-olds, compared to the nineteen percentage point margin they gave Reagan in 1984. Thomas B. Edsall and Richard Morin, "Democrats Make Inroads on Reagan Coalition," *Washington Post,* November 9, 1988, A9.
5. Max Farrand, ed. *The Records of the Federal Convention of 1787,* vol. II (New Haven, Conn.: Yale University Press, 1966), 33. Clinton Rossiter, ed., *The Federalist Papers* (New York: New American Library, 1961), 437.
6. Quoted by Edward S. Corwin in *The President: Office and Powers,* 4th ed. (New York: New York University Press, 1957), 332-333.
7. Michael R. Beschloss, *Mayday: Eisenhower, Khrushchev, and the U-2 Affair* (New York: Harper & Row, 1986), 3.
8. This history is more fully told by Michael Nelson in *A Heartbeat Away* (New York: Unwin Hyman, 1988).
9. In the most recent and extensive round of historians' rankings of the presidents, Johnson was rated a failure, Tyler and Fillmore as below average, and Arthur as average. Robert K. Murray and Tim H. Blessing, "The Presidential Performance Study: A Progress Report," *Journal of American History* 70 (December 1983): 535-555.
10. Ibid. Roosevelt and Truman were rated near-great, Johnson above average, Ford average, and Coolidge below average.
11. Joel K. Goldstein, *The Modern Vice Presidency* (Princeton, N.J.: Princeton University Press, 1982), 72-75; Nelson, *A Heartbeat Away,* 91.
12. Paul C. Light, *Vice-Presidential Power: Advice and Influence in the White House* (Baltimore: Johns Hopkins University Press, 1984).
13. Quoted by Jules Witcover in *Marathon: The Pursuit of the Presidency, 1972-1976* (New York: Viking, 1977), 361.
14. A broader treatment of vice-presidential selection may be found in Michael Nelson, "Choosing the Vice President," *PS: Political Science and Politics* 21 (Fall 1988): 858-868.
15. Goldstein, *Modern Vice Presidency,* 123-132.
16. The survey data on which these conclusions are based may be found in George Skelton, "Dukakis Lost Own Issue—Competence," *Los Angeles Times,* November 9, 1988, 23; E. J. Dionne, Jr., "The Debates: Revival for Democrats," *New York Times,* October 7, 1988, 10; Dionne, "Bush Runs Ahead in Popular Vote," *New York Times,* November 9, 1988, 13; Robert Shogan, "Democrats' Losses at Polls Laid to Staleness of New Deal Creed," *Los Angeles Times,* November 9, 1988, 23;

John Dillon, "Scanning Election Results for Future Trends," *Christian Science Monitor,* November 23, 1988, 1; and Tom Sherwood, "Doctor Temporarily Silences Bentsen as Voice for Democrats," *Washington Post,* November 10, 1988, A39.

17. One political constraint can restrict the presidential candidate's ability to choose wisely: the need to unite the party. For example, feminist organizations threatened to withhold their support from Mondale in 1984 unless he nominated a woman to be vice president. Still, such pressure is not irresistible: Dukakis ignored efforts to place Jesse Jackson on the ticket in 1988.

18. Thomas B. Edsall and Richard Morin, "Super Tuesday's Showing," *Washington Post National Weekly Edition,* March 14-20, 1988, 37.

19. George Sirgiovanni, "The 'Van Buren Jinx': Vice Presidents Need Not Beware," *Presidential Studies Quarterly* 18 (Winter 1988): 61-76.

20. Harold W. Stanley and Richard G. Niemi, *Vital Statistics on American Politics* (Washington, D.C.: CQ Press, 1988), 229.

21. Dionne, "Bush Runs Ahead in Popular Vote"; and Skelton, "Dukakis Lost Own Issue." The *Los Angeles Times*/CNN poll showed Reagan to be slightly more popular (60 percent) and Bush to have run even better among those who liked Reagan (83 percent). William Schneider, "Solidarity's Not Enough," *National Journal,* November 12, 1988, 2853-2855.

22. John P. Roche, "The Electoral College: A Note on American Political Mythology," *Dissent* 8 (Spring 1961): 198.

23. Farrand, *Records of the Federal Convention,* vol. I, 68.

24. Ibid., vol. II, 31.

25. As George F. Will notes, the theory is associated with political consultant Horace Busby. Will, *The New Season: A Spectator's Guide to the 1988 Election* (New York: Simon & Schuster, 1987), 96-97. See also James Q. Wilson, "Realignment at the Top, Dealignment at the Bottom," in *The American Elections of 1984,* ed. Austin Ranney (Durham, N.C.: Duke University Press, 1985), 308-309.

26. See, for example, Nelson W. Polsby and Aaron Wildavsky, *Presidential Elections: Contemporary Strategies of American Electoral Politics,* 7th ed. (New York: Free Press, 1988), 279; and Wallace S. Sayre and Judith H. Parris, *Voting for President: The Electoral College and the American Political System* (Washington, D.C.: Brookings Institution, 1970), 61.

27. Polsby and Wildavsky, *Presidential Elections,* 276.

28. Lawrence D. Longley and James D. Dana, Jr., "New Empirical Estimates of the Biases of the Electoral College," *Western Political Quarterly* 37 (March 1984): 168-170.

29. Michael Nelson, "Liberals Quit 'College,'" *Politicks and Other Human Interests,* November 22, 1977, 22-24.

30. This method is more fully explained and defended by Michael Nelson in "Partisan Bias in the Electoral College," *Journal of Politics* 36 (November 1974): 1033-1048.

31. Paul Taylor and David S. Broder, "In the Closing Days, Dukakis Is Betting on 18 States," *Washington Post National Weekly Edition,* October 24-30, 1988, 12-13; Elizabeth Drew, "Letter from Washington," *New Yorker,* December 12, 1988, 133-134.

32. Austin Ranney, "What Constitutional Changes Do Americans Want?" in American Political Science Association and American Historical Association, *this Constitution: Our Enduring Legacy* (Washington, D.C.: Congressional Quarterly, 1986), 277-286.

33. Author's calculation. Ironically, such biases have existed in the past, but were not noticed. See Nelson, "Partisan Bias in the Electoral College."
34. Fourteen of twenty-four years if the Democrats retain control of Congress in 1990, which is very likely.
35. Paul Allen Beck, "Incomplete Realignment: The Reagan Legacy for Parties and Elections," in *The Reagan Legacy: Promise and Performance,* ed. Charles O. Jones (Chatham, N.J.: Chatham House, 1988), 163,
36. Kristi Anderson, "Generation, Partisan Shift, and Realignment: A Glance Back to the New Deal," in Norman H. Nie, Sidney Verba, and John R. Petrocik, *The Changing American Voter* (Cambridge, Mass.: Harvard University Press, 1976), 74-95; Robert S. Erikson and Kent L. Tedin, "The 1928-1936 Partisan Realignment: The Case for the Conversion Hypothesis," *American Political Science Review* 75 (December 1981): 951-962.
37. Kevin B. Phillips, *The Emerging Republican Majority* (New Rochelle, N.Y.: Arlington House, 1969).
38. Beck, "Incomplete Realignment," 167.
39. See Walter Dean Burnham, *Critical Elections and the Mainsprings of American Politics* (New York: W. W. Norton, 1970).
40. Ibid.
41. Schneider, "Solidarity's Not Enough," 2853.
42. After 1980 Republicans became net losers of open seats in both the House and Senate. Stanley and Niemi, *Vital Statistics on American Politics,* 169.
43. Morris P. Fiorina, "The Reagan Years: Turning to the Right or Groping Toward the Middle?" in *The Resurgence of Conservatism in Anglo-American Democracies,* ed. Barry Cooper, Allan Kornberg, and William Mishler (Durham, N.C.: Duke University Press, 1988).
44. Gary C. Jacobson, "Meager Patrimony: Republican Representation in Congress After Reagan" (Paper delivered at the conference on the Legacy of the Reagan Presidency, University of California, Davis, May 24-26, 1988).
45. Ibid. Jacobson has amassed data from a long series of *New York Times*/CBS News polls.
46. Such issues did not prevent both kinds of voters from supporting Bush almost unanimously, just as they had supported Reagan. "The Static Dynamic Electorate," *Washington Post National Weekly Edition,* November 7-13, 1988, 15.
47. Corwin, *The President,* 1st ed., 171; James MacGregor Burns, *The Deadlock of Democracy: Four-Party Politics in America* (Englewood Cliffs, N.J.: Prentice-Hall, 1963).
48. Benjamin Ginsberg and Martin Shefter, "Political Parties, Electoral Conflict, and Institutional Combat" (Paper delivered at the annual meeting of the American Political Science Association, Washington, D.C., September 1-4, 1988).
49. During the nineteenth century, when the presidency was a much weaker institution, approximately one Supreme Court nomination in four was rejected by the Senate.
50. The three rejected nominees were: John J. Parker (1930), Abe Fortas (to be chief justice, 1968), and Homer Thornberry (1968). For a review of the *vive voce* nominations, see Henry J. Abraham, *Justices and Presidents: A Political History of Appointments to the Supreme Court,* 2d ed. (New York: Oxford University Press, 1985), chaps. 8-10.
51. Quoted by David M. O'Brien in *Storm Center: The Supreme Court in American Politics* (New York: W. W. Norton, 1986), 52. Certain senators were sufficiently powerful to enforce a more assertive view of senatorial courtesy. In his own case,

said Democratic senator James Eastland of Mississippi, "[T]he senator nominates and the Senate approves." Quoted by Robert H. Birkby, "The Courts: 40 More Years?" in *The Elections of 1984,* ed. Michael Nelson (Washington, D.C.: CQ Press, 1985), 250.

52. Indeed, so great was the expectation that the branches would share common partisan control that even when they did not, cooperation on nominations remained the norm. Neither party would see an advantage in introducing conflict when each expected to benefit, more often than not, from cooperation.

53. One might just as easily add to the current rather than the preceding period the 1968 rejections of Fortas and Thornberry, two nominees of Democratic president Lyndon B. Johnson, since they occurred in the expectation that the Republicans would win the presidency but not the Senate in the 1968 elections. The four rejected nominees since 1968 were Clement Haynsworth (1969), G. Harrold Carswell (1970), Robert Bork (1987), and (counted as rejected although technically not nominated) Douglas Ginsburg (1987).

54. Martin Shapiro, "The Supreme Court's 'Return' to Economic Regulation," *Studies in American Political Development* 1 (1986): 91-142; Mark Silverstein and Benjamin Ginsberg, "The Supreme Court and the New Politics of Judicial Power," *Political Science Quarterly* 102 (Fall 1987): 371-388.

55. In Pennsylvania, for example, Reagan left six vacancies unfilled for more than two years.

56. David M. O'Brien, "The Reagan Judges: His Most Enduring Legacy?" *The Reagan Legacy,* 67-75.

57. Judging from their reaction to the appointment of Antonin Scalia to fill the seat vacated by Warren Burger in 1986, Senate Democrats probably would not reject the nomination of a "qualified" conservative to the Court if a conservative justice, such as Byron White, died or retired.

58. Abraham, *Justices and Presidents,* 46.

59. The results of the 1970 survey of law professors, historians, and political scientists are reported in Abraham, *Justices and Presidents,* 377-379.

60. Ronald K. L. Collins, Peter Galie, and John Kincaid, "State High Courts, State Constitutions, and Individual Rights Litigation Since 1980: A Judicial Survey," *Publius* 16 (Summer 1986): 141-162.

61. Ranney, "What Constitutional Changes Do Americans Want?"

CONTRIBUTORS

Rhodes Cook is senior writer for the *Congressional Quarterly Weekly Report*, where he has covered politics and presidential campaigns since 1976. He is the author of *Race for the Presidency* (1987), a major contributor to CQ's *Guide to U.S. Elections*, and the author of *Dollar Politics* (1981).

Jean Bethke Elshtain teaches political science at Vanderbilt University. She is the author of *Public Man, Private Woman* (1981) and *Women and War* (1987).

Erwin C. Hargrove teaches political science at Vanderbilt University. His books include *Presidential Leadership, Personality and Political Style* (1966), *The Power of the Modern Presidency* (1974), *The Missing Link: The Study of Implementation of Social Policy* (1975), *TVA: Fifty Years of Grassroots Bureaucracy*, with Paul Conkin (1984), *The President and the Council of Economic Advisers*, with Samuel Morley (1984), *Presidents, Politics, and Policy*, with Michael Nelson (1984), and *Jimmy Carter as President: Leadership and the Politics of the Public Good* (1988).

Gary C. Jacobson is professor of political science at the University of California, San Diego. He is the author of *Money in Congressional Elections* (1980) and *The Politics of Congressional Elections*, 2d ed. (1987) and the coauthor of *Strategy and Choice in Congressional Elections*, 2d ed. (1983).

Michael Nelson teaches political science at Vanderbilt University. A former editor of the *Washington Monthly*, his articles have appeared in numerous scholarly journals and popular magazines. He is editor of *The Presidency and the Political System*, 2d ed. (1988) and *The Elections of 1984* (1985), coauthor of *Presidents, Politics, and Policy* (1984), and editor of Congressional Quarterly's *Guide to the Presidency* (1989).

Thomas E. Patterson is professor and chair of political science at the Maxwell School of Citizenship and Public Affairs at Syracuse University. His books include *The Unseeing Eye: The Myth of Television Power in National Elections,* with Robert D. McClure (1976), and *The Mass Media Election: How Americans Choose Their Presidents* (1980).

Paul J. Quirk teaches political science at the University of Illinois at Chicago. He is the author of *Industry Influence in Federal Regulatory Agencies* (1981) and coauthor of *The Politics of Deregulation,* with Martha Derthick (1985), winner of the Louis Brownlow Book Award of the National Academy of Public Administration.

Francis E. Rourke teaches political science at Johns Hopkins University. He is the author of several books about executive branch politics, including *Secrecy and Publicity: Dilemmas of Democracy* (1961), *Bureaucracy and Foreign Policy* (1972), and *Bureaucracy, Politics, and Public Policy* (1978).

John T. Tierney teaches political science at Boston College. His books include *Organized Interests and American Democracy,* with Kay Lehman Scholzman (1986), and *The U.S. Postal Service* (1988).